For...
Nalini, who is no more

and
our grandchildren:
Gaurav, Shivani and Anisha,
Kiran and Tara

and
their parents:
Apoorva and Ruchi
Sona and Josh

"Give me your tired, your poor,
Your huddled masses yearning to breathe free,
The wretched refuse of your teeming shore.
Send these, the homeless, tempest-tossed to me,
I lift my lamp beside the golden door!"
—Emma Lazarus, from a poem inscribed on the Statue of Liberty, 1883

"Yes, East and West, and North and South, the palm and the pine, the pole and the equator, the crescent and the cross—how the great Alchemist melts and fuses them with his purging flame! Here shall they all unite to build the Republic of Man and the Kingdom of God. Ah, Vera, what is the glory of Rome and Jerusalem where all nations and races come to worship and look back, compared with the glory of America, where all races and nations come to labour and look forward!"
—David Quixano, a character in Israel Zangwill's play, The Melting Pot, 1908

The life so short, the craft so long to learn!
—Hippocrates, Greek Physician, c. 460–370 BC

The past is a foreign country: they do things differently there.
—L.P. Hartley, The Go-Between, Hamish Hamilton, 1970, p.17

All remembrance of things past is fiction and this fiction has been cut ruthlessly and people cut away just as most of the voyages are gone along with people that we cared for deeply. Only they knew certain things. Other people are not there as people are not there in life afterwards although, to themselves, they are always more there than anyone.
—Ernest Hemingway, A Moveable Feast, Scribner, 2009, p.229

Table of Contents

Foreword *by Alice M. Rivlin*

I first got to know Natwar Gandhi when we worked together in the second half of the 1990s to rescue the District of Columbia from financial meltdown. The nation's capital city was close to bankruptcy—in imminent danger of being unable to pay its workers and provide basic city services. This catastrophe had multiple causes and did not occur overnight. The District's population had been declining for decades. First the white middle class and then the black middle class escaped to suburban Maryland and Virginia, leaving behind affluent neighborhoods and vast areas of the city with deteriorating housing, boarded-up stores and predominantly low-income residents. Despite its eroding tax base, the District was responsible for providing not only city services such as education and public safety, but also services normally provided by states, such as prisons and motor-vehicle licensing.

The D.C. government served both residents and commuters, as well as millions of tourists and visitors. Adding to the fiscal strain, two-thirds of the people who worked in the city lived outside the District, mostly in the surrounding suburbs, and Congress prohibited the District from taxing the incomes of nonresidents, which states with income taxes routinely do. A downtown office boom that had brought money into city coffers in the 1980s ended and the recession of the early 1990s hit the city hard. These underlying challenges, combined with mismanagement, over-hiring and failure to collect taxes brought the city to the brink of fiscal collapse in early 1995.

I was then serving as director of the Office of Management and Budget in the Clinton administration. Since I lived in the District and had chaired an earlier commission on its finances, I became the point person for the federal response to the city's fiscal emergency. Partisan political tension was running high because the Republicans under Newt Gingrich had just won control of the House of Representatives to the dismay of the Clinton administration. But, with the help of the District Congressional Delegate Eleanor Norton and Northern Virginia Republican Congressman Tom Davis, we worked successfully with the new Republican leadership and quickly put in place a federal law creating a Control Board with temporary power to override the locally elected government and restore the capital city to solvency. The new law also created a powerful new permanent position, an independent chief financial officer (CFO) for the District of Columbia, perhaps the crisis' most lasting contribution to fiscal responsibility in D.C.

The five-person board, under the leadership of economist Andrew Brimmer, plunged into the tough, unpopular tasks of cutting spending, fixing tax assessment and collection, and reducing the city's payroll. We convinced Anthony Williams, then CFO of the U.S. Department of Agriculture, to become the District's first CFO, and he recruited Gandhi—an experienced accountant and senior official of the General Accounting Office—to become the D.C. tax commissioner. Many of his GAO colleagues thought he was crazy to abandon the prestige and security of his position for the chaos of the District, but fortunately he ignored their advice.

The District of Columbia's fiscal turnaround was remarkably successful, and Gandhi played a crucial role in that success, first as tax commissioner and then as CFO. In 1999, Williams surprised many of us by deciding to resign his CFO post to run for mayor. After his election, Gandhi was chosen as CFO, a post he held for 13 years, serving with Williams and two subsequent mayors. I took over the Control Board chairmanship when Brimmer wanted to return to private life. In 2001, I had the unusual experience of closing a government agency that had done its job well and was no longer needed. By then the District was able to balance it budget, submit clean audits, and borrow money at reasonable rates due to a strong bond rating and solid fund balance. The nation's capital was beginning to struggle with the problems of all successful cities—growing population, traffic congestion, rising rents and property values, and gentrification's pressure on the poor—but the financial crisis was definitively over.

When I met Gandhi, he was a respected figure in the accounting profession, who worked easily with business leaders and government officials. I did not guess—and only learned later—that he had grown up in a poor family in an isolated village in western India, and struggled to get an education and learn English. He arrived in America with seven dollars in his pocket, worked hard to obtain a Ph.D. in accounting and break into American academia, and ended up thriving at the GAO. I would also not have guessed that he had another career as a poet, who published in his native language, Gujarati.

There are many sides to Natwar Gandhi, and they are engagingly displayed in this book. His is an American dream story, but not without missteps and setbacks. I admire the fact that he opens this memoir with his worst professional moment, the discovery of an embarrassing financial fraud that escaped detection in his own agency. That is an unusual way to start a memoir, but Gandhi is an unusual man. I have been privileged to know him and hope you will enjoy making his acquaintance as you read this book.

Dr. Rivlin was the first director of the Congressional Budget Office, 1975-83;
director of the White House Office of Management and Budget, 1994-96;
vice chair of the Federal Reserve System, 1996-99; and chair of the D.C. Control Board, 1999-2001.

Introduction

A FATEFUL DAY

November 7, 2007, was supposed to be the most glorious day of my professional career. Born in a dirt-poor village near India's west coast, I arrived in the U.S. with $7, studied hard, and worked harder to arrive at a moment when all of my struggles and accomplishments would be recognized, even honored.

That morning I put on a freshly ironed white shirt, my best suit and black shoes especially polished for the day. My wife, Nalini, put on her most beautiful saree and favorite jewelry that she had brought from India. Our two adult children were also well dressed. I planned to take my family and a few friends that evening to Washington's historic Willard Hotel for a glittering event at which *Governing Magazine* was honoring me with its prestigious "Public Official of the Year" award, established to "recognize and celebrate exceptional public leadership."

I was going to receive the award at a gala ceremony also honoring Christine Gregoire, governor of the state of Washington; Fabian Nunez, speaker of the California Assembly; William White, mayor of Houston, Texas; and William Bratton, chief of police of Los Angeles, California. I could hardly wait till evening, when I would be honored as a distinguished public servant among these luminaries.

The day failed to unfold as I had hoped.

Very early that morning, as I was polishing my shoes, FBI agents knocked on the door of Harriet Walters, a mid-level official in the District of Columbia's tax office. They roused her from bed and arrested her on charges of masterminding a major embezzlement scheme. They accused her of conspiring to siphon off $50 million in tax receipts over the course of nearly 20 years—under the noses of the agency's leaders, including myself. For the past decade, I had been Harriet Walters's boss, first as tax commissioner for the District, then as its chief financial officer.

That afternoon the U.S. attorney for the District of Columbia held a press conference to provide details about the investigation into the corruption. City leaders lined up behind him included Mayor Adrian Fenty and me, the city's CFO. The ever-aggressive Washington media attacked the District's young mayor and accused him of a lack of vigilant management. How could such embezzlement go undetected for so many years?

Ignoring protocol, I rushed to the microphones and faced the cameras.

"It's not the mayor's fault," I said. "If anyone was responsible, it has to be me. I was in charge of the tax office."

Under the District's unique governance structure, the CFO controlled the entire financial administration, including its tax office. "I am the CFO. Therefore, I should be the one held responsible."

Suddenly the bright lights and TV cameras turned on me, and I was hammered with rapid-fire questions from reporters. So much for the day that should have been my crowning achievement.

———————

Ever since I moved to Washington in 1976, I had dreamed of being the focus of a press conference. I had imagined the president appointing me to direct a major federal agency. I would stand there enjoying my 15 minutes of fame. Press photographers would click their cameras as I listened to endless encomiums coming my way.

This press conference on November 7, 2007, however, was not the one that I had imagined. It basically appeared to end my dreams. Nothing good could come of this attention. I was being branded as a negligent manager under whose eyes a mid-level bureaucrat had been able to commit major embezzlement. The next day, and for weeks to come, *The Washington Post* and other papers carried news of the scandal on their front pages. I was an object of derision. The *Post* skewered the city government in editorials and depicted me in a derisive political cartoon. The scandal made news for what seemed an eternity. What I had foreseen as my 15 minutes of fame instead became 15 months of infamy and agony.

During those dark days, it was a foregone conclusion that I was a dead man walking. Every day I arrived at the office expecting a new revelation about the ever-expanding scandal. The pressure on me was so great that some of my friends and well-wishers thought I might emotionally unravel, that I might just throw in the towel and leave the city.

I didn't. I couldn't. I persevered. In the end, it is nothing short of a miracle that I survived the scandal and remained the District's CFO for six more years. I provided crucial financial leadership during the Great Recession, when the District was under severe financial duress along with most state and local governments.

How did I manage that?

First of all, it was a matter of professional pride. I was determined not to let the scandal define me. If it happened on my watch—which it did—I would do whatever it took to fix it. Second, I wanted to restore my reputation. When I had joined the

District in 1997 as its tax commissioner, the tax office was mostly broken. Practically nothing worked. The city was insolvent—it had run out of cash. But after more than a decade under my watch, the District was financially stable, flush with cash, its reputation on Wall Street restored. I was not going to let this scandal be the last word on my tenure in the city.

People often ask how I survived such a professional calamity.

Simple. I have an immigrant's survival instinct. I have been through worse in my life. From my earliest days, I swam against the tides of traditional Indian culture. No matter what they say, Indians generally worship money and material success. We are a smart, disciplined and shrewd people, but we can be crass.

We measure success by the size of one's bank account, the number of rooms in one's home, the make of one's car. That's why my father urged me to become a successful businessman in Mumbai—to make money, show it off and send it home to support the family.

"Make money, not poetry!" he would yell at me. I recoiled and rebelled.

Blame it on Abraham Lincoln. And Walt Whitman, Wallace Stevens, Emily Dickinson and Ralph Waldo Emerson. And above all Mahatma Gandhi. They were my heroes; I wanted to be like them.

Gandhi was a rather a curious case. In his autobiography, he presents a self-deprecating portrait of himself. As a young boy he was afraid of darkness. He was not a particularly good student. He barely made it through his bar exam in London. He could not argue his first case in court because he was too timid. He failed as a lawyer in Mumbai and left to go to South Africa to see whether he could make a living there. Some years later when he appeared before the Indian National Congress to present a resolution, he could not speak in front of such a gathering. His autobiography is a rich catalogue of his weaknesses and failings, particularly in his early life. Reading it as an impressionable young boy, I wondered... *If such a weakling could become the Mahatma, why not me?*

While my more enterprising peers in Mumbai were immersed in commerce, I was steeped in American literature and biography. My eyes were set on people like Lincoln, who changed the world for the better, rather than on those who made millions from building and selling a better mousetrap.

My ambition was to be a man of consequence. As a professor at the University of Pittsburgh, I wanted to be more than just an academic. I wanted be like Harvard economist John Kenneth Galbraith, a much-celebrated writer and public-policy intellectual, who was once President Kennedy's ambassador to India and a major player in the Democratic Party during the 1950s and '60s. At the General Accounting Office, I strived to have an impact on public policy. My aim was to make a positive difference in the world. I refused to be ignored.

———————

In the age of Donald Trump's "Make America Great Again," survival instincts have become a necessity for Asian immigrants, among many others. On February 22, 2017, a young Indian software engineer named Srinivas Kuchibhotla was having a drink after work at his favorite bar in a small town southwest of Kansas City, where he and his wife had made their home. A disgruntled former Navy man named Adam Purinton confronted him and his friend, shouted racist slurs and said "get out of my country" before shooting Kuchibhotla. A few weeks shy of his 33rd birthday, he died of his wounds. Later Purinton pleaded guilty to first-degree murder and was sentenced to life in prison. India's minister of external affairs tweeted: "I am shocked at the shooting incident in Kansas in which Srinivas Kuchibhotla has been killed. My heartfelt condolences to the bereaved family." That was cold comfort to his mother, who said: "Now I want my younger son, Sai Kiran, and his family to come back for good. I will not allow them to go back."

No doubt Kuchibhotla's tragic death is a sign of the times. All of a sudden, a climate of fear has spread across immigrant communities, including among South Asians who have made this country their home. His widow, Sunayana Dumala, asked on her Facebook page: "Do we belong here? Is this the same country we dreamed of and is it still secure to raise our families and children here?"

I confronted that question in 1965 when I contemplated my prospects in the teeming streets of Mumbai. Like Kuchibhotla, I was itching for adventure. For me, an impoverished young man, the answer was clear: Go west, young man—go to America! I boarded an Air India flight in 1965 on a one-way ticket that took me across the oceans, not knowing when, if ever, I would return.

But why did I choose America? Why not elsewhere in the West? Millions of Indians have migrated to Canada, Great Britain, Australia and even to non-English-speaking countries of Europe. Some have even gone to Russia! Similarly, some Indians have also made their home in the burgeoning economies of East Asia or the Middle East. In an earlier era, they had gone to Africa to make their fortunes.

I chose America because more than any other country it has the tradition of accepting and absorbing immigrants. It gives them a chance to remake their life and I got that chance for a life that would otherwise have been wasted in India. Here, at last, what matters is what I know and can do and not where I come from or how I look or what my hereditary lineage is.

For an immigrant, America is heaven if you know what you want to do with your life and are willing to work at it. Only in America can an Asian immigrant like me become the chief financial officer of the nation's capital. This nation's generous people open their hearts and doors to immigrants and let them pursue their dreams. And that is why America is still the most favored destination for tens of millions around the world. The best and brightest as well as the tired and poor come to America, invited or not. Surveys show—and images from the evening news confirm—that people want to come here even when risking their lives.

My story is both cautionary and instructive, difficult yet uplifting. Ultimately, it is a harrowing tale of how to survive in India and succeed in America. It was an uncertain beginning, in some ways even more difficult than immigrants face today. In this winter of American discontent, when a presidential candidate rode into the White House based in part on his anti-immigrant rhetoric, it is rather quaint to say, as I do, that "America is still the promised land for immigrants." Especially when Indians and Asians have been targets of some of the worst violence against America's newcomers.

In singing America's glory, I am not ignoring what is bad and ugly here. Like anyone I also see crime, drugs, social promiscuity, homelessness, profound economic inequality, racial discrimination and, above all, its toxic, special-interest-driven tribal politics that have debased the public square. And, yes, I too feel the sting of discrimination—crank calls from crazies telling me to go back home. But where would I go? This is my home, now and forever!

Most Americans take their country for granted. I don't. I know better. I am from the Old World, where America is still the place to go. When I hear people denigrating America, I am reminded of a poem by Ray Bradbury:

America
We are the dream that other people dream.
The land where other people land
When late at night, they think on flight
And, flying, here arrive
Where we fools dumbly thrive ourselves.

Refuse to see
We be what all the world would like to be.

How dumb! Newcomers cry, you are mad! They shout,
We'd sell our souls if we could be you.
How come you cannot see the way we see you?

You be the hoped-for thing a hopeless world would be.
You are the dream that other people dream.

I am a citizen now, and celebrate July 4th. But the day of my biggest celebration each year is October 10th. On that day in 1965, I landed in America. That is my Independence Day. Here's how I found my way to America and achieved the American dream.

Chapter 1

GROWING UP WITH BOOKS, MOVIES AND DREAMS

There is no record of my birth, but I do have an approximation of my birthday.

Early one morning when I was about 5 years old my mother came to the foyer where I was sleeping with my brothers. "Get up, Natu," she implored. Natu is short for my given name, Natwarlal, one of the numerous names of Lord Krishna, the most popular Hindu god. "Your Kaka is going to take you to school today." Kaka is how I addressed my father whose name was Mohanlal. Similarly, I call my mother Baa, for Shantabahen. My grandfather Jivanlal would be addressed as Bapa while I called grandmother Manibahen, Maa.

She bathed me, dressed me in a special outfit of new kurta—a loose Indian shirt that she was saving for a special occasion—and took me to a corner in her room where she kept a framed picture of Kankai, our family goddess. The Hindu pantheon has numerous goddesses in addition to hundreds of gods. Our family would pray to our goddess Kankai for good luck when we began something new, like starting a business or enrolling in school.

My mother prayed and asked me to bow down and pray as well. I did not understand what the fuss was all about, but did what she asked. Then she fed me a little breakfast of sweets to celebrate the auspicious day and sent me on my way.

Kaka held my hand and we started walking the 10 minutes to school. My elder sisters were amused to see me dressed up. "Wow! Look at our little brother!" I also had a little shoulder bag that contained a slate and a few pieces of chalk to write with. There were no pens or pencils, nor any notebooks. Kaka, a man of few words, walked without speaking to me. If my mother had not alerted me that he was going to enroll me in school, I would not have known where I was going.

Kids in the neighborhood were amused to see me in special clothes. As we walked past, they laughed and made fun of me. "Hey, Natu, where are you going all dressed up?" one asked. Quipped another one: "Don't you know he is getting married today?" The third one exclaimed, "No, no, he is going to Mumbai!"

Not all the kids in town went to school. Many went straight to work doing minor chores in shops, farms and family businesses. They would start working as young as 9 or 10. No one bothered to think of that as child labor. One of my own brothers dropped out of school soon after he was enrolled so Kaka could put him to work as a gofer in our family shop.

Kaka and I walked through the town bazaar, empty and silent at this early hour. The shutters were closed in our shop, a small grocery store that my father had inherited from my grandfather. Other stores sold household goods, clothing and sundry merchandise. We rushed past so Kaka could complete my school enrollment and quickly return to open our store for business.

It took us about 10 minutes to reach the elementary school. I had passed by the building a hundred times without ever setting foot inside, a bland two-story affair. Like most public buildings in town, it was old and dilapidated. The door to the principal's office was open. A shabbily dressed peon in short pants motioned us inside. The principal was seated by his desk. He appeared older than Kaka and his mouth was full of paan, a betel leaf filled with jam and tobacco that Indians chew, particularly at the end of a meal as a mouth freshener. He was not clean shaven and wore a dhoti and dirty shirt. His long green topcoat hung in the corner.

The office walls were barren. No pictures or photos hung on the expanse, badly in need of a coat of paint. The floor needed a good sweeping and the few pieces of furniture needed dusting. The windows were wide open to the strong breeze that blew papers off the desk. Pieces of stone were used as paperweights. Walking into the principal's office, I was a little apprehensive. What was I expected to do? What if the principal did not like me? Suppose he would not admit me? What about the teachers? Some were known for meting out corporal punishment. If they punished me, what would I do? If word of my punishment were to reach my parents, they would be disappointed! I had a good reputation. People would say, "Natu is a good boy! He would do no such thing!"

Without exchanging any pleasantries, Kaka briskly told the principal, "I want to enroll my son in the school."

"What is your son's name?" he asked. That was easy for my father.

"And when was he born?" My father looked out the window. Frankly, he did not know my birthdate. But he had to come up with a date that would make me 7, the required age for enrollment. He didn't know my age, but knew that he wanted me out of the house.

"October 4, 1940," he said. That became my birthday. And Kaka was on his way to open the shop.

The principal completed the paperwork and escorted me into the classroom, which was as shabby as his office. He interrupted a class and said to the teacher, "I have a new student for you. His name is Natu." That was it. I was enrolled in school and assigned a teacher.

After that encounter, the date of my birth never came up as long as I lived in India. There were no birthday celebrations in our household. I celebrated my birthday for the first time when I came to America; thanks to a bureaucratic moment, I have one.

This much I know: I was born in a small town called Savarkundla in Gujarat—a state in western India—at home with the help of a midwife. There were no hospitals or maternity homes. I was the third child and first boy among seven surviving children. I had two elder sisters who had never enrolled in school. The birth dates of the three brothers and one sister who followed me in school were based on that which my father had made up for me. He and the school official would add a year or two to my alleged birthday, and that would be their birthdates.

Decades later, when I sponsored nine members—six adults and three children—of my extended family to come to the United States, only the children had their birthdates properly recorded, because they had been born in Mumbai. For the adults, I had to have a town elder sign an affidavit certifying their birthdates. This was long before the age of Trump and extreme vetting; otherwise they would never have made it into the U.S.

During my first decade growing up in our small town in western India, the world convulsed. World War II engulfed Europe, Asia and Northern Africa. The Nazis murdered millions of Jews, along with Catholics and Gypsies, in the Holocaust. When I was born, India was still part of the British empire, so from birth until I reached age 7, I was a subject of the United Kingdom.

In 1942 Mahatma Gandhi continued his nonviolent crusade for Indian independence by launching his Quit India Movement in Bombay (now Mumbai). The major port and most Westernized city of India, Mumbai is the commercial hub of the country. It is about a 24-hour train ride east of our village, yet neither Gandhi's movement nor the world war made a ripple in Savarkundla—until August 15, 1947. On that morning, as soon as I arrived at school, the teacher told students to hurry up and get ready to go to the town center. We arrived to see India's tricolor flag unfurled by a local Congress Party leader who had gone to jail for his role in the independence movement. Students sang India's national anthem, *Jan Gan Man*. We all took the day off to go home and celebrate. From then on, August 15th became a national holiday.

The next time I remember being excused from school and brought to the town center was January 30, 1948, the day that Mahatma Gandhi was killed by a fundamentalist Hindu activist who thought the old man was being too good and lenient to Muslims. I did not know much about Gandhiji, as he was reverentially called, but at the meeting I heard a lot about the father of our nation, as he was also known, and what he had done to liberate the country.

I left the meeting and went straight to the town library, where I borrowed Gandhi's autobiography. A literary masterpiece, it is written in simple Gujarati, his native language and mine, and one of India's 22 official languages, each with a full-fledged literature of its own. I found Gandhi's experiences in London and South Africa fascinating. He had gone to London to study law and later to South Africa to practice it. Mahatma Gandhi became my hero that day. I wanted to know everything about him. Our small-town library might not have the latest novels, but it certainly had numerous books about Gandhiji. They were all in Gujarati. All of them were published by Navjivan Press, which Gandhi himself had founded in 1929. One set of books that particularly appealed to me was Mahadev Desai's diary, which ran to several volumes.

Desai was Gandhi's personal secretary from 1917 through 1942, when he passed away. During these years he kept a detailed diary of Gandhi's life—James Boswell to Gandhi's Samuel Johnson. The picture of the Mahatma that emerges from the diary is that of a stern taskmaster who demands the last ounce of energy not only from himself but also from all of those around him. Every waking moment must be accounted for and devoted to public service—and to India's freedom struggle.

In one telling episode, while traveling together, Gandhi forbade Desai from going on a sightseeing tour of a nearby natural wonder—Gerosoppa Falls, the second-highest waterfall in India. Why? Because that would be a frivolous waste of time when so much work was yet to be done for India's freedom!

Gandhiji had and continues to have a profound influence on me. Years later I learned that my father had also been deeply influenced by him. In fact, Kaka had joined the independence movement and gone to jail while he was in school in a provincial capital. Going to jail for independence was considered a badge of honor in those days. Gandhi himself, like most leaders of the Indian independence movement, spent years in jail.

Though the Mahatma and I share the same last name, I am not related to him, nor for that matter to any of the famous Gandhis—Indira or her son Rajiv. People often want to know, yet Gandhi is a fairly common name, signifying a trader who sells perfumes. Gujarati Indians are well-known for their entrepreneurial zeal and mercantile skills. My Gujarati brethren have ventured all over India and the world setting up shops and businesses of all varieties.

On January 26, 1950, India became a republic with its own constitution, under which it has a bicameral legislature with a duly elected president, prime minister and parliament. It was a remarkable day in India's tumultuous history, but for us children, it was just another holiday from school.

––––––––

Savarkundla, where I spent my entire childhood, can be called a town only charitably. About 20,000 of us lived in the pair of villages—Savar and Kundla—separated by the Navali River, more like a stream than a river and nothing like the size of the

Ganges. Still, it was our central water supply. We went there to bathe and wash. For drinking and cooking, water was brought in from the river by the women of the house. I recall my mother and sisters lugging buckets to and from the riverbanks.

I was born into a place with no paved streets, no electricity, no telephones and no running water. There were no cars. Cows were considered sacred and roamed freely through the streets. We touched them for good fortune and spiritual cleansing. They were food for our souls, not for our bellies. I grew up in a vegetarian world; a morsel of meat never passed my lips.

The cows were joined by cats, dogs, goats and donkeys in the streets. Dangerous animals such as lions, tigers and leopards lived deep in Gujarat's Gir Forest, some 200 miles away. Bullocks hauled carts with heavy loads. The few horse buggies were used only sparingly, for special occasions like weddings. The only doctor in town used them to make house calls. Yes, in those days in India, doctors made house calls.

We had no discernible seasons beyond hot and dry summers followed by monsoons. The summer heat was unbearable. Since there was no air-conditioning, we learned to endure the heat. It was not at all uncommon to see bare-chested adult men and naked children walking the streets.

The natural world in and around our village held beauty, but we didn't engage the environment either at school or home. We had no connection to birds, animals, flowers or forests that would enrich our lives beyond the practical aspects of exploiting the environment. Villagers cut down trees for cooking fuel. The chirping of birds was a common sound, but I could not distinguish any birds except peacocks and crows.

Along the riverbanks I strolled by roses, lilies, lotuses, hibiscuses and jasmine, but do not recall any flowers being brought into our house to liven up the place, not even during the weddings of my two elder sisters. Wherever I walked, wherever my eyes settled, dust, dirt and filth were under my feet and in my sights. Children would excrete in the streets, which would not be cleaned for days. Even adult men urinated openly. I would watch people sweep their houses—then throw the rubbish in the street. All of this would turn into stinking filth and mud during the monsoon season. Our town had no sewage facilities; sanitation was manual and rudimentary. We would wait for the searing summer sun to dry everything, and life would go on.

Every morning a train stopped at the one-room railway station. It brought yesterday's newspapers from Mumbai and Ahmedabad, the biggest city of Gujarat. The town librarian would pick up the papers and take them to library. Sometimes he would miss picking them up and collect them the following day. The newspapers would give me a chance to devour a glimpse of life beyond my town.

The railway station had a tea stall where villagers waiting for the train could sip tea and have a smoke. They would puff *bidis*, a cheap, handmade local version of cigarettes. We could spot visitors from Mumbai, because they smoked cigarettes made mainly by the city's Imperial Tobacco Company. It wasn't hard to pick out the travelers from Mumbai. They wore socks and shoes. Their shirts and pants were properly ironed. They carried perfumed handkerchiefs in their pockets. And they sprinkled an occasional word or two of English into their conversations. I thought of these visitors as sophisticated people who came to town along with the newspapers. They were "cool," so I used to hang around them. I wanted to talk, walk and dress like they did. I even fancied smoking cigarettes like them!

Buses and a single-track rail line connected the town with the outside world. Passengers generally showed up early at the station to buy tickets. The stationmaster was usually late opening the ticket window, causing a mad rush among passengers to buy tickets. There were no lines. Occasionally fights broke out, even though there was always room for everyone on the train.

Just as the daily train delivered people to and from our village, the movie theater transported me from the doldrums around me. I will never forget *Devdas*, a movie that came to town when I was about 15. It was a love story adapted from a famous Bengali novel of the same name. One of the most celebrated Indian actors of all time, Dilip Kumar, played the hero who failed to marry his childhood sweetheart and fell into deep despair. In his depression, he turned to drinking and frequenting Calcutta's red-light district, where he found a compassionate courtesan who took care of him. Ultimately, the hero tried to make his way back to his childhood sweetheart, but he died at her doorstep.

My heart broke with his. I yearned for love, for adventure—for escape! The tragic ending of the story deeply affected me and I remained melancholy for weeks. Life seemed pointless. For days I barely talked with anyone. Seeing me sad and depressed, my mother grew worried: "Natu, what is wrong with you? Are you not feeling well, son? Are you feverish?"

"No, I am fine." I didn't want to discuss the movie with my mother or, for that matter, with anyone else. It was an intensely private affair. I was sure that she would not understand.

"It is just a movie!" she would say. But for me, it was everything.

Movies with tragic endings were rare. In Bollywood movies—Hindi cinema—things always work out in the end. The hero gets his girl and everyone lives happily ever after. Almost every Bollywood movie is a musical, full of song and dance. We used to memorize the songs and sing all day. The village theater was a ramshackle building with simple wooden benches of the sort one would find in an old American gym. Too often the benches were full of bugs ready to attack us as soon as we sat down. I expected the discomfort, but it never stopped me. As at the train station, people did not form lines; there was always a mad rush to buy movie tickets, interrupted by occasional fights.

I never got involved in fights. I didn't have the guts. I would patiently wait and, as soon as the theater doors opened, join the crowd racing for seats. But I rarely got one because I wouldn't fight. So, I would stand for the duration of the movie, which could last as long as three hours. I did not mind. I got so engrossed in watching movies that nothing else mattered to me.

Keep in mind, Savarkundla had no electricity. The movie projector operated thanks to an old, noisy generator, so loud that it was often difficult to follow the dialogue. But I didn't care. I went to movies to see beautiful Bollywood actresses dancing and falling in love with their heroes. Sometimes the generator would shut down in the middle of a movie. Pop! The screen would go dark. I would file out with the others, wondering whether our hero would get his girl or not.

Every week a new movie would arrive and take us to the glamorous world of Mumbai, the most cosmopolitan metropolis of India, with its wide boulevards, restaurants, colleges, asphalt roads, neon lights and, above all, beautiful people. After every movie, I would dream about Mumbai and wonder when I would go there. But first I had to sing. At the end of each movie, the Indian national anthem was sung. A giant national flag waved on the screen while the anthem blared from the loudspeakers. The idea was to promote patriotism, which was quickly ebbing as people turned to more mundane things after independence. The government mandated that audiences stand and sing the anthem. It was hilarious to see people rushing to exit as soon as the anthem began.

Years later, "Time to sing the anthem" became a Gujarati euphemism for "It's time to go."

————

Every morning my father and I shopped for the food for our family's meals. Buying fresh vegetables was a daily affair, since there was no refrigerator at home as there was no electricity in town. We would stroll through the small bazaar, and Kaka would choose among tomatoes, string beans, eggplants, cucumbers, cauliflowers, onions, cabbage and spinach. Then I would take the produce home for my mother to cook. Little shops were arrayed on both sides of a dirt road. In them town folk did their daily shopping for grains, nuts, oils, tea, sugar, vegetables and other provisions.

To celebrate special occasions such as the Hindu New Year's Day, Kaka would buy sweets. When in season we would feast on mangoes, a luxury in our household. I loved mangoes and wanted him to buy them every day during the season. But Kaka was frugal and mangoes were expensive, particularly those that came from other states.

If Mahatma Gandhi was my star and idol, my high-school teacher, Mukundbhai, was my guide, the single saving grace in the town's decrepit school. I remember walking into class and seeing him for the first time. A light-skinned man of medium height who parted his hair sharply in the middle, Mukundbhai was always well dressed and carried himself with a confident bearing. He spoke eloquently and in complete sentences, unlike the other teachers, who were in general quite slovenly. Most were old and did not have a college degree or any teacher certification. All that was needed to be a teacher was a high-school diploma and, equally important, some influence in the state education ministry. Of all the teachers, Mukundbhai was the only one with a master's degree, and in literature, which is what he taught us. He got me hooked on literature, particularly poetry. If not for this one great teacher, I might not have made it out of the village.

Mukundbhai explained Gujarati literature to us with great verve. He talked about Gujarati novelists such as Ramanlal Desai and K.M. Munshi, and I would rush to the library to get their books. If the books he recommended to me were not available in the town library, he would lend me his own copies. Our school had no library, but Mukundbhai had one of his own! He made poetry and Sanskrit meters come alive for me. Thanks to him, I started experimenting with metrical poetry even during my high-school days.

One day Mukundbhai talked about a famous poem called *Meghdoot* (*The Cloud Messenger*) by India's greatest poet, Kalidas. In this long poem, the hero asks a cloud to carry a poignant message to his beloved, from whom he is separated. When I learned that the poem was in Sanskrit, I went to Mukundbhai after class and told him, "Sir, I don't understand the poem. It is in Sanskrit, but I would like to read it."

"No worries," he said. "I will give you a Gujarati translation." He quickly produced the book and gave it to me.

I was so charmed by the poem's beautiful meter (*mandakranta*) and elegiac tone that I quickly produced a poem in the meter and took my scribbling to Mukundbhai. He was surprised that I could do such a thing and said to me, "Natwar, you will be a poet!"

This was the first time that anyone had called me by my proper name. No lazy abbreviation like "Natu" for Mukundbhai, of course. His prediction about my future, however, was a bit off the mark. Though I retained my love for Gujarati poetry and published three volumes of poetry later in life, I would become an accountant.

Years later, when being honored by my hometown in India, Savarkundla, for my work as CFO of Washington, DC, I was overjoyed to learn that Mukundbhai was to be honored at the same ceremony for his excellent teaching. I went to greet him at the ceremony. In his 90s, he was stooped and hard of hearing. Still, he recognized me. "I am very proud of you!" he said. He had read about my work in Washington in the newspapers.

"Do you remember you taught me Sanskrit meters?" I asked him. "And predicted that I would be a poet someday?"

He nodded.

I said, "I have published a book of poems—all sonnets and in meters that you taught me." With a twinkle in his eyes, he said in a barely audible voice: "I have a copy of your book, too."

Beyond Mukundbhai, what I remember about other teachers is not so good. The odor from the headmaster's long green, unwashed jacket was unbearable. He wore the same jacket every day with no shirt underneath and would show up unshaven, as did many teachers, all of whom were men.

Once hired, a teacher was in for life. No one ever got fired. It was a safe and easy job with regular pay and not much work. The science teacher would do a chemistry experiment and then discount it by saying, "It is all *maya* (illusion)!" The arts teacher would ask us to draw something—and to keep quiet so he could doze off undisturbed, which distinguished Mukundbhai even more. The other teachers envied him. Even the school principal showed him deference. He was a humorist and the only teacher to publish articles that were later collected in a book.

Even with Mukundbhai, though, I can't say that school was a joy. The two school buildings, one for elementary and the other for middle and high school, were simple, drab structures with grimy walls that seemed never to have been washed or painted. During the heavy rains, students had to be sent home because the roofs leaked. I remember leaving school one day to escape water pouring through, yet at home I found buckets placed throughout our house. Its roof was no better.

To be clear, these schools were not full-fledged educational institutions of the sort that one would find in almost any American town. There were no extracurricular activities, no libraries, no cafeterias, no gyms, no organized sports, no field houses, no auditoriums. We had to go to a nearby provincial town to take our final exams to graduate.

Every day in every class, a group of students sat in the last row, separated from the rest of us. They were the untouchables. These students might not have looked different in dress or demeanor, but they were the lowest of the low in our town—and all over India. I grew up in Hindu society, where people were categorized and divided according to a strict caste system, the unshakeable iron frame of Hindu society. You were born into a caste, which determined your fate on earth. There was no movement up or down. At the top were the Brahmins: the priests and teachers. They were followed by Kshatriyas, the warriors and rulers. Then there were the Vaishyas—farmers, traders and merchants—and the *Shudras*, the laborers. The untouchables, often called the Dalits, were at the bottom. Gandhis—my family and the Mahatma's as well—were Vaishyas.

The untouchables lived in a separate section at the edge of town and did their work—handling carcasses, sweeping streets, cleaning latrines, removing filth—comprising all sorts of "dirty" stuff assigned to them by the caste system. They were not allowed to participate in any of the town's collective activities, such as prayer meetings where Hindu saints would come and preach. The untouchables were not allowed to go to temples or draw water from common wells. No one seemed to see them. Town life went on as if they did not exist. They were like the weather—just there—and lived in their own world. All five castes attended school, but the rest of the students rarely if ever talked or played any games with the Dalit kids. I never had an untouchable acquaintance, much less a friend.

Mahatma Gandhi made it his life's mission to remove untouchability from Hindu society. He considered it a stain on Hinduism and made a Herculean effort to integrate untouchables into the larger society. After he returned home as a hero of the successful mass movement against apartheid in South Africa, Gandhi established the *Sabarmati Ashram*, his first communal abode, in Ahmedabad. He invited an untouchable family to live there. This scandalized the city. His donors stopped funding the ashram. But Gandhi was determined to integrate untouchables into the larger society no matter what the cost. He called them *Harijans*, children of God. He held his prayer meetings, as well as official meetings of the Congress Party, in areas where untouchables lived. Through the sheer force of his personality, Gandhi made Hindu priests open their temples to untouchables. It is because of him that a highly educated untouchable named Dr. B.R. Ambedkar was appointed to chair the committee to draft the constitution of India that outlawed untouchability.

Like Mahatma, I fully realized the injustice that was done to untouchables only after I left India. When I came to the U.S. in the mid-1960s, through sheer accident I landed at a black college in Atlanta. The city was a hub of the civil-rights movement that was gaining strength at the time. It was also the home of the Ebenezer Baptist Church, where Martin Luther King, Jr., and his father preached.

In Atlanta, I learned a lot about how blacks had been subjected to the cruelty of slavery and how it had taken a catastrophic civil war to abolish it. I also learned that systematic discrimination against blacks continued long after slavery was abolished. It occurred to me then that that is what we Hindus had been doing to untouchables through the centuries, except that our discrimination was cleverer. In America, blacks were discriminated against because of the color of their skin. In India, an untouchable looks more or less like any upper-caste Hindu! A subtler antenna was required to identify an untouchable person.

Though untouchability has been outlawed, it still continues in understated form, particularly in villages. Today, about 160 million untouchables have been relegated to inferior lives through no fault of their own but merely because of their tainted birth. Our school also had a few Muslim children. Muslims lived in their own separate area. They had their *masjid*—their mosque, or place of worship—and cemetery there. The only time they ventured prominently into town was during their annual Eid procession. In my 17 years in town, I never experienced or heard of any Hindu-Muslim discord. The communities lived separately but peacefully.

———

I still remember doing my lessons under the dim light of a kerosene lamp. Around the mid-1950s, electricity was being brought into the town, though not widespread. Only a few well-off people and businesses could afford it. Our family could not. With electricity came radio. The municipality bought a huge Murphy radio the size of today's microwave oven and connected it to loudspeakers placed throughout the town. We hungrily listened to movie songs broadcast from a radio station in Ceylon, today's Sri Lanka. Prudish All India Radio would not broadcast Bollywood songs lest they corrupt our young minds! As in the Soviet Union, the radio network broadcast speeches of ministers on such weighty issues as improved steel production and pending agricultural reforms—all equally boring, yet I hungered for news. No wonder we turned to Radio Ceylon.

Every evening I would stand beneath a loudspeaker and listen to the All India Radio news piped in from faraway cities like New Delhi and Mumbai. I wanted to discuss what I heard about current affairs, literature and culture, but with whom might I talk about these things?

I clearly remember one evening in late 1954 when the radio announced the death of the renowned novelist Desai. He had written numerous novels in which the handsome hero was influenced by Mahatma Gandhi, and had dedicated his life to selfless public service and the independence of India. I had read all those novels that were available in the library. Indeed, I wanted to be a writer like Desai. Shocked to hear the news, I wanted to rush out and tell someone, to share my grief. But who could I talk to? Neither Kaka nor Baa nor any adults in the house—or in the neighborhood for that matter—would know much of anything about this novelist, much less grieve his passing. I had to wait till the following day to share the news with Mukundbhai. He, of course, had read most of what Desai had written.

———

As I was coming of age and beginning to understand politics, a young socialist named Navin Ravani burst upon the scene. He was always well groomed and wore an ironed white shirt with long sleeves, ironed blue pants and black shoes. He was constantly glancing at his wristwatch, as if he had to go somewhere. Young and idealistic, he was a charismatic speaker. Ravani emerged almost out of nowhere and challenged the old guard by running for mayor against the Congress Party candidate who had been managing the city ever since independence. Town folks were impressed with Ravani's guts and audacity. He captured their imagination and their votes. Our town had never seen anyone like him before.

Though I was too young to vote, I was fascinated by Ravani. After one of his public meetings, I went to him and said, "I want to work in your campaign." Instantly, he gave me a bundle of pamphlets and said, "Good—go distribute these. Quick." They were announcements of his next public meeting. When Kaka found out what I was doing, he quickly put an end to it. He didn't want me to get into any trouble. Ravani became mayor in a landslide. It was such a big event that it made the Mumbai papers. Socialists from everywhere came to town to learn how he managed to defeat an entrenched and deep-pocketed Congress Party candidate. Unfortunately, Ravani's mayoral reign was short-lived. The old-guard politician outwitted him by getting the Congress Party-dominated state government to supersede his municipal authority by taking over. There was nothing Ravani could do but protest. In India, state governments have supervisory authority over local governments. The governor, with the advice and consent of the state legislature and chief minister of the state, can dismiss a duly elected mayor.

This sordid affair further alienated me. I wanted to get the hell out of town. Reading books or occasionally going to the movies were escapes for me—and liberating experiences as well. For those few hours, I was in Mumbai or elsewhere, anywhere except Savarkundla. But alas, these were only temporary reprieves and soon I was back in my dismal town. I found everything around me—my family, school, neighborhood, town—quite ordinary, boring and suffocating. I looked for the kind of dashing characters that I read about in novels and saw in movies—people who could be my role models, who would inspire me to do great things. But there were none. Everyone and everything seemed small-minded.

The famous novelist V.S. Naipaul's description of small Caribbean islands aptly described our town: "Small places with simple economies bred small people with simple destinies." I did not want to be confined to a simple destiny. I had ambitions. Like Mahatma Gandhi, I wanted to go abroad and study and be a leader of men. Like many leaders of the independence movement, I wanted to be involved in politics. Some days I wanted to be a novelist like Desai. Other days I wanted to be a poet like Kalidas. In short, I wanted to be relevant. I wanted a life of consequence. I hated the insignificance that surrounded me in my little town. But first, I needed to leave.

———

When I was growing up, Savarkundla was in the doldrums. It had no industry except one. Scales for weighing were manufactured on the riverbanks, but the scope of the industry was quite limited, employing only a few families of ironsmiths. Our own grocery store was losing money. Kaka would not change with the times and offer new products or sell goods on credit. With the changing scene, his routine life was fast crumbling and my grandfather's savings were eroding. Kaka wanted me to follow the example of my cousin Amritlal, who had moved to Mumbai and made his fortune. He helped his family financially. Kaka wanted me to do the same. People with ambition had no choice but to leave town. Kaka also wanted me to leave immediately for Mumbai, even before I finished high school. But word came from our Mumbai relatives that I should at least finish high school. Nevertheless, my future beyond Savarkundla was beginning to take shape.

In the meantime, I found solace and escape in books. The town library was heaven. Hungry to know more about the world beyond my little town, I devoured newspapers and magazines. I would lodge myself in the library every free hour I could find and get lost in a wider world. The librarian would collect the newspapers that came about 24 hours late via train from big cities like Mumbai and Ahmedabad, then carefully separate the pages and put them in a rotating glass case. People would stand on both sides to read the newspaper pages. At most the papers consisted of four to six pages, and I would read every line on every page. Staffed with one librarian and stocked with relatively few books, it was not a library in any modern sense. Its ramshackle benches were full of bugs, just like those in the theater. But it had books and that was enough for me. Sometimes I felt that the books were there only for me. I would voraciously read Gujarati novels, short-story collections and poems.

I would take a book or two and disappear upstairs in a room in our house that was used mostly for storage. The room had no windows, and daylight poured through a roof full of cracks and holes. It was heavenly for me except in monsoon season. There, in the midst of dusty sacks of grain, I would lodge myself and get lost in the book at hand.

The only problem was that the books in the library were under lock and key. To let me check out a book, the librarian had to find the right key, get up, go to the right shelf and retrieve the book. He did not like that chore and hated me for making him do that. This lazy man was rarely shaven and always shabby, his short-sleeved shirt only half buttoned. His hairy chest was always visible since he never wore an undershirt.

In 1957, after finishing my final exams and while waiting for the results, I had nothing much to do except read. One day I approached the librarian and asked for a specific book—the autobiography of the great Gujarati novelist Munshi, who was also a prominent Mumbai attorney and significant figure in drafting India's constitution. I greatly admired him and wanted to be like him when I grew up.

Without even looking at me the librarian said: "The library does not have it. We will order it!" Yet I had seen it in the glass bookcase.

"But of course, we have it," I said. "I will show you where it is!" He did not like being caught in a lie. He reluctantly went to the bookshelf, retrieved the book, dumped it in my lap and gave me a stern look that I will never forget. Soon after procuring the book, I went to our shop to see if my father needed any help before I went home to start reading it. Right behind me was the librarian. He angrily confronted my father.

"Your son is spending too much time in the library," he shouted. "He's asking for too many books!"

"What are you talking about?" Kaka asked.

"You heard me right," the librarian said. "Your son is a nuisance in the library. Don't you have things for him to do in the shop?"

My father turned to me. "Why are you spending so much time in the library?" he asked. "You should be helping me mind the shop." Kaka assured the librarian that I would no longer be spending so much time in the library. That evening Kaka told my mother, "It is about time we send Natu to Mumbai. Next week—perhaps tomorrow, if you can get him packed and ready." My mother and I had no say in the matter. She put together a small luggage bag with a few clothes, and I was on the train the next day to Mumbai. Kaka was right: The librarian would not have to worry about me anymore. For that day at least, the librarian had the last laugh.

––––––––––

As I look back on my childhood years in Savarkundla, they were suffocating and boring; above all, I was lonely and quite unhappy. Yet those years instilled in me the habit of reading books, particularly biographies of the great and near-great that fired up my imagination and inspired me. I learned to dream, aspire and strive to reach my potential. All of that has stayed with me till this day.

Chapter 2

A FAMILY OF STRANGERS

During my first visit back to India after I migrated to the U.S., I was taking an early-morning jog in Mumbai when I passed Kaka, who looked like such a forlorn soul. I stopped in my tracks and turned around. The streets were jammed, even at that early hour with people going to work or returning from their night shift, but I kept my eyes on him and pushed my way forward, exclaiming "Kaka!"

Surprised, he turned to look at me. Our eyes met.

"What are you doing out so early, son?" he asked. "It is not safe. Mumbai is a different city now than when you were here. Go home to our place."

The year was 1974. I had finished my doctoral dissertation at Louisiana State University and been awarded my Ph.D. degree. Nalini and I had moved to Pittsburgh, where I had taken a job as an assistant professor at the University of Pittsburgh. I was on a tenure track to become a full professor and had dreamed about accomplishing this ever since I'd started teaching in the U.S.

Nalini and I had bought a house near North Park, a lovely area in suburban Pittsburgh. Our son, Apoorva, was now 4; his sister, Sona, had turned 1. My parents had never seen our children except in photographs. They were particularly eager to see their first grandson, who would carry the family name forward. I thought that it would be an ideal time to return to India. This would be my first visit since I'd migrated to the U.S. I had left India a defeated man. Now I would be returning as a man of accomplishment, the first in our extended family to have completed college and earned a doctorate. I wanted to share the joy and pride of being "Dr. Gandhi." A doctoral degree, a faculty position at a major American university and, above all, a fine family with a son and daughter, which overjoyed Nalini as our first son died soon after he was born in Mumbai some 10 years earlier.

Now I even had enough income to help my father. Kaka was still struggling financially. I also dreamed of bringing my parents to America and showing them the New

World. So the four of us—Nalini, the children and I—flew to New York and boarded an Air India plane for Mumbai. We landed a day later in the middle of the night. The whole family was waiting for us at the airport. We went through the exhausting Mumbai customs process, which required bribing officials at every stage.

When my mother saw my son, she rushed over and hugged him tightly. Tears rolling down her cheeks, she said, "At last I see my dear, dear grandson! How lucky I am!" Then she handed him to my father: "Look at him—how handsome our grandson is! He is going to carry the Gandhi name forward!" My father also became emotional, hugging all of us—a very unusual gesture for him.

My parents were living in a two-room flat in Borivali, a distant Mumbai suburb. Three of my brothers and one sister lived with them. Almost apologetically Kaka said, "As you can see, there is not enough room for all of us here." So he found us a nearby flat owned by a distant family member. It took us a few days to recover from the jet lag and get used to the new environment, particularly the ubiquitous mosquitoes. I tried to visit all of the places where I had worked and lived in Mumbai. My regular morning jog helped me to get reacquainted with those places—and reminded me of what I had left behind.

It was on one of those mornings that I encountered my father on his commute to work.

He repeated himself: "You shouldn't be out so early, son. It is not safe. Mumbai is a different city now than when you were here. Go home."

"But what are *you* doing out so early?" I asked. "Should you not also be home now?"

"I am going to work," he said. "I go early so I can get a seat on the train. During rush hour, trains are so crowded that it is very difficult even to board. And I never get a seat." I reached out and put my hand on his shoulder. "Please, Kaka," I implored. "Give up your job. It is too much for you. I am making enough money now. You don't have to work anymore. I can support you."

He said he would think about it and began walking toward the station.

Weeks later, as soon as I returned to the U.S., I got a telegram from India: "Kaka passed away this morning. Massive heart attack." I was devastated, with a profound sense of guilt. I couldn't help him when he needed me the most. I had failed. I took the first available flight back to Mumbai. A speeding taxi took me home. I found my mother sitting alone in the dark two-room flat, forsaken and downhearted. I broke down and wept uncontrollably like a child in her lap. As I write this, tears well up in my eyes.

In some ways, my fleeting visit with my father was a reflection of our family life in Savarkundla. We never sat down to dinner together. There were no dinner-table conversations. There was no dinner table. For that matter, there were no chairs. At mealtimes we sat cross-legged on a mat in the kitchen. We ate in shifts because the kitchen was too small to accommodate all of us. If Kaka was home when the meal was ready, he ate first so he could rush back to the shop. Should my grandfather Bapa arrive, he took priority in seating. Then came the children, two or maybe three at a time.

"Eat fast," my mother Baa would say. "Others are waiting." My poor mother would be the last to eat. Obviously, conversation was not part of our dinner ritual. It was more like a cattle call. In addition to Kaka and Baa, 12 other people lived in the house. Our extended family consisted of my parents, my paternal grandparents, my father's uncle and his wife, a widowed aunt who had lost her husband soon after she'd married him at the age of 15, and us—the seven surviving siblings.

There were not enough rooms in the house to accommodate everyone. Adults slept in rooms but with the doors open. Children slept in the foyer and courtyard. The house constantly needed repairs. The leaky roof desperately required fixing, yet monsoons came and went, and the same buckets were always set out in the same rooms. The barren walls, with no pictures or photographs, badly needed painting. Though we lived in such intimate proximity, we were like a collection of strangers thrown together. When adults talked with one another, the conversation was always short and perfunctory. Little joy was ever expressed. It is little wonder that I never really bonded with anyone, including my parents.

I had two older sisters, one younger sister and three younger brothers. Girls were not typically sent to school at the time and my older sisters never went. What was normal for girls was that the elders would find husbands for them when they reached puberty. Bapa played an active role in finding husbands for my older sisters. In a nearby town he found two young men from respectable families of our caste. My sisters had no say in the matter. They were expected to follow the wishes of their elders, move in with their husbands' families and make new lives for themselves.

Both of my brothers-in-law had finished high school. One of them went to work in his family's pharmacy, while the other went to Mumbai. He did quite well and brought his family, including my sister, Bhanu, to Mumbai. When I eventually went to Mumbai, I stayed with them until I found my own accommodations. Bhanu's case was rather tragic. She bore five daughters in succession without producing a son. Among paternalistic Indian families, for a woman not to produce a son is very unfortunate. After each girl, Bhanu kept hoping for a son, but it was not to be. The birth of the last two girls—twins—pushed her into a deep depression. Bhanu felt that she was cursed. She began consulting all sorts of preachers and religious quacks to remove the curse.

Finally, she gave birth to a sixth child and this one was a boy—but by that time she had developed paranoid schizophrenia and eventually died a tragic death.

Most members of my family, including my parents and two elder sisters, are long gone; my three brothers and a sister remain, but I am in contact with only one brother and the sister. I support another brother financially, although have not seen him in years.

––––––––––

Of all my relatives, my father's case is the most puzzling to me. The truth is that I never really got to know him. He was a man of few words. I can't remember a single conversation with him that had lasted more than few minutes. There were no father-son outings—no going on a picnic or taking a walk to the river, let alone an out-of-town trip. Kaka inherited a retail grain shop from Bapa. It might be more accurate to say that my father took over the shop when his father could no longer keep it up. As the eldest son, I often accompanied Kaka to the shop. He would busy himself organizing sacks of various grains and keeping the books as he waited for customers. Many a time, Kaka and I would look at each other as we waited. Sometimes this would become quite uncomfortable for me, so I would ask, "Kaka, may I go home? I have some homework to do." He would look vacantly at me and shrug his shoulders. We both surmised that no more customers would appear that day. I would quickly leave the shop before Kaka changed his mind and assigned me a chore.

Over time, fewer and fewer customers stopped by. Other shopkeepers catered to them by offering varied goods, such as tea, sugar, nuts, cottonseeds, oil and the like. They also provided customers credit. Not Kaka. In changing times, my father refused to change. Even so, keeping the shop overwhelmed him and he had little time for us. I am not saying that Kaka had no fatherly affection or love for me and my siblings. It's just that he showed no outward signs and there was no bonding between us.

––––––––––

At the age of 17, I completed high school—the first in my family to do so—and was ready to take my graduation exams. Our town was too small to hold exams, so local students had to go to Bhavnagar, a nearby provincial city, to take them. This presented Kaka with a dilemma. I was too young to go on a train by myself. Someone would have to accompany me to the exam center. It might seem to be the perfect trip for a proud father. But not for Kaka. The trip would have required four days' lodging in Bhavnagar since the exams were spread over that period of time. Apparently that was too much for him and he declined to go. Suddenly I was faced with the prospect of not graduating because my father refused to take me. Despondent at possibly missing my exams, I ran into Vinoo, one of my friends, and told him of my plight.

"My father is taking me," he said. "Maybe you can come with us." Vinoo's father, Haribhai, was a well-known school teacher in our village. I mentioned the possibility to Kaka.

"Go with Haribhai and Vinoo," he said, "and stay with them for four days."

But he refused to approach Haribhai and ask him to take me to the exam center, leaving that formality to me. Sheepishly, I approached Haribhai.

"Sir," I said, "may I go to Bhavnagar with you? My father has pressing business that keeps him here."

Without a moment's hesitation Haribhai replied, "Of course you can come with us. Vinoo would like that. Tell your father not to worry. We will take good care of you."

During the train ride and stay in Bhavnagar, I clearly saw how much Haribhai cared for Vinoo. He woke Vinoo up early each morning, made special tea for him, and sat with him in case Vinoo had any questions as he studied for his exam. I was very envious, but Haribhai gave me the same nice treatment. So this is what fatherhood could be!

––––––––

It was as if Kaka had resigned from his parental duties. He seemed to have little interest in rearing his children, especially when it came to education. Worse yet, he took no interest in making sure that his children got married. In a country where dating was practically absent, it was left to parents, particularly the father, to find a suitable match for his children. But that was too much trouble for Kaka. Thus two of my younger siblings—one brother and one sister—never got married and were deprived of life's basic sexual needs. Since they didn't have enough gumption of their own, they lived a damaged life full of anger, frustration and deep hurt. The rest of my brothers and I had to fend for ourselves in the marriage market. Had it not been for my grand-father, my two elder sisters would not have been married.

Kaka seemed to have lost interest in life. The question was why—I always wondered what had turned him so inward, so focused on a failing business, so uninterested in his family. All that mattered to him was the shop. He would spend all day there, come home, eat and go to bed. He didn't read books or newspapers, never went to movies or did anything to entertain himself or the family. He took no vacations. He had no friends with whom to unwind. Rumor has it that he had been a pretty good flutist in his school days, but I never saw or heard the flute during all of my years at home.

One day I overheard a conversation that provided some insight. A friend of the family, who had come to visit from Mumbai, had known my father in his younger days. "Remember when Mohanlal was a revolutionary?" the friend asked my mother. "He joined India's independence movement under the influence of Gandhiji and even went to jail!" My father—a revolutionary?! I couldn't see it and listened intently.

"Yes, and Bapa was quite upset about it," my mother said.

Bapa, my grandfather, had no interest in seeing his son join Mahatma Gandhi's struggle for independence. Bapa had sent Kaka to boarding school in a nearby town because the tiny village where he grew up had no school. My grandfather was grooming him to be a successful businessman, not a revolutionary.

Learning that his son had been detained, Bapa immediately went to the boarding school and delivered a few choice words to the headmaster. Then he went straight to court, paid the necessary fines, got Kaka released, brought him home and put him to work in the family shop. No more education. No more revolution. Bapa wanted to make sure that his son stayed confined to his way of life. Without further delay, he got him married. He figured that the responsibilities of running a household would rid him of his rebelliousness. It worked. Soon my oldest sister was born. Then another sister, and then I came along. More children followed. The taming of Kaka was complete. I never heard him talk about his revolutionary days, how he joined the independence movement, how he got thrown into jail or how Bapa got him out of it. I learned about it only when my mother bragged about Kaka to a visitor. How I wished that Kaka would talk to me about his participation in that struggle, how and why he went to jail, what was it like to be there with his fellow revolutionaries. I wanted him to talk about Gandhiji and the influence that he had on him. It was not to be.

––––––––

By the time I was born, Kaka was deeply immersed in the family business. Running the shop was his principal and only preoccupation, just as his father had wished. My father was set in his ways, as his father had hoped. And my father had the same future in mind for me: make money, raise a family, help him in his old age. Kaka wanted me to leave school as soon as possible, go to Mumbai and start earning money to help him out. Little did he know that, as it turned out, I would be an abject failure at making money.

Word came from relatives in Mumbai that I should at least finish high school before migrating to the big city. Kaka had to wait a few more years before sending me off. But as soon as I finished my final exams, without waiting to hear the results, he put me on a train to Mumbai. A complaint from the town librarian helped push forward my leaving! I was spending too much time in the library. The shop continued to lose money. Before it failed, Kaka gathered my mother and siblings and moved the family to Mumbai, where he thought he might be able to make a living, eventually by accepting a job with a relative.

I have always wondered what heartbreak that Kaka, once a revolutionary, must have endured late in life when he had to start all over in Mumbai. All of his sons were failures in the way that Indians judge their sons—taking care of their parents in old age by relieving them of their financial burden. Alas, none of us made any money to do that. In a circumstance that I regret to this day, by the time I was ready to assist him financially, it was too late as he was four months from death. Except for his early years in the Indian independence movement, Kaka lived an uneventful life, tending to the family shop into his midlife. Then came his frustrating later years in Mumbai. It was drudgery for him, with no help from any of us. I never saw him laughing out loud or enjoying any moments of success.

That said, he was a steady provider. He kept his frustration to himself and never took it out on any of us. It was not uncommon at that time for frustrated men to beat their wives or children. In fact, one of my cousins, a highly ambitious Congress Party politician, routinely cursed and beat his wife in anger. She, a gentle woman, took it as punishment that she deserved. Kaka, despite his frustration, never took to drinking, smoking or cursing. I never heard him raise his voice; he never beat any of us, even when we misbehaved. And he never talked about his frustrations with me or, for all I know, with anyone else. He suffered silently. I had no ill feeling toward Kaka at the time. Indeed, I was proud of him. I used to brag that he had participated in India's independence movement and gone to jail for it, which was considered a badge of honor. More important, my father provided life's essentials by keeping a roof over our heads, making sure that we were fed and maintaining peace in the house. Though devoid of visible love, our home was safe and secure.

Life was not a bumpy ride with Kaka; there simply was no ride. We lived in separate worlds. Even when I left for Mumbai, all he could say when he dropped me off at the railway station was: "Stay with your sister until you find your own place. Your brother-in-law will meet you at Bombay Central Station." And then he walked away without waiting for the train to depart. Apparently he did not think that at 17 I was too young to go by myself on a 24-hour railroad journey that involved changing trains. He had never bothered to train us to do things on our own. Sink or swim was his unspoken mantra!

––––––––––––

If my father's story is sad, my mother's is no better. While Kaka was away all day minding the shop, she was taking care of a large family consisting of grandparents, distant relatives and, of course, her seven surviving children. As if this weren't enough, one day my grandmother broke her leg. It was monsoon season and water was everywhere; she slipped, fell and cried out for help. Baa rushed to her and tried to help her stand, but grandma could not. I had just come home from school and Baa frantically said, "Natu, go and get Kaka from the shop. Grandma has broken her leg!"

When I got there, Kaka was busy haggling with a customer. I told him what had happened. He showed no emotion but said, "Tell your mother I will be there shortly."

I ran back home. Hours passed and there was no Kaka. The pain was unbearable for grandma, who was now crying loudly. Baa again told me to rush to the shop. "Tell your Kaka to come home immediately. Grandma is crying!" Kaka was not happy to see me.

"I told you to tell them I was coming!"

"But grandma is crying! Baa wants you to come now."

"All right, I am coming," he said and told me to mind the shop while he was gone. "There is always something!" He did not want another problem. But this was to be my mother's problem till my bedridden grandmother died. Until that happened, however, grandma's needs had to be attended to while she lay in bed. Baa had to do it all—bathe her, dress her, feed her, clean her chamber pot. This went on for years. There was no help for Baa. We were not rich enough to hire someone to attend to my grandmother or help mother with the numerous household chores. I never saw her resting or relaxing, or take a day off. She always had work to do. Like Kaka, she seemed to have no friends with whom to gossip or unwind. She rarely ventured out of the house, much less out of town. I never saw her dress up for anything. As far as I knew, she had no wardrobe or jewelry to speak of. One great delight in the life of an Indian mother is to be a mother-in-law and lord it over the daughter-in-law who will take over all the household chores and relieve her of that burden. Unfortunately, that did not happen for Baa.

After my marriage, my wife and I were mostly in Mumbai and then the U.S. Two of my younger brothers and their wives also lived in Mumbai. So there was no one to shoulder my mother's burden. When Kaka and Baa moved to Mumbai, she had to continue running the household, albeit in a new, even more difficult setting. Like Kaka, my mother would be viewed as a parental failure according to modern standards. She never sat down and told stories or read children's books to us. How could she? All of her time was consumed doing household chores. Besides, she was illiterate.

In many ways, Baa's story is typical of most women of her time in small Indian towns and villages. They usually were married off young by their parents to men they neither knew nor had seen. They had no say in the matter at all. They were expected to leave their parents' home and go live with the husband's family for the rest of their lives. By today's standards, my parents' marriage would be considered strange. There were no outward signs of love or affection. I never saw Kaka bring Baa a gift—a saree, jewelry, flowers, anything. I never saw them celebrate an anniversary or birthday, or even go out together. I never saw them hug one another, share a joke, laugh together or even talk intimately. When they talked, it was for a few minutes, usually about some household matter.

My parents paid little attention to their children, yet their parental behavior was quite normal by the standards of the day. To lament now that they failed as parents would be to apply modern standards of childrearing to a different era and a vastly different social milieu.

Haribhai, the father of my friend Vinoo, with whom I went to Bhavnagar, was an exception. But he was a teacher who realized the importance of education. Most people expected children to grow up by themselves. Indeed, children were constantly encouraged to get out of the house and play with other kids and not be nuisances at home.

To write critically of one's parents is blasphemy among Indians. Indian sons are expected to take care of their parents like the legendary Shravan, who heroically took his aged parents on pilgrimages to holy places by carrying them in baskets suspended from a bamboo pole borne across his shoulders. And here I am criticizing my elders for not being good parents. Blasphemy, indeed!

––––––––––

Before I left for Mumbai, I was so immersed in my world of books and magazines that I had minimum contact with the world around me. I was a loner and made few lasting friends. At home I would seclude myself in an upstairs room reading romantic novels and had little interaction with other members of the family. In many ways, not forging lasting bonds with family members made me fiercely independent and autonomous. The lack of close parental involvement early in my life forced me to face the world on my own, which gave inner strength that helped me survive some harrowing years in Mumbai and many vicissitudes in the U.S. as well. Beyond the lack of bonding, our family had very little sense of its history. I know nothing about my maternal grandparents; my mother never talked about them. And though my paternal grandparents lived with us, I knew virtually nothing about their parents, not even their names. Nor did I know much about the aunts and uncles who lived with us and whom I saw daily.

The family practiced religion only ritualistically. In a small corner of our home my mother every day would light a little lamp in front of a deity, the family goddess. My father did the same in his shop at daybreak. These rituals were the extent of their religiosity. No one in the family went to temple regularly or ever went on a pilgrimage to any of the Hindu holy places. Nor did we ever invite in any of the holy men who went from house to house showering their blessings. And we never attended any of the religious revivals to which masses thronged to hear saints preach from ancient scriptures.

No one else in the family read. There were no books, not even the standard religious tracts, in the house. And if members of my family were not readers, they certainly were not writers of letters. Though I left home at 17 and stayed away nearly all my life, very little correspondence passed among us. The only letters that I got from my father were simple cursory notes about sending him money. If storytelling is the essential activity whereby elders pass along family history to the young, there was none of that in our family. I never heard fairy tales from my grandmother or from anyone else.

In many Indian families, elders sing early morning prayers called *prabhatiya*; these rhythmic songs become part of family lore. Children wake up hearing them and they in turn share them with their children. That did not happen in our household. One might say that Kaka, Baa and the rest of the family lived a dreary life, every day the same as every other. Still, it was a life of stability and predictability. There was no drama. I never heard adults in the family arguing or quarreling about anything. When I hear about the ACE (Adverse Childhood Experiences) phenomenon that prevails in many American families where adults quarrel, fight and separate—and how it all affects the behavior of children when they grow up—I am actually thankful for the dullness of the family I grew up in. As I write this, I wonder how the occasional arguments that Nalini and I had impacted our children.

———————

Late in her life, I was able to bring my mother to the U.S. She stayed with us for a few months, but soon returned to Mumbai. She found it difficult to adjust to the new environment, especially with its harsh winter. During a period when heavy snow made it impossible even to go to the mailbox, she said, "Natu, I want to go back home. How soon can I go?"

"Baa," I said, "the snow will be shoveled quickly, or it will all soon melt. Can you wait just a few months? I want to show you America. It is very scenic. We are going to Niagara Falls as soon as winter is over."

She looked at me. Her sad, vacant face said it all: It was time for her to go. Despite all the issues of running a household on her own in Mumbai after my father's demise, she thought it better to be in an environment that she was familiar with than in the U.S. There she could walk to the bazaar and do her shopping and greet people. She could go to the temple and pray—a practice that she had taken up later in life. Here she was homebound and felt like a prisoner. I gave up.

"If that is what you want, Baa, I will arrange for you to go."

Soon thereafter I drove her to New York. As she was about to board the Air India flight to Mumbai, I bowed down and touched her feet, a Hindu custom of respect for the elderly. She hugged me close and began crying softly. I couldn't control myself either, and also started crying. She began wiping tears off my face, kissing me and saying, "Don't cry, son, don't cry. God bless you, son. Live long, son. Live long!"

Before I knew it, she was on the plane. I felt like rushing after her and accompanying her to Mumbai, but I stood there until the plane took off. And that was the last I saw of her. On the drive back to Washington, I was filled with a deep sense of remorse. How terribly I had failed her and my father! I wanted Baa to stay with us in America. I wanted her to see its beauty, to enjoy American luxury of a kind that she'd never had. Above all, I wanted her to enjoy her grandchildren a little longer, particularly our son, the sole male child in the family to carry the Gandhi name forward. But all that was not to be.

At that stage in her life, she was simply too tired to go on. She seemed to have had enough. Despite having four sons and three daughters-in-law, there was no one in India except my unmarried sister to take care of her as she approached the end of her life. My sister told me that Baa stopped eating, as if she was hungering to die. She told my sister not to wake her if she was sleeping late. One day she simply slept too late and slipped into an easy death.

When the news of Baa's death came, I rushed home, but for what? My strongest living link with India was gone. I was not emotionally attached to any of my surviving siblings. I reached home in Mumbai in the middle of the night. I went to Baa's room in the back of the apartment, empty and dark. Suddenly I broke down. An immense sense of guilt came over me again. But there was nothing I could do about it now. Years later I helped finance a women's wing in the town's charitable hospital in her name. A minor act of expiation.

Chapter 3

THE ROAD DIVIDES IN MUMBAI

The train platform in our small town was teeming with travelers the morning I left home for Mumbai. I had been to the station many times to watch in awe as people boarded the train for faraway destinations. I always wondered when I might have a chance to do so. Now it was my turn. Now I was the traveler. My father and I walked wordlessly through the quiet streets toward the bustling rail yard. By sunrise the air, already steamy and fetid, sat on my shoulders like a wet scarf. At the station Kaka asked me to wait outside while he went in to buy the ticket. He came out after some time and handed me a small piece of paper that said MUMBAI in capital letters.

"Don't lose it," was all he had to say. We waded into the throng of people having tea and chatting. "Put it well inside your trouser pocket!" My father seemed annoyed. He'd had to wait at the ticket window. The stationmaster had been late, as usual. Kaka had a few choice words about him and turned to me.

"Listen carefully, Natu," he said. "You change trains at Viramgam Junction, then stay on until you reach Bombay Central Station. Your brother-in-law will pick you up. I will send him a telegram. Go with him and stay with your sister until you find your own place. Oh well.... The train is late as usual!"

At that my father walked away and left me alone on the platform.

———

The day had begun on a more nurturing note. My mother awakened and guided me to the corner of our house where she kept a picture of Kankai, our family goddess. She lit a small lamp as she did every day. She looked at me with sadness in her eyes.

"Son," she said, "bow down to Kankai. She will look after you in Mumbai." Baa held me in a tight embrace and cried softly. Then she gave me a bag containing snacks. "Eat this when you are hungry," she said. "Don't buy anything from vendors—that will make you sick."

I bowed down and touched her feet as usual. I did the same for my grandparents and other elders in the house. They all blessed me, and I was off on my life's

26

most important journey. In time I came to realize that my journey to Mumbai was as momentous as my passage to the U.S. some eight years later.

––––––––––––

Apparently, it was not that special for my father. I watched him walk away. Would he turn around and wave? Rush back and give me a hug? Impart a few words of wisdom? No and no and no.

That was the end of my life in Savarkundla, the place where I was born and raised, the place from which I desperately wanted to escape. This was my moment and yet I was deeply apprehensive. I knew what I was leaving behind, but beyond what I imagined from movies and legend, I had no idea what to expect. I was just 17 years old and had never been anyplace else except Bhavnagar, the nearby town I had traveled to for my final high-school exams. But I had gone there with my friend Vinoo, and his father had taken care of me. Here I was, all alone, taking a 24-hour train journey to a place where I had never been. I did not know when the train would reach Viramgam Junction, or how I would change trains when I got there.

When the train finally arrived at the Savarkundla station, the chatting passengers turned into a roiling mass of humanity rushing toward the train. Half-carried, half-running, I pushed onto a car and found a seat. I looked around but did not recognize a single face. I settled down and placed my mother's bag of snacks on my lap. I felt for the ticket, still safe in my pocket. The car was crowded with all sorts of people, mostly men. Judging from their dress, conversation and behavior, most were farmers, cowherds, laborers, office clerks and such. There was also a group of old people accompanied by a holy man, apparently going on a pilgrimage. They were singing *bhajans*, Indian prayer songs, and invited the rest of us to join them in singing.

Hawkers entered the car and moved from passenger to passenger, trying to sell all manner of stuff, including snacks and soda. Every time the train stopped at a station, they switched to the next car. The same was true of the beggars, who were more persistent and told sob stories to try to persuade passengers to give them money.

An older man had taken the seat next to me. A slightly pudgy fellow of medium height, he had a kindly face that instantly inspired calm. He was dressed in the traditional *dhoti*, *kafani* and *bandi*, the traditional dress that Gujarati men wear nearly every day. A *dhoti* is a rectangular piece of unstitched cloth wrapped around the waist and legs and knotted at the waist; a *kafani* is a loose shirt worn under a sleeveless jacket, the *bandi*. Kaka wore the same kind of clothing every day, but this man's clothes, unlike Kaka's, appeared clean and washed. He was also clean-shaven. From his demeanor, I took him to be a Brahmin, perhaps a teacher. He held a string of rosary beads in his hand and seemed to be praying in a very soft voice with his eyes closed.

As soon as he opened his eyes, I leaned toward him. "Sir," I asked, "how long before we reach Viramgam Junction?"

"Are you going to Mumbai?" he asked. He could read the confusion on my face. "I am going there, too. Stick with me, boy!" He even offered to share his small sack of food. After our lunch, he went back to his prayers and beads. Though we were sitting next to each other, that was the extent of our conversation during the journey.

Luckily, I brought a book that I'd borrowed from the town library. It was the autobiography of a famous writer that had gotten me into trouble with the librarian and hastened my departure for Mumbai. The librarian apparently never missed it, since I never heard from him. I guess he was happy that I was no longer in town bothering him for books.

Having settled into the train, I looked through the window at the landscape rushing past. The trip from my village to the big city takes a route in the shape of a question mark around Khambhat Bay, off the Arabian Sea. We headed north and curved west around the bay before heading south along the coast. The landscape was mostly barren, with only a few trees, stray cows, dogs and buffalos. I saw farmers working in fields and women carrying pots of water over their heads. The train stopped often at towns with names like Nadiad and Surat. I did not get off at any of the stations, afraid that I might not be able to get back to the train in time and it would leave without me, also afraid that I might lose my seat. I would get up only to take bathroom breaks. Finally, after all the excitement of the day, I fell asleep.

———————

For as long as I could remember, I'd wanted to go to Mumbai. I yearned to escape my town's smallness, dirt roads, filth and petty quarrels. I wanted to be cosmopolitan! The Mumbai that I had read about in books and seen in Bollywood movies fascinated me. A crime thriller titled *CID* remains etched in my memory. The year was 1956 and I was about 16. It became a hit movie of the year. What I liked most about it was its iconic song, *Yeh Hai Mumbai Meri Jaan* ("This Mumbai Is My Life"). My friends whistled it constantly. It was performed on-screen by Johnny Walker, a legendary Bollywood comedian. In the movie, Walker sings it on the wide pavement of Chowpaty, a sea-facing residential area where visitors from all over India came to glimpse Mumbai's rich and famous. Walker gets on and off of a horse-driven carriage singing the song, while in the background one sees ocean waves, beautiful mansions, strolling tourists, rushing cars and people simply enjoying themselves.

In Bollywood movies I saw the Mumbai of wide boulevards, asphalt roads, tall buildings and towers, colleges and universities, air-conditioned theaters, a museum, zoo, gardens, the Taj Mahal and other five-star hotels and restaurants, English newspapers, Dalal Street and the financial district, national and international banks, insurance companies and much more. I was fascinated by it all.

I wanted to go to Brabourne Stadium, where cricket matches were played; when radio came to our dusty town, we would stand in the town square and listen to running commentary on test matches being played there. The names of legendary cricket players like Vinoo Mankad, Vijay Merchant and, above all, Jasu Patel, who held India's Test-bowling record for 40 years, were engraved in my memory. Now I wanted to see these great players in action. From books and movies, I had learned a lot about Mumbai's sophisticated people, well-dressed and well-mannered, conversing in English. I'd seen couples going hand-in-hand into restaurants. I couldn't take my eyes off of girls in their swimsuits at the famous Juhu beach. I'd seen smart ladies in Western dresses working in offices and talking freely with their male colleagues. I'd seen finely dressed young men and women going to colleges. Oh, how I wished I could join them!

I'd seen fast-moving commuter trains bringing hundreds of thousands of suburbanites into the city every day and streetcars called trams. I'd seen automobiles, even foreign-made brands such as Impala and Mercedes. I'd seen people hailing yellow cabs and swiftly getting in and out of them. This was the Mumbai of movies and books—and the stuff of my dreams. I was charmed and wanted to go there. I was hardly alone. The mantra for young men in our village was: "Go west, young man—go to Mumbai!" Even though it was in fact south from where we were!

―――――――

"Get up, boy," my seat neighbor said, waking me from a sound sleep. "We have to change trains." The train had reached Viramgam Junction. I collected my bag and followed him. We switched platforms and waited—among hundreds of others—for the train to Mumbai. Again, I joined the mad rush when the train arrived. Luckily, I managed to stay together with my new acquaintance. We found seats. I was relieved, settled and safe for at least the next 12 hours when the train would reach Bombay Central, where I hoped my brother-in-law would receive me.

A full 24 hours after we departed Savarkundla, the train reached our destination. In the cavernous Bombay Central terminal, thousands of people were jostling and milling about. I had never seen so many people in one place. And they were quite different from what I was used to seeing in my town. They all seemed to be rushing somewhere, speaking languages that I could scarcely understand.

"Do you have someone to receive you here?" the passenger who took care of me during the journey asked.

"Yes," I replied. "My brother-in-law is supposed to meet me."

"Good luck," he said and then disappeared in the crowd. I wish I had known his name and at least thanked him for what he did for me.

I realized in that moment that I did not remember what Harkishanbhai, my brother-in-law, looked like. I had seen him only once, many years ago, when he had come to marry my eldest sister. I hoped he would be able to find me in the midst of all those people. I found an empty spot and looked around. Out of nowhere a man approached and reached for my bag.

"Let's go!" he said.

It was my brother-in-law. No pleasantries there. Like Kaka, he was a man of few words. We got into a taxi. Not only was it my first-ever taxi ride, I had never set a foot in a car. I was thrilled. And scared.

Though I had dreamed about Mumbai all my life, and read about and seen it in the movies, the actual experience of the city was something that I could not have imagined. The sheer size of it was overwhelming. I stepped into the street and saw throngs of people of all kinds rushing to go somewhere. They spoke languages that I had never heard before and scarcely understood. And there was the deafening cacophony of traffic—cars, trams, double-decker buses, taxis, horse buggies and hand carts all making unbearable noise in their efforts to find space on the narrow streets. Street vendors hawked their wares at the top of their lungs. Even though the municipality of Mumbai declared itself a "Silence Zone," horns blared everywhere.

During my first days in Mumbai, I took long walks along the city's wide boulevards and marveled at its monuments and museums that I had seen only in films. I gazed at statues of great figures of India's past, about whom I had learned in history books. Like a kid at a candy store, I pressed my face against the windows in Mumbai's fashionable downtown, known as Fort. The windows of travel agencies were among my favorites, showing posters of exotic places like New York, London and Rome. I would stand outside famous hotels and restaurants to see if I could recognize any famous people walking in and out. I was too timid and, of course, too poor to go inside. My first ride on one of the city's crowded commuter trains was a thrill. So was my first-ever ride in an elevator.

One of the greatest pleasures for me was the ability to see—and meet—at literary gatherings some of the Gujarati writers whose books I had read. An especially memorable gathering for me took place at the renowned Cowasjee Jahangir Hall in 1957, my first year in Mumbai. Prominent Gujarati poets gathered there to recite their poetry in an extravaganza that lasted almost three hours. I was familiar with the works of nearly all the poets on the stage, though I had never seen them before. Now here they were in person, reciting their poems. I was thrilled—but still too shy to go up and talk with any of them.

Though New Delhi was the nation's capital, Mumbai was the most important city in India. One of the country's most populous, it was a metropolitan center that attracted people from all over India seeking to make careers and fortunes. It was and still is India's financial capital and home to the headquarters of major national and international banks and trading houses. Like New York, in addition to being the financial center of the country, with its vibrant performing-arts and literary scene it is the cultural capital of India. It is also known as the home of India's movie industry, second only to Hollywood in the production and distribution of movies.

It was and still is the most Westernized city in India. It also played a significant role in the political arena until 1947, when India became independent. The Congress Party that ruled independent India for many years was founded in Mumbai in 1885. Over the years, the city has been home to India's who's who, including its top industrialists, financiers, bankers, artists, actors and actresses, producers, writers, editors, publishers, educators, opinion-makers and many others. And now I was to live in their midst.

My exuberance soon evaporated beginning with my less than auspicious living situation. My sister Bhanu's family shared a crowded apartment with her in-laws. It was a large extended family like my own. My reception there was rather cool—clearly, I was not a welcome guest. There were only three small rooms. Only the front one allowed daylight in. To see anything in the other rooms, a light bulb had to be on all the time.

"Natu will sleep in the hallway," Harkishanbhai told my sister.

I surmised that I should leave the place as soon as possible, but where would I go? None of our other relatives had volunteered to take me in. I had no money to stay in a hotel, of course. The more important and urgent question, however, was where I would work. I had no idea how I would find a job. I had many distant relatives in Mumbai but no one who might help me find work. I had no college degree. I had very little familiarity with English since all my education thus far had been in Gujarati. I also had no knowledge of the city's geography. But I did have some fragile family connections. Harkishanbhai took me to Nathabhai, a distant relative who worked in Mumbai's famous Mulji Jetha cloth market. He had been a senior accountant in a textile firm for years.

"Natu has just come from Desh"—a term used to refer to provinces or native villages—"and needs a job," Kishanbhai said. "Would you please hire him?"

Nathabhai was a lanky man, poorly dressed in unwashed *kafani* and *dhoti* and a black cap with a worn-out rim. He was smoking *bidi*, a cheap local version of cigarettes. He looked me over intently, as if my future hung by a thread on his good will, but was initially hesitant. "I don't think we have a space here for one more person," he said. "We are overstaffed as it is."

Then he must have seen the hope mixed with fear in my eyes.

"Here is what we will do," he said. "Natu could come and work here and learn a few things about the trade and be of some use to us. But he will have to behave. It is hard work—and there will not be any pay, of course."

"I assure you Natu is a good boy," Kishanbhai said. "He will do whatever you ask him to. There is no need to pay him. He is staying with us." He must have figured this was a first step in getting me out of the apartment.

My very first position in Mumbai: an unpaid gofer! I had no choice in the matter. In fact, I was delighted. A job, however menial, would get me out and about. I would have a chance to see and meet people and learn more about the city. More importantly, I would learn something about the trade. I remembered Kaka's mission in sending me to Mumbai. He wanted me to learn a trade and then start my own business, make money and help him financially.

———————

"Hey, boy! Go and get me some tea!" That's how my boss greeted me my first day on the job. Sudama, the shop peon, took me by the hand. "Come with me," he said. "I will tell you where to go for tea for the boss man! He likes ginger and special spices in his tea. People at a particular tea stall know it." He took me to the stall and introduced me to the man who was making tea. "We have a new boy in the shop. He will come here to fetch the tea for the boss man. Okay?"

At the time, Mumbai was the country's chief textile manufacturing and distribution center. Until the mid-1970s, most of India's textile trade was conducted at Mumbai's Mulji Jetha cloth market. It was the largest textile bazaar of its kind in Asia. More than a hundred years old, the market had about a thousand shops doing brisk wholesale business in all sorts of textiles produced in mills all over India. If you were in the textile business, you had to be there. I had to be there because I had no choice.

When I went to work in the market, small shops nearly all the same size were strewn along its many narrow alleys. The alleys crisscrossed each other so haphazardly that it was nearly impossible to track your way back to where you started. It was very easy for a newcomer to get lost in that maze. I often did, and had a hard time finding my way back to the shop where I worked.

On one occasion Nathabhai asked me to deliver an invoice to a shop just a few alleys away. I delivered the invoice, but then could not find my way back. I was too embarrassed to ask anyone for help. Ultimately, Sudama was sent to find me. When he did, I was almost at the other end of the market. "What happened to you, Natu?" he asked. "I was looking all over for you!" On the way back, he pointed out several signposts that would lead me to the shop. Gradually I became familiar with the market's geography and learned the likes and dislikes of my superiors, but I was still not paid any salary. I had no idea how the business of buying and selling textiles was done. All I did was run errands throughout the day.

I was at the bottom of the firm's totem pole, which had owner at the top, of course. Between him and me were several layers of people, every one of whom had the right to order me around. And order they did. If any of them wanted tea or snacks, to have goods brought from a warehouse, a letter mailed, an invoice delivered or movie tickets bought, I was there. I had to show up early before everyone else to sweep and clean and get the shop ready for business. I was also the last one to leave.

In the shop hierarchy even Sudama was above me. He became my guide and guru. "Stick with me," he said. "You will be alright!" A thin man of pleasant demeanor, he had been working at the shop for years. There was no expectation that he would ever rise above his lowly position, though it did not seem to bother him. Sudama belonged to the large group of people known as *ghatis*, meaning they come from *ghats*, or mountains. They are servants who work in shops and at homes all over Mumbai. Generally uneducated, they would leave their families in the mountains and work in Mumbai doing menial household and office chores. They might visit their families once a year.

A few months of working in the market as a gofer dashed all my hopes of making it big. Like countless others from all over India, I had come to Mumbai to make my fortune. I started out full of ambition and high hopes; however, my daily existence as a gofer was full of hurts and humiliations. Many migrants like me had been there for years, but they still struggled and were as distant from their dreams as they had been the day they arrived. Given the frustrated souls all around me, what chance did I have of making millions there? At the rate I was going, I would be lucky even to get a paying job. Any thought of my making money in the market was laughable.

Frustrated and tired, I thought of returning home. But what would I do there? There were no jobs and nothing much to do. That's why Kaka had sent me to Mumbai in the first place. Also, there were his hopes that I would start making money and relieve him of his burden. But how was I to make money when I didn't even have a paying job?

Kaka kept sending letters asking how long it would be before I started my own business and made money and sent him some! He was oblivious to the fact that I had a job that did not pay and was living off of my sister.

Despite my severe frustration, I realized that I had some potential connections through relatives I met at weddings and other community gatherings. At one of the weddings, a well-dressed gentleman of approached me. "Natu," he said, "I heard that you had just come to Mumbai. Let me know how I can help you!" He introduced himself as Ratibhai and said he was a distant cousin. I had a vague recollection of his story. He told me that he was very grateful to my parents, who had taken him in and cared for him when he was orphaned at an early age. As a child, Ratibhai had lost both of his parents in a flu epidemic. He was orphaned, alone and bereft. My parents had brought him into our crowded quarters and taken care of him until he left Savarkund-la for Mumbai. All of this had occurred before I was born, so I never knew but had heard of him.

In Mumbai, Ratibhai had worked hard and educated himself, going to college and earning a business degree. After working for a few years in a trading firm, he started a business buying and selling printing equipment. Ratibhai was a self-made man. He managed to procure licenses to import printing equipment from Germany before the Indian government severely restricted imports of all kinds to promote indigenous industry. The law grandfathered in existing licenses, which became scarce commodities and could be traded. Reliable German machinery was in great demand and Ratibhai had hit the jackpot. He did not import printing equipment but just traded licenses—and became rich!

A tall, handsome man, he was always neatly dressed. Most men in the market were dressed in *dhoti*, but Ratibhai wore freshly ironed pants and a bush shirt. He always had on socks and shoes and not the slippers worn by most traders. He had an impressive bald head, much like that of Dwight Eisenhower, who had just won his second term as president of the United States.

I told Ratibhai of my frustrations with the job in the market.

"If you want to make something of your life," he said, "you should go to college"—the route he had taken. His business degree helped him get a job where he could learn a trade. Then he'd ventured out on his own. "Get out of the market," he told me. "It will ruin you!" But how? "Here is what we will do," he replied. "You teach my kids. Instead of paying a tutor, I will pay you. That will take care of your college fees and other expenses."

I knew that I could tutor Ratibhai's kids—a boy and a girl, both high-school students—and still take care of college studies; in fact, I was enthralled by the prospect. I still had to find a place to live, since I could not stay at my sister's place any longer. It would also be difficult to study in that cramped apartment.

"Stay at the community hostel," he advised. "That's where I stayed." We belong to the Kapol Bania community. Generally known as industrialists and businessmen, our community is also considered civic-minded, with a philanthropic presence in Mumbai. The rich of the community have built student hostels, educational and charitable institutions, affordable housing and sanitariums for the benefit of the community's poor. He enrolled me in a Kapol community hostel that was built to house college students from the provinces who had no place to stay in the city.

———————

But what about Kaka? My father was adamantly opposed to my going to college, as that would delay my making money for at least four years. He needed help urgently. He thought my going to college was a waste of time and money and not at all necessary for making money. Kaka had numerous examples of people like my other cousin, Amritlal, who did very well in Mumbai without ever going to college. When I told this to Ratibhai, he laughed. "Look around," he said. "For every Amritlal you will find a thousand others who are still slaving at menial jobs in the market because they don't have adequate education." I told him that Kaka would be very upset. "Don't worry," he said. "I will take care of your father."

I told Ratibhai that, because I had a strong literary bent and had dabbled in poetry while in high school, I planned to enroll in an arts college and major in literature. "Have you lost your mind?" he said. "Who is going to give you a job if you major in literature? If you want a job, get into accounting. That will get you a good job and ultimately a career." Since he was my benefactor and a shield protecting me from Kaka, I dutifully followed his advice and enrolled in Mumbai's well-known business school, Sydenham College of Commerce. I left the textile market and found living quarters at the community hostel.

Kaka was very upset and deeply disappointed. His hopes that I would soon start making money and help him were dashed. He stopped sending me letters. With Ratibhai's help, I became an aspiring and eager collegian.

Chapter 4

NO COUNTRY FOR YOUNG MEN

Within my first few weeks of study, I could see that I had committed a major blunder. In Sydenham College, as in all other Mumbai colleges, instruction was in English. I had only rudimentary knowledge of the English language and could read and write in it only perfunctorily.

College textbooks were the first books in English that I'd ever seen. All the books I'd read from the town library at home were in Gujarati, my mother tongue. Now, though I studied the college textbooks diligently, I had a hard time grasping the subject matter. I had to keep an English-Gujarati dictionary at hand as I went from page to page. Even worse, I couldn't follow professors' lectures in the classroom. Afraid that I would make a fool of myself trying to speak in English, I couldn't muster enough courage to ask a question in class.

How would I pass examinations that were all in English? I couldn't tell Ratibhai that I wanted to give up college. What would I do then? Go back to a menial job in the textile market? Leave Mumbai and go back to my hometown? None of these options was viable. My only solace was that I was not alone in this predicament. Many other students from the provinces also lacked proficiency in English. I could see them struggling, too. We were all in the same boat. The only answer for me was to sweat through the books and classes and learn English as best I could. The lack of English proficiency in classes sometimes led to humorous situations. For example, a professor of industrial organizations often talked about "fatigue" caused by long hours and night shifts. In Gujarati, the word sounded like "faatee-gyue," which meant something that had been torn apart at the seams! So every time the professor uttered the word "fatigue," we Gujarati students would burst out laughing.

When a professor learned that Deboo, a convent-educated student who often spoke in class, was sick, he said, "Poor Deboo!" I wondered why the professor called Deboo "poor" when he was in fact rich—he was chauffeured daily to the college while most students made their way on crowded trains. Basic fluency in reading and writing English would come in due course, but conversational inadequacy haunted me for a long time. Within a year I learned enough English to understand professors in class-rooms and study textbooks—with the help of a dictionary, of course. By the end of four years, I was able not only to pass my exams but to do so with good grades.

My college years were rewarding but not much fun. Most mornings I was busy tutoring Ratibhai's children. That helped pay for my tuition and hostel fees. But I was always short of money and had almost none for incidental expenses. I could rarely afford to go to the college canteen for a snack. I bought no new clothes or shoes, simply making do with what I'd brought from home. Because I was new to Mumbai, I needed to make new friends. My raggedy footwear and rumpled dress, inadequate conversational skills, unfamiliarity with the Mumbai scene—all of this made it difficult to initiate conversations, particularly with sophisticated students from Mumbai and other cities. Many of my classmates were from Mumbai and some were educated at convent schools, so they were proficient in English and knew their way around the city. They would go to cricket matches, watch Hollywood movies, wear fancy clothes, smoke cigarettes and eat at expensive restaurants. A very few even had girlfriends. One could easily distinguish them from us shy, shabbily dressed provincials.

Soon after joining the college, I noticed that there was a Gujarati literary wall where students could post poetry and other writings. Everything on the wall was hand-written. After a few months, I gathered enough courage to approach a student who was pasting new material on the wall and introduce myself. I told him in Gujarati, "I write poetry and would like to put some poems on the board. How do I do it?"

"Give me your poems," he replied. "I will put them up. I am the editor. My name is Navin Jarecha."

We quickly bonded. Though Jarecha also came from the provinces, he had none of my inhibitions. Always sure of himself, he moved about the college halls freely and even dropped unannounced into the office of professor of Gujarati Murli Thakur. He exuded confidence and dressed smartly in a traditional Indian *kafani lengha* dress that was always ironed and, on his feet, wore fancy *chappals*, a kind of slipper. He too wrote poetry. At lunchtime we would share our poems and I would share his lunch! He was lodging with his sister in a distant Mumbai suburb, and she would send him off daily with lunch, a *tiffin*.

Through Jarecha I met another student poet, Meghnad Bhatt, the son of Harishchandra Bhatt, a distinguished Gujarati poet whose work I knew. The three of us became good friends and read each other's poetry daily. Jarecha and Bhatt played significant roles in my life. It is because of the former that I migrated to the U.S. And it was the latter who helped me get my first paying job.

Bhatt passed away in his early middle years. Jarecha became a dear friend and remains so to this day, about which more later. I have always marveled at my chance encounter with him and how it changed my life profoundly for the better!

My poems were written in sonnet form and in difficult Sanskrit meters that I learned from Mukundbhai during my high-school days. At college, professor Thakur saw my poems and asked to see me. "Gandhi," he said, "you should keep writing. I see a poet in you. Please don't give up on poetry!" His encouragement helped me to feel good about myself for the first time. His was the only professorial contact outside of the classroom I had during my college years.

The rest of the professors were for the most part deeply disappointing. They would come to class, lecture for about an hour and then not be seen until the next class. There was no classroom discussion between students and professors, no questions asked or answered. And there was rarely any contact outside the classroom. Nor was there any attempt on their part to see whether students understood what they were teaching. It was all a one-way street. This was typical of Indian colleges—students learned little if anything in the classroom.

I remember one professor who yawned frequently during his lectures. He was a prominent regional writer who stayed up late to do his writing—thus his frequent yawning. Students used to guess about the number of pages he had written the night before based on his yawns in class. We had a professor of English who accomplished the major feat of making George Bernard Shaw's *Pygmalion* seem boring! Not until I saw the movie *My Fair Lady*, starring Audrey Hepburn and Rex Harrison, did I realize what the play was all about. Some professors wrote books that were adopted as textbooks, generating substantial side income for them. On close examination, it was clear that they did little original research or writing but instead loosely plagiarized American or British textbooks. There was no rigorous research requirement or "publish-or-perish" regime for acquiring academic tenure, no evaluations by students of professors' classroom effectiveness. Tenure was usually granted on the basis of seniority. Once tenured, the professor, good or bad, was in until mandatory retirement age.

Worse yet, their knowledge of the subject matter was theoretical and dated. Most seemed to have memorized their lectures out of their own college textbooks. Hardly any independent thinking or research took place. Nearly all parroted what they had read in books published in the West.

Even professors of accounting who were practicing chartered accountants never brought real-life cases to class to illustrate a point. They simply showed us how to record journal entries and tally a balance sheet, and that was that. The idea that there was a larger purpose to accounting was alien to them. They were glorified bookkeepers and taught us to be like them—bookkeepers! No one attempted to link classroom teaching to the outside world. Current affairs were never discussed in or out of the classroom. During the late 1950s and early '60s, India was going through five-year plans to chart its economic development. Yet nary a word about that was mentioned in an economics class! Though we were students of commerce, we hardly knew what Indian commerce was. We knew how to answer the questions on our exams. The answers were in the guidebooks that we memorized and faithfully reproduced. So we passed the exams and duly became commerce graduates!

———————

Equipped with an accounting degree from the best commerce college in India, I could not find a job in Mumbai! I had high hopes that I would quickly be hired by a big bank or insurance company. Those hopes were soon dashed. The brutal reality was that there simply were not enough jobs to go around for a burgeoning population of jobseekers. There was no help from the college, either. Unlike American colleges and universities, there were no placement bureaus or job counselors advising graduating students on how to go about placing themselves in good jobs. No potential employers came to the college campus to hire the best and brightest. It was all a buyer's market. As graduates, we were on our own.

———————

My college friends Jarecha and Meghnad graduated two years ahead of me. Bhatt had some high-level connections at the headquarters of Mafatlal Industries, a well-known industrial house with numerous textile mills in its fold, and was quickly hired there. The fact that he could get such a plum job gave me hope that I could do the same when I graduated. Once, when I asked Jarecha over coffee how his job search was going, he calmly said, "I am not looking for job. I am getting ready to go America for an MBA!" That took my breath away! I knew his family relatively well and couldn't comprehend how he could afford to go to America. It seemed an outlandish enterprise for someone in his moderate economic condition. "Did you win a lottery or what?" I asked. "Or are you that rich and I just did not know it?"

He explained the situation to me. His father, Mafatlal, was of modest means but had high hopes of sending his son to America. He was a teacher in a small town in Gujarat but also an enterprising community activist and organizer. He had a reputation for selfless service. Mafatlal had come to Mumbai to raise funds for Jarecha. He approached the community's rich barons and asked them to fund his son's education abroad. He explained that times had changed and the caste needed to emphasize higher education and foreign studies. His son would be the first in his community to go to the U.S. That would encourage others to follow his example. Indeed, once there, Jarecha would facilitate others' going to America.

Given his reputation for probity and integrity, Mafatlal was able to convince the community leaders, who banded together and raised enough money for Jarecha's studies in the U.S. Once the money was secured, Jarecha got busy preparing to go to America. During the '50s and '60s, going to America was still a mysterious adventure to Indians. Even more mysterious was obtaining admission to one of the thousands of universities and colleges spread across the vast continental nation. There were consultants in Mumbai who, for a sizable fee, would help aspiring students sort out such issues as which university would be most suitable, how likely would a student be to get admitted there, whether it was affordable, how to get a scholarship and other aid, what subjects a student should pursue, what the weather was like where the university was located, and so on.

Jarecha found a consultant who quickly got him admitted to Atlanta University. A travel agent helped him secure a passport, visa, appropriate clothing and boat passage to New York. All of this happened at lightning speed. Things move fast in India when you have money. The appointed day of his departure came. A farewell ceremony was held at a fashionable restaurant where the bigwigs of his community who footed the bill for Jarecha's overseas education crowded onto the stage, pushing the guest of honor into the corner. I was invited at Jarecha's insistence. Could such an event ever be held for me?

I went to Mumbai's Ballard Pier to bid Jarecha farewell as his boat set sail. It was a cargo ship with a few passenger quarters. Jarecha invited me up to his cabin. I was in awe. I had never been on a ship before. Walking back from the pier, I began dreaming of going to the U.S myself. If Jarecha could go, surely there was hope for me. However, I soon realized the difference between our situations. While his father had worked hard to raise funds for him to go America, my father was eagerly waiting for me to send him money.

––––––––––

It was two more years before I finished my studies. As soon as I graduated, Kaka began sending letters again inquiring how long it would take for me to get a job and send him money. So I got busy. I would start my day poring over the want ads in the *Times of India* looking for job openings for commerce graduates. For the few such openings I found, I would begin applications with "Respected Sir." I had no typewriter—even if I had one, I didn't know how to type. And there were no Xerox machines at the time in India. So I handwrote each application in legible letters and walked to the *Times* building downtown to drop them in a huge shiny box outside the building. My carefully crafted and beautifully handwritten applications usually generated no positive response. It was as if they had disappeared into some giant black hole. Foreign companies, usually American or British, sometimes responded with form letters containing a polite *no*. After months of applying, I still had no job.

A hundred or so applications into the process, I realized that was not the way to get a job. Yes, I obtained a few interviews, but the result was still the same: Unless I had someone inside pulling strings for me, there would be no job no matter how well qualified I might be or how good I'd been in interviews. My dilemma was how to find someone to pull those strings. Sadly, I did not know anyone who could help. The only people I knew were my college friends Jarecha and Bhatt. Jarecha was already in the U.S., but Bhatt was still in town and handsomely employed at Mafatlal Industries. I wondered if he could pull strings for me at Mafatlal.

When I approached him, he bluntly told me that there were no possibilities in his office, but one of his colleagues had just left to join Thomson & Taylor, a new American-style department store that had recently opened. The store was looking for accountants. He might put a word in on my behalf to his friend Mehta. He warned me that the salary would be low, but it would be a start. I pleaded him to do so. I rushed to see Mehta at the store and told him that Bhatt had sent me. After a brief conversation, Mehta casually said, "You can start tomorrow." I was hired as a junior accountant with a monthly salary of Rs.150 or about $22 at the then-prevailing exchange rate. Today it would be more like $3! Ultimately, what my laboriously crafted hundred-plus applications could not accomplish was done through a friendly call and a cursory interview.

———

Getting a job was half the battle for me in Mumbai. The other half was finding a place to live. As soon as I graduated, I had to leave the hostel. Since I did not want to impose on my sister again, where could I go? A group of us departing boarders banded together and rented a flat that was available only for a few months. It was a stopgap measure, but a breather that I could use. I had no other place to go and no money for a *pughree*, a large chunk of money that had to be paid upfront even to rent a place. I gladly moved into the flat with four other people, but knew that I would soon have to find a place of my own.

After a few months, time had come to move out. But where to go? One of us came back with a solution. If we joined the law school, we could live in its dorm. So we rushed to Government Law College and applied for admission. Fees were nominal. We quickly got in and asked for residence in its dormitory. Unfortunately, it was not what we had expected and was far away in Bandra, a Mumbai suburb. They were old dilapidated army barracks that were converted into dorm rooms, in such bad shape that we all had to sign papers saying that we stayed there at our own risk. The college would not be held responsible if a roof were to collapse and we got hurt! Yet what choice did we have? After a month, as we were having a leisurely lunch one Sunday in the cafeteria, a peon rushed to tell us that a barrack had collapsed. We ran to see which one and if anyone was hurt. Unfortunately it was ours. Soon we moved to another barrack hoping that it would be sturdier and safer.

Mumbai was a Mecca for jobseekers from all over India. As a result, it had become one of the most populous and crowded cities in the world. Its official population was around five million in 1960, in 2017 around 21 million, though the unofficial count would be far greater. As hundreds of new inhabitants arrived daily, there was no way to geographically expand the city to accommodate them. Mumbai is essentially an island. It could expand somewhat north and east but was bound on the south and west by the Arabian Sea.

People lived in far suburbs and commuted long distances, spending an hour or two in crowded trains each way every day to and from work since most jobs were in the south of the city. During the early '60s there was a tremendous shortage of housing. How would I find enough *pughree* money to rent a place in the crowded city? There were no 30-year mortgages or other installment lending plans in India at the time.

———————

After a few months working at Thomson & Taylor, I realized that the department store had a limited future in Mumbai. The city was not yet ready for an American-style store. So I decided to search again for a better, more stable job. The store was run by a young man who had just returned from the U.S. Armed with an MBA, he thought he could start a revolution in retail in India. He dreamed of starting a chain of stores like Macy's in major Indian cities. He convinced his rich father to invest a large sum of money to buy an existing pharmacy and convert it into a department store. Keeping the store's books, I could see that this ship would not sail far. While the American-trained MBA was preparing fancy flowcharts and rosy scenarios in his secluded office upstairs, store workers downstairs were running the store into the ground. Pharmacists were pilfering expensive medicines daily with the connivance of security guards who got a cut of the loot. The staff rationalized this thievery the way workers in some expensive restaurants do: It was the only way they could supplement their low wages. Besides, the owner would never miss the stolen items anyway.

In my desperation to leave the store, I made two false starts—first deciding to become a life-insurance agent and next taking a job as a journalist. Within a week of embarking on each of those careers, I realized that they were ill-advised steps and quickly returned to the store. Selling life insurance is a difficult enterprise in India, where it is family tradition to take care of the elderly. Moreover, people are generally fatalistic. In my first day on the job, my supervisor at the agency suggested that I draw up a list of friends and relatives and visit each one to explain the benefits of buying life insurance.

Nathabhai was the first person on my list whom I approached. Early one Sunday, I appeared at his door. I wanted to catch him before he went out. He was surprised to see me so early and without any notice. Alarmed, he asked: "Who died? Is it your father?" Telephones were not yet common, and he thought I must have bad news to share to have shown up so early on a Sunday morning. I told him there was no bad news, that I had come instead to share good news about buying life insurance. Then I plunged into the sales pitch that the agency supervisor had taught me. He listened carefully, then he shook his head and said, "When you left the market to go to college, I thought you would amount to something. You'd work for a bank or some big company. But here you are trying to sell insurance to unsuspecting people on a Sunday morning. What is wrong with you?"

I was taken aback by his bluntness but got his point. That was the end of my one-week career as an insurance agent. Luckily, I had not resigned from the store. When I returned there, my kindly supervisor, Mehta, asked why I had not shown up for a week.

"We were all worried about you, Gandhi! Were you sick? How are you feeling now?"

"I'm sorry, sir," I said. "I was quite sick and had no way to reach you! I do not have easy access to a telephone."

"Don't worry," he said. "Just don't work too hard!"

It also took only about a week for me to realize that I was not meant to be a journalist. Sure, I had a flair for writing and was quite familiar with Gujarati literature. Given this, I thought that I would do well. I approached the editor of a major Gujarati newspaper and told him that I would like to be a journalist. He said, "I have no opening at the newspaper, but could use you on the staff of a Gujarati monthly that I am editing on my own." I readily accepted the job but soon learned from other staff members that the editor tended to exploit people who worked for him. Indeed, they were surprised that I would even consider working there since I already had a commerce degree. They said that I could easily qualify for a good job at a major bank or large American company where my salary and benefits would be substantial. Pondering the working conditions and the shabby environment of the office, not to mention the meager salary with no benefits, the glamour of being a journalist quickly wore off.

I went back to Thomson & Taylor, where again I thankfully had not resigned. I made up a story to account for my week-long absence and resumed my daily routine. But at the same time, I continued to search for a better job. I resumed applying for jobs on an almost daily basis despite my earlier experience with the application process. First thing every morning I looked at the *Times* want-ad section in search of openings that fit my background. Even though responses that I received were generally discouraging, I kept sending applications.

One day I got a response not in the form of a letter but a personal visit. A stranger showed up at the store asking for me. He introduced himself and told me that he would like to talk about an application I had sent a few weeks earlier for an accounting job in the local office of a South Indian textile mill. Among all of the applications that I was sending out, I had forgotten this one.

The man took me out for coffee and I asked him to tell me about the job. He said a mill agency needed a Gujarati accountant who could keep books in English. The majority partner in the firm was from Andhra Pradesh, a state in the south of India, who had little understanding of Gujarati, the language in which the books were kept. He wanted the books to be kept in English and auditable. A Gujarati junior partner was keeping the books and was not always diligent about it. They were in such disarray that they couldn't be audited. Because of this, it was difficult for the senior partner to know whether the firm was making a profit and, if so, how much.

My visitor, Bhanubhai, told me the senior partner had seen my application and résumé. A smallish man who snuffed tobacco while talking, Bhanubhai was a neighbor of the senior partner. "If you want the job," he said, "it is yours. You could start immediately!" He offered me almost twice the money I made at the store. The only problem was that taking the job meant going back to the Mulji Jetha market, which I had left five years earlier. I told Bhanubhai that I had not had a particularly happy experience working there before. He quickly said, "Gandhi, your office would actually be outside the market. You will be the chief accountant. You will no longer be a gofer. Indeed, you will have a gofer of your own to run errands for you!"

The most attractive part of the new job was that its one-room office had a bathroom and a facility to sleep in overnight. I apprised Bhanubhai of my predicament: I was renting a flat that I would have to vacate soon and would have no place to stay. Would the mill agency agree to my sleeping in the office until I found something suitable? "Don't worry," Bhanubhai said. "I will make that happen. Will you take the job?" Without a moment's hesitation I said, "Yes!"

I was immensely relieved. I quickly signed up at a nearby community kitchen that provided two meals daily for a reasonable fee. Though I agreed to take the job, I did not resign from Thomson & Taylor. I took a week's leave to try out the new job. I had learned my lesson; if this job did not work out, I wanted to go back to the store. The senior partner was so eager to have me work there that he bent over backwards to accommodate all my needs. The junior partner, on the other hand, viewed me with a suspicious eye.

After my evening meal following my first day on the job, when I returned to the office to sleep I found two elderly gentlemen also getting ready to make their beds. They were surprised to see me. I explained that I had permission from the boss to sleep in the office. They didn't like the idea of sharing the space with me, but had no choice.

Besides, I told them, they needn't worry—my arrangement was temporary and I was actively looking for a place to live. I knew, however, that it would take a long time for me to accumulate enough *pughree* money to rent my own place.

Given the severe housing shortage in Mumbai, it was quite common for men to leave their families behind in the provinces and go back once a year to visit them for a week or two. My fellow office boarders were in their late 50s and had come to Mumbai as teenagers. They had gotten married during their occasional visits back home and had children. But they had lived apart from their families all their adult lives. Upon retirement, they would go back to their villages. Hearing their stories, I slept only fitfully for several nights, fearing that I might fall into the same trap. Would that be my fate?

Occasionally, the two boarders would invite me to accompany them to Falkland Road, Mumbai's red-light district. I had seen references to it in a poem about Mumbai, but that was all I knew of it. I had no desire to go there on my own, of course. And if I went with my fellow boarders, I feared that my superiors might find out about my nighttime adventure and I could lose my job, which meant that I would also lose my place to sleep. Besides, I had plans to get married that I had not yet shared with anyone.

Chapter 5

ROMANCE TO REALITY

While reading all of those romance novels in the attic of our house in Savarkundla, I created for myself an alternative universe in which lovely girls fell madly in love with me. I saw many such romances in Bollywood movies. There was little chance for romance in Savarkundla.

There were only three girls in our high school. They would come to a class full of boys, leave with the teacher and retreat to the girls' lounge. There were no exchanges between boys and girls beyond a stolen glance or two. Social taboos prohibited any interaction. In my 17 years in Savarkundla, I never spoke with a girl other than my sisters, and even those conversations were cursory.

One reason for going to Mumbai was to satisfy my intense curiosity about girls. I had watched young men and women fall in love in Bollywood movies—holding hands and strolling freely together on beaches and in the streets and going to movies and restaurants. Filled with the youthful urge to seek the company of young women, I wondered if Mumbai would bring romance into my life.

Yet after four years of college in the big metropolis, I had not had a single girlfriend or even a female acquaintance. I was so inhibited by my lack of urban sophistication that I'd never approached a girl. I also had no money to take a girl out to a fine restaurant or movie.

Dating was still basically nonexistent in Mumbai. Few girls enrolled in commerce college, and those who did sat segregated up front. They were generally rich, convent-educated girls who spoke fluent English. Given my poor conversational English, I lacked the courage to go near them. There were hardly any girls with whom I could converse in my native language; Gujarati girls mostly went to arts colleges.

To alleviate my loneliness, I often went to my uncle's place in Vile Parle, a Mumbai suburb. He was my mother's brother and I called him Mama. He and his wife, Mami, had special affection for me. I was always welcome in their two-room apartment. Mama had had a hard time settling down in Mumbai. After several false starts, he got a clerk's position at a fountain-pen manufacturing company owned by a rich man of our caste.

He was also able to secure a two-room flat in an apartment building built for needy caste members. Next to Mama and Mami was the Vora family. There were three sisters and three brothers; the eldest brother was married and had three children. The entire extended family lived in a crowded, two-room place—one of 12 two-room apartments in the building.

All of the residents belonged to our Kapol Bania caste and lived in extended families. Doors were always open during the day. People moved in and out of each other's apartments without hesitation. There was very little privacy. Conversations could easily be heard from adjoining apartments.

During my frequent visits to Mama's place, I developed a liking for Nalini, the youngest of the Vora sisters. She was of average height and had a brown complexion. Though perhaps not beautiful by Bollywood standards, she was nice looking. Moreover, she showed interest in me and was eager to talk. She was my first-ever female acquaintance outside of family, and I always looked forward to seeing her. Pretty soon Nalini became the reason for my visits to Mama's place.

Our conversations were never one-on-one but always in the company of others. Every time I went to Mama's place, Nalini would come on some pretext or other and smile at me. As I left she would say, as if speaking on behalf of everyone there, "Natu, when will we see you again?" Nalini's parents had passed away years earlier, and the responsibility for seeing that she married belonged to her elder brother, Vajubhai, who had seen me often at Mama's place. We spoke occasionally and developed some familiarity. He was actively looking for an appropriate mate for his sister. In time, Vajubhai approached Mama and proposed that Nalini and I be married. Mama broached the subject with me.

"Yes," I replied instantly, "but please tell Vajubhai I do not have a room in Mumbai—I sleep in the office!"

"Oh," Mama responded, "he knows that. But he still would like to go ahead. What do you think?"

"Okay," I said. "Tell him I am ready to get engaged but not to be married yet. First I want to have a good job and get a permanent place to live."

———

Nalini's family considered me an ideal prospect for her. I was a commerce graduate with a job, while Nalini had hardly finished high school. To them I was a big catch. Nalini had no say in the matter, but I assumed she was happy about the arrangement. She later told me that she agreed because she wanted to get away from her elder brother and his family. To them she was a burden. In India's age-old arranged-marriage system, marriages are for families. The bride and bridegroom are just the vehicles by which the families are united. Their consent is not always sought, nor does it matter.

Given the shortage of eligible boys in India, a girl's family is nearly always looking for a good young man. As soon as it locates one, the elder of the family approaches the boy's family and proposes marriage. If the boy's family—particularly his father—agrees, then the engagement is finalized.

The marriage follows intricate negotiations about the dowry. If the girl does not bring the agreed-upon dowry or it is judged to be not enough, the young bride is punished when she goes to live in the in-law's house. In rural India, the punishment could be as extreme as bride-burning, disguised as suicide. Though illegal in any form, this sort of bridal punishment is still going on in India.

In our case, Vajubhai was acting as the family elder and Nalini's surrogate father in approaching Mama and proposing her hand in marriage to me. Mama was acting as a surrogate father for me since Kaka was in Savarkundla and took little interest in what I was doing in Mumbai except to see whether I was making enough money to support him financially. So Nalini and I became engaged. It seemed so easy and natural.

Those were the days of my high patriotic fervor and Gandhian simplicity. I was a minimalist and a reformer, too. While millions were going hungry, how could I spend money on a wedding feast? After all, from our limited contacts, I believed that Nalini cared for me and I cared for her. And that was all that mattered—the rituals and formalities of a traditional wedding ceremony seemed superficial. I thought it would be a minor revolutionary act to dispense with all that and settle instead for a civil ceremony. Since I was a reformer, I refused a dowry in any form, what I considered a retrograde tradition that should be abolished.

After the engagement was finalized, Vajubhai had second thoughts about delaying the marriage. He suggested that if I could not get a place by the time Nalini and I were married, she could go to Savarkundla and stay with my parents. It was not at all uncommon for young brides to stay with in-laws in the provinces until their husbands were able to settle down in Mumbai. After all, I was living with boarders at the office whose wives were living in villages with their in-laws.

Vajubhai pushed for an early wedding date. I informed Baa and Kaka of the impending marriage and told them that I wanted to forgo the traditional Hindu ceremony and associated festivities, including the feast, in favor of a simple civil wedding. So spoke that modern man and reformer in me! Besides, I had no money and no help in Mumbai to arrange an elaborate wedding anyway.

Back in the village, my parents did not celebrate. Kaka was deeply disappointed in my inability to support him financially. He showed no interest in my engagement or wedding. Baa was very unhappy that I wanted to forgo a traditional Hindu wedding ceremony and have a civil ceremony that would only involve signing a few documents.

And that is what I decided—no horse for the bridegroom, no wedding procession with women singing, no band declaring the arrival of the groom and his party, and certainly no feast at which parents would bask in glory following the wedding. I even refused to dress up in special clothing for the wedding. I wanted to get married in plain, everyday clothes—a simple *kafani lengha*, loose Indian shirt and pajama-like pants. I invited no friends and only a few relatives.

Kaka was indifferent, but Baa was deeply hurt and unhappy. She wanted her eldest son to be married amidst the fanfare of a lavish wedding ceremony. She wanted to bask in the motherly glory of her first son's wedding. This should have been a great festive occasion in her otherwise lackluster life. She refused to attend the wedding. As it turned out, it was best that she didn't show up. The day's difficulties might have foretold what was to come later in my married life.

———————

Still living in the office, I got up early on the morning of May 6, 1962. I wanted to get to the bathroom, bathe and get ready before my fellow boarders rushed in. Because I dressed normally, they did not have any idea of what was going to happen that day. Wanting to keep wedding guests to minimum, I hadn't told them about or invited them to the ceremony. I had to get an early start to meet the wedding party at a relative's place in Matunga, a distant suburb. From there we would all go to Nalini's place in a van. When I went to the train station, the platform was bustling with people trying to beat the rush hour. I missed the first train to Matunga because it was so crowded that I could not get in. I couldn't let the second train go, so I pushed through the crowd of rushing people, causing my clothes to be rumpled. I didn't want to be late for my own wedding!

I got to the relative's place on time, but there was no van to take us the 15 miles to Nalini's place where the wedding papers were to be signed. I set out on foot to look for it. There were no cellphones in those days. Luckily, I was not dressed in special wedding garb, or I would have looked silly searching frantically for the van in Mumbai's chaotic morning rush hour. At last I found it and raged at the driver. "You gave me the wrong address!" he shot back.

Worse yet, it was also the wrong kind of van! I thought I had booked one that reasonably would pass as a luxury vehicle in India. Instead, it turned out to be a small, beaten-up bus used to transport rural people long distances. It did not even have enough seats. The bridegroom and a few men stood while the bus tried to make its way through Mumbai's nightmarish traffic, the driver honking all the way, which took the place of the celebratory music that usually accompanies wedding processions in India. Nalini's family was worried that something bad had happened and began searching for the van at their end.

We finally reached our destination some two hours late. Instead of being astride a horse, the bridegroom was walking, all disheveled and not dressed ceremonially. The court officer there to officiate the wedding was unnerved by our tardiness. He had other appointments that day. Neighbors were curious about what was happening: They had never seen so many people coming to the building together at one time. We were eventually all gathered in my in-laws' cramped, two-room quarters. A traditional wedding in India involves elaborate ceremonies that usually take days—my two sisters' weddings had taken three days each. My court-sanctioned civil ceremony was over in a matter of few minutes. That hot day in 1962, Nalini and I signed a few papers and were wed.

Nalini later told me that she was pleased to marry me because it got her out of her brother's unwelcoming place. Of course, she didn't have much choice in the matter. Vajubhai had decided that she should get married to me, and that was that. He wanted her out of his place. Now he had one less person to worry about. But what about me? Why did I get married? It was not love in the modern sense. Nalini and I knew each other only superficially and certainly not intimately. We'd never had a serious conversation about anything, much less about getting married. I had never touched her, much less kissed her. So why? I guess it must have been my intense, youthful desire for female companionship and need to quench my sexual thirst. I also thought, given my precarious financial situation, that no one else would be interested in me. Whatever the case, I got married, one of those impetuous things that generally only the young and immature do. In my cockiness, I thought that I could manage it. In fact, it was akin to the way the distinguished poet T.S. Eliot described his own rash decision to marry: "Youthful indiscretion."

For our short honeymoon, Nalini and I took the train to Matheran, a hill station near Mumbai. Kaka, who had come to the wedding alone, took the train back to Savarkundla. He was not pleased that I was "wasting" money on a honeymoon. But I had read so much about honeymoons in romantic novels that I was not going to pass up this once-in-lifetime opportunity.

There was another, more practical reason for going to Matheran. We had no place of our own to stay overnight in Mumbai. I couldn't take Nalini to the office and spend our wedding night there with other boarders.

On the train to Matheran, Nalini and I looked at each other and did not quite know what to do. Until then I had never touched a girl, much less kissed one. To release my sexual tension, I used to go to Hollywood movies. Indian censors didn't allow kissing scenes in Bollywood movies. To see those beautiful actresses being kissed by dashing heroes was a treat. Clark Gable, Humphrey Bogart, Cary Grant and Marlon

Brando were doing all the kissing for me. Every Sunday afternoon, I became a Gable-like lover. I would line up at Mumbai's Metro cinema for a matinee. There I once saw *Pillow Talk*, starring Doris Day and Rock Hudson. Following the show, I learned that a sequel, *Lover Come Back*, was to play next, so I took a little lunch break and lined up again for the sequel. I never had enough of Kim Novak in *Vertigo*, Grace Kelly in *Rear Window* and *Dial M for Murder*, or Eva Marie Saint in *North by Northwest*. I saw each of these movies several times!

Now that I was married, I could touch and kiss a girl. Our honeymoon was a welcome respite from the harrowing reality of Mumbai. For a few days, I forgot my problems and had a wonderful time with my new wife. Being a hopeless romantic, I brought a book of love poems to read aloud to her. Poor Nalini. She had little interest in romance. Being utterly practical, she worried about what would happen to her when our brief honeymoon was over.

Since we had no place in Mumbai, we had agreed that Nalini should go to Savarkundla and stay with my parents until I found a place in Mumbai. My family members were total strangers to her. Nevertheless, we left for Savarkundla the day we returned from Matheran. On the train to Savarkundla, I was quite apprehensive about the reception we would get at home, especially since Baa was quite hurt by the way I got married. I had deprived her of all the joy an Indian mother would experience on her first son's wedding. My fears were unfounded. As soon as we saw Baa, we bowed down to touch her feet and show our respect. She hugged us both and started crying. These were tears of joy. At last, there was something joyous in her life. "Son," she said, "you brought me a *bahu*"–a daughter-in-law–"a lovely *bahu*! How lucky I am."

All the traditional Hindu rites and rituals that we had avoided in the civil cere-mony in Mumbai were imposed upon us by Baa. A Hindu priest was brought in to perform them. There was also a feast of the sort that I had ruled out in Mumbai. I couldn't say no to any of these. I didn't want to hurt her any further. Besides, now I was in her territory and she was in charge. After a week at home, I was relieved that Baa seemed mollified.

She welcomed Nalini with open arms and showered much attention on her as the first daughter-in-law in the family. Baa took Nalini to meet neighbors and relatives, telling them, "Look, Natu brought me a *bahu*!" With Nalini's arrival in the household, Baa's status was enhanced. She was now a mother-in-law–a big deal in a traditional Indian household. Now Baa had someone who would look up to her, follow her guid-ance and relieve her of daily household chores.

The day before I was to leave for Mumbai, Nalini cried and cried. "When will I see you again?" she asked. "When will you call me back to Mumbai?" I assured her that I would find a place for us to live there soon and her stay in Savarkundla would be only a few short months long. I understood my new bride's dismay and disappointment. She would have to make her new life without her husband, in the midst of people whom she had never met in a place that she had never been. Beyond that, she had to live with no electricity, no running water, no paved streets and without many other things that she was used to in Mumbai. I was the only connection that she had with this strange new world, and I was leaving her there. All I could do was tell her that I would try to get her back to Mumbai soon. But I knew it to be a false promise. I told Kaka the same thing, since he was still eager to see our family settled in Mumbai. Despite my promise, I knew all too well that it would be nearly impossible for me to find accommodations anytime soon in Mumbai. What had I done?

On the train back to Mumbai, the reality began to dawn on me. I had been single and carefree and didn't have to worry about anyone else. But now I was married and responsible for Nalini. How could I even think of getting married while still without a good job and place to live? Even if I had those, what was the rush? Why did I not wait? But I was only 22. What did I know of life then? Had I not rushed into marrying Nalini so soon, my life would have been on a different trajectory. I could have avoided most of my harrowing Mumbai problems. Ratibhai was disappointed that I had not leveraged my eligibility as a desirable marriage prospect into a residential flat or partnership in a business. In fact, that is what he had done. He'd married a rich landlord's daughter, and his father-in-law instantly provided a two-room flat in one of his buildings in a desirable Mumbai suburb. Ratibhai didn't have to pay any *pughree*. Another cousin of mine was able to get a partnership in his father-in-law's business. Beyond all of that, Nalini had hardly finished high school. A college-educated girl might have been of some financial help. Nalini came from a poor family and required my support. Now my fear was that I would end up just like my fellow boarders at the office, visiting a wife and children left behind in the province for a week or two once a year.

How would I cope? I couldn't sleep for days and felt trapped.

My financial situation in Mumbai was precarious. I was making about 200 rupees a month, roughly $30 in those days and about $4 in today's currency. It was not enough to live on in Mumbai, much less to save and send money home. I would never be able to do what Kaka expected. He wanted me to take care of the family by getting everyone settled in Mumbai, the way my cousin Amritlal had. The more I worked in Mumbai, the more I realized that I would never make that kind of money without going into some sort of business. But how did one get into business? I had no knack for business of any kind, nor any entrepreneurial skills or zeal. As an accountant, my day was spent keeping books and working with auditors. That kept me away from what I needed to know most about doing business—buying and selling and getting to know suppliers and customers. By getting an accounting degree, I had acquired a sort of "trained incapacity." I was incapable of doing anything except keeping books. To go into business, one also needed seed money. I had none. But how could I explain this to Kaka, who kept sending me letters asking for money?

Back in Mumbai, I was a changed man. While before I was free and full of enthusiasm, going places and visiting people, now I shied away. I even stopped going to Mama's place. Though Nalini was hundreds of miles away, I felt her presence all the time. I knew that I had to somehow find a room somewhere in Mumbai so she could come back. Nalini's letters arrived almost every other week. She wanted to know how long it would be before she could return to Mumbai and stay with me. Unfortunately, I had no answer. I fully understood her disappointment. After all, it was not too much for a young bride to ask to stay with her husband after the wedding.

More than a year passed. She was even more desperate to join me. During that time, I visited her only once. We both wondered what sort of married life it was in which the couple is separated soon after wedding. I felt profoundly guilty, but what could I do? Nalini came up with an idea. Rich benefactors of our caste had built sanatoriums near Mumbai's Chowpaty Beach, as well as in distant suburbs, to temporarily relieve sick people of the damp and dirty air of the city's congested areas. How about living together temporarily in a Mumbai sanitarium? Some of her relatives in similar straits had used this alternative. These facilities, however, were available only for three months at a time, and only to those who were certifiably sick and had permanent living quarters in Mumbai. Getting a doctor's certificate was no problem—that was always available for a price. But how to prove that we had living quarters in Mumbai? For that we convinced Nalini's elder sister Tara to apply for us, as she had a one-room apartment in one of Mumbai's most congested areas. She obliged, and we were admitted to our first sanitarium for three months in a distant Mumbai suburb. Now Nalini could join me in Mumbai.

We agreed that I would meet her halfway at Viramgam Station. This would be our first time living together in Mumbai as husband and wife. I was quite excited. At the appointed day and time, I reached Viramgam and looked for her. To my surprise I found my father and Manu, one of my younger brothers, standing there with Nalini. For a moment, I thought they had come to Viramgam only for a ride and would go back to Savarkundla on a return train. I was wrong.

"Manu will go with you to Mumbai," my father said.

Not quite understanding what I'd just heard, I asked "What?"

"Yes," he responded. "Manu will go with you."

"But you do not understand, Kaka," I said. "This sanitarium arrangement is temporary—it is only for three months. I don't know what will happen next. Nalini might have to go back to Savarkundla!"

"In that case, Manu will come back, too," Kaka said. "But you will take him with you now."

"But what will he do there?" I asked.

I didn't want to take my brother to Mumbai. I was looking forward to being with Nalini alone. We had yet to enjoy living together as a married couple. I didn't want an interloper with us. From Kaka's perspective, though, there was nothing wrong with sending Manu to Mumbai to stay with me until he found something on his own. It was the same way he pushed me out of Savarkundla and told my sister to take me into her cramped place in Mumbai. It didn't matter whether my sister and her in-laws liked the idea of my living with them or not. Similarly, it didn't matter to Kaka whether I liked Manu living with us or not. I didn't. But it was my duty to take him to Mumbai and help him settle. In fact, it was normal to expect those who were better off to help relatives in need. But I was not better off and in a very problematic situation myself.

"You don't understand," Kaka said. "I am tired of your brother. I can't manage him anymore. You will find something for him to do in Mumbai."

Not grasping Kaka's dilemma with Manu, I asked: "What about his schooling? How could he miss school for three months?"

"Well," my father responded, "he has dropped out of school. And he is not going back. He's just hanging around the house. He is a nuisance to your mother. You will have to take him to Mumbai and keep him there!"

I was furious. Kaka was pushing Manu on to me. "Okay," I said. "I will take him—but not today. I'll take him only when I have secured a permanent place to live."

Kaka suddenly broke down and wept. I was taken aback.

Nalini intervened. "Okay," she said. "We will take Manu with us. Don't worry, Kaka."

I relented, too, and could see that Kaka was at the end of his rope. Nalini and I boarded the train to Mumbai with Manu in tow. Kaka took the train back to Savarkundla and washed his hands of my brother. So much for our marital bliss.

―――――

The sanitarium that we were admitted to—in a distant Mumbai suburb—was spacious with two rooms and wide windows that let in lots of sunshine and fresh air. It had a separate kitchen, bathroom and front yard with a large banyan tree and a well from which we could draw water and bathe ourselves. An outhouse was nearby. It was a far cry from the densely crowded tenement of inner-city Mumbai. It had all the necessary amenities of a place of convalescence. At last, Nalini and I had a bedroom of our own so, for the first time, we could enjoy life as man and woman. We set up our temporary household by borrowing a few essential things from relatives. The joy of getting a nice place to live, however, soon evaporated. Now I had two people to worry about: Nalini and Manu.

My brother could barely read or write. Who was going to hire him? When I suggested that he get a gopher's job like the one I had in the beginning, he declined. He thought that he deserved better. Manu was more of a burden to Nalini than to me, since I would leave in the morning for the office and come back late in the evening. He would stay home all day, not venturing out unless someone was with him. Nalini and I rarely got any quality time to ourselves.

However, we had a bigger problem than what to do with my brother. The clock was ticking on our stay at the sanitarium. What would we do at the end of three months? What else but ask for an extension? We found a bigwig in our community who was a distant relative and begged him to pull some strings for us. It worked. We got an extension for another three months—with a warning that there would be no more extensions.

Then where would we go? Nalini told me unequivocally that she would not go back to Savarkundla. The probability of my generating enough *pughree* money to rent a room in Mumbai was negligible. The only alternative was to look for another sanitarium. In fact, we found two of them near Chowpaty Beach, one of the most exclusive areas of Mumbai. We quickly applied using Tara's name again and the same medical certificate. It worked. When our extended time was up we shifted to the Chowpaty sanitarium. This too was spacious, with two rooms, a bathroom and kitchen. Besides the necessary amenities, it had the added benefit of being near Chowpaty Beach. Tourists came from all over India to stroll on the wide pavements that served as a boardwalk and enjoy the sprawling Indian ocean. Vendors sold snacks until late at night. Among the beach's attractions were giant statues of the leaders of India's independence struggle, as well as a favorite of newlyweds: horse-and-buggy rides—one of which Nalini and I enjoyed. One side of the beach was lined with old British-style mansions filled with elegant flats where Mumbai's rich and famous lived. While enjoying the new sanitarium and the nearby beach, I was looking ahead. As soon as we moved in, I quickly applied to another sanitarium nearby. Luckily, we got into that one, too.

Now we were secure for at least the next six months, but I knew that we were running out of sanitariums. Of course, the sanitarium people could see the game we were playing. Both of us looked healthy and showed no signs of the illness that the doctor had certified us as having. We discovered that most people in the sanatoriums shared our predicament. We would exchange notes about how much time was left and where to go next. Sometimes we lost neighbors overnight and new neighbors appeared in their place. Once we ran into the same neighbors in two different sanatoriums. Apparently, we had the same list of places to apply. We also discovered that most sanitarium buildings were old and dilapidated. The last one we occupied was downright dangerous. The roof was supported by pillars placed throughout the building, including one in the middle of each of our two rooms. We had to sign an agreement not to sue the sanitarium if it collapsed and we got hurt. I finally concluded that this sort of nomadic existence was unsustainable.

Living in Mumbai's sanatoriums had its moments, though. We had to remember our varying identities as we moved from place to place, borrowing names of relatives who obliged us by applying for us. We also had to alert friends and relatives about our changing identities when they came to visit us. As suggested above, Nalini's sister Tara had applied for us at our very first sanitarium, which led to a humorous situation. There is a widely popular mythological story of a Hindu king, Harishchandra, and his wife, Taramati, or Tara for short. The king is known for never lying and always keeping his promise. In an attempt to test his truthfulness, God pushes him to the extreme, but the king passes the test and goes to heaven with all of his subjects. As new residents of the sanitarium, Nalini was impersonating her sister Tara. Neighbors humorously referred to me as Harishchandra, the truthful king, not realizing that our residence there was under false pretense. Yet we carried on gamely as Taramati and Harishchandra!

Some of these sanatoriums were located in desirable parts of Mumbai. And despite some that were old, the level of cleanliness and lack of congestion made living in them worthwhile, especially the two near Chowpaty Beach. Both places were within quick walking distance of Bhartiya Vidya Bhavan, a major arts and cultural center. Many literary, cultural and political figures visited and spoke at events there. I rarely missed these events if they were free. Thus I got to see, albeit at a distance, some of the luminaries of the Indian cultural and political world. In a sense, this life was like scenes that I had seen in the movies coming true for me. Among the luminaries who appeared was my childhood hero K.M. Munshi, the well-known Gujarati novelist and prominent lawyer who had helped draft the Indian constitution and was the founder of the cultural center. I had read his autobiography and always wanted to be like him. A man of fair complexion, he was elegantly dressed in a white *dhoti*, long coat and Gandhi cap. He walked briskly to the stage and spoke in clear English. Among all of the speakers, he alone had his speech printed and handed out. I secured a copy but couldn't make my way through the mad rush of people to get it autographed. Still, I felt quite privileged to see him in person and hear him speak.

———————

As my search for stable living accommodations continued, I had a radical idea. How about looking for a job elsewhere and leaving Mumbai? That would solve our housing problem once and for all. As I explained our predicament to Nalini, all of a sudden I broke down. I felt humiliated and helpless, knocked out like a defeated boxer described by Gay Talese in *A Writer's Life*:

"You realize... what has happened to you. And what follows is hurt, a confused hurt—not a physical hurt—it is a hurt combined with anger. It is a what-will-people-think-hurt.... The worst thing about losing is having to walk out of the ring and face the people."

I lost my self-respect. I was ashamed to go to social gatherings or meet friends and relatives. Among all the people I knew, I was the only one who couldn't make it in Mumbai. I failed even in the most elementary things—I couldn't get a respectable job despite my commerce degree or a place to live, however modest. All I wanted was a small room. That would have been enough. I cursed myself. Why did I get married without a place to live? Without a good job? Why did I get married so young! Why did I not wait?

I wondered if there was some kind of curse on me. All of my friends and relatives in Mumbai had permanent places to reside. But not me. How strange it was that millions came to Mumbai to make their fortunes, yet I was thinking of leaving empty-handed and defeated!

How to reconcile my failure in Mumbai? In many ways, Mumbai is like New York. E.B. White famously said that those who wanted to come to New York had to be lucky to be fulfilled. Otherwise the city would destroy them. "No one should come to New York to live unless he is willing to be lucky." This was true of Mumbai as well. I simply wasn't lucky. I wanted to get out before the city destroyed me! But as I reconciled myself to leaving Mumbai, I was determined to come back. I did not want this defeat to define me. As to how I would come back, I had no idea.

Nalini was taken aback at seeing me cry. She instantly agreed with the idea of moving out of Mumbai. She too was tired of shuttling from place to place, not knowing where we would go next. And what if we did not get a place for the next three months? She didn't want to go back to Savarkundla and be away from me. She wanted us to start a family. So I got to work, furiously applying for positions in the major cities of India. The *Times* carried vacancy announcements from all over the country. I applied for an accounting job with a chemical factory in Bhopal. The health hazards of working in chemical factories were not widely known at that time. Even if I'd known them, what choices did I have? I was called by the chemical company's Mumbai representative for an interview. I must have impressed him because I got the job instantly. It paid enough for me to rent a furnished house. Unlike Mumbai, there was a shortage of qualified people in provincial cities. I accepted the job immediately and settled on a date of departure from Mumbai. Nalini started packing what little we had.

I decided to make a few rounds among friends and relatives to inform them of our decision to leave Mumbai. Kaka, of course, did not like this. What about his plans to move the whole family to Mumbai? What would happen to my brother, who was already living with us? I didn't care. All I wanted was to be with Nalini in a relatively permanent place and enjoy our married life together. Besides, she had suffered enough.

The other person who didn't approve of my plan to leave Mumbai was Ratibhai, my erstwhile guardian. He reminded me that people came to Mumbai from all over India to make their fortune—and I was leaving it? "What future will you have in Bhopal?" he asked. I wondered aloud: "What future do I have in Mumbai?" Indeed, I didn't see a future for me in Mumbai. Besides, I was tired of moving every three months not knowing where I would go next. How long could I keep moving at this pace, even if I were to find a new sanitarium? This kind of nomadic existence was tormenting and unsustainable.

"Why don't you rent a room somewhere?" Ratibhai asked.

I replied, "Where is the *pughree* money? I have no money."

Ratibhai understood my predicament. I needed *pughree*—a large down payment—even to rent. With my meager salary I was also unlikely to generate any savings in the foreseeable future.

"I will return to Mumbai once I have accumulated some money and established myself in a profession," I told him.

"Look here, Natu," Ratibhai said. "I don't want you to leave Mumbai. Going to Bhopal even temporarily is not a good idea. Go find a room and I will pay your *pughree*. For heaven's sake, don't leave Mumbai."

I was taken aback by his generosity. "I'm very grateful but have no idea when I might be able to pay you back."

"Don't worry," he said. "Pay me back when you can. But for heaven's sake, don't leave Mumbai!"

I was overjoyed and rushed to find a real-estate broker who could help us find suitable accommodations. This was the second life-changing event in which Ratibhai played a critical role. Without his help, I would still be a gopher in the Mulji Jetha market. He had saved me from that, encouraged me to go to college and helped pay for it. Now he was saving me from going to work in a chemical factory in Bhopal, the city where decades later a catastrophic accident at a Union Carbide plant killed 4000 people. With the help of a real-estate agent, I found a one-room apartment in Kandivali, a distant Mumbai suburb, for a *pughree* of 2,500 rupees, about $40 at today's exchange rate. Ratibhai said he would give me 2,000 rupees and asked that I raise the remaining 500 on my own. But I had no savings and approached Nathabhai, the relative who had hired me when I first came to Mumbai, and explained my dilemma. He instantly gave me money and we got the "room," one of several designed as servants' quarters behind

a bungalow. No matter. We bid goodbye to our sanitarium neighbors, who congratulated us on our good fortune. Now we didn't have to move every three months. It was
just one small room, but it gave us a permanent place to live in Mumbai.

Kaka was delighted. He immediately sent my sister to live with us. We were expected to find a husband for her. To accommodate her, we installed a wooden partition in
the room so she could sleep on one side and Nalini and I on the other. My brother,
who was still with us, would sleep in the hallway outside.

As we settled down in our one-room abode, I wondered: Is this what I had bargained
for? My idea of marital bliss was all derived from the reading of romantic poems of
Gujarati literature. I myself had written a few poems glorifying the love and happiness
of newly married couples. None of that marital bliss was there in our early life together.
It is as if all that world of romance crashed the day I got married. What happened?

Chapter 6

OUT OF INDIA

May of 1964 was a momentous time in India. On May 27th, Jawaharlal Nehru, India's first prime minister, died. He had become prime minister on August 15, 1947, when India became independent, and served 17 years until his death. He had been a fixture of Indian politics since 1929, when he became president of the Indian National Congress. Indeed, much of post-independence India was ruled by members of the Nehru dynasty as prime ministers—first Jawaharlal, then his daughter Indira and then her son Rajiv.

The country was in deep shock. A weeklong national mourning period was announced. The country came to a stop. Shops, restaurants, banks and businesses were closed. People were mournfully wondering: Now what? Most had never known India without Jawaharlal Nehru at the helm. A new chapter was about to open in India's tumultuous history.

May was also a momentous time in our lives given that we secured a place to live in Mumbai. Henceforth, my life would no longer be nomadic. Now I would be a normal resident of Mumbai who went back home to the same place every evening, day after day and year after year.

With a secured place to live, I became a full-fledged *Mumbaiwala*, a householder in Mumbai. But with the salary I was making I couldn't afford rent, food and transportation, let alone any form of fun or entertainment. Searching for ways to supplement my meager salary, I looked for part-time work in the want-ad section of the *Times of India*. One day I came upon an ad by someone seeking a tutor to teach his unlettered son English and acquaint him with some general knowledge. I immediately called upon him.

His name was Mr. Mehta. He was a prominent citizen who ran a highly successful family business. I went to see him in his spacious, air-conditioned office located in the Flora Fountain area in the heart of Mumbai's business district. As I entered the office I was greeted by a secretary, who seated me in the reception area and offered me coffee. The office was well-organized, the staff well-dressed and the ambiance soothing. A lot was going on, but without the hustle and bustle normal to most offices in Mumbai. Fresh copies of several newspapers and magazines were displayed on the coffee table.

As I sipped my coffee, a well-dressed man with a fair complexion and impeccable manners strode out of his office. "Mr. Gandhi?" he said. "Please come in." And he took me into his office. It was the first time that anyone had called me Mr. Gandhi!

Leaning back in a swirling chair behind his desk, Mr. Mehta quickly looked over my résumé and said, "I am glad you came by, Mr. Gandhi. My son Piyush has been quite sick for a long time and had to drop out of school. Now he is fine but has missed several years of schooling. He is quite street-smart but not educated the way you and I are. He needs to improve his general knowledge and acquire some basic English. Can you work with him?"

"Yes, sir. What do you want me to do?"

"Oh, nothing much, just sit with him for an hour every day and read the *Times* aloud. That will make him aware of what's going on in the world and help him stay abreast of current affairs. It will also improve his English. If you do this much, I will be very grateful to you!" No one had ever treated me with such professional courtesy in Mumbai or elsewhere.

"Of course I can do it," I replied. "When do you want me to start?"

"I will pay you 100 rupees a month," he said. "If I see improvement in Piyush, I will give you more."

And then he called his son, who was sitting in the next room. He was a young man wearing a starched shirt, pants and well-shined shoes. He appeared to be in his late teens. "Yes Dad?" he asked.

"This is Mr. Gandhi. He will come to our flat every morning and teach you. He will start next week."

The son looked at me suspiciously. "All right," he said and walked out. Mr. Mehta added, "You can teach him some manners, too!"

———

In a celebratory mood, I went out to a nearby restaurant called *Chaaya* and ordered a good meal, a rare treat to celebrate my moment of good fortune. I read the *Times* every day anyway. Now I would read aloud to the young man and get paid for it. This was easiest hundred rupees I'd ever made! At today's exchange rate it would be just two dollars, but it was a big help to me at the time. As I was enjoying my meal, my old friend Doshi walked into the restaurant. I was surprised to see him. "What are you doing here, Doshi?" I asked.

"I just had a meeting with someone who needed a tutor," he said. "He told me that the job was just filled. He had hired a tutor only moments earlier. I should have gone sooner." Doshi apparently had read the same ad that I had!

The tutorial job took me every day to Malabar Hill, a far corner of Mumbai where the rich and powerful lived. I would wake up around 5 in the morning. Nalini would get up with me. As I bathed and got ready for the day, she made me breakfast—a simple Indian meal of *chapatti* bread and vegetables, and tea, but in substantial portions since I wouldn't eat again till late afternoon.

I would leave home at around 6 for the 15-minute walk to Kandivali station. The streets would be busy with milkmen and newspaper carriers rushing to finish their deliveries, and mill workers returning from their night shifts. And there were souls like me whose days started early. At that hour in the morning, the trains would still be crowded. Mumbai never sleeps and people were always either going to work or returning home. I would take the train to Grant Road station in central Mumbai. Before boarding, I would get a copy of the *Times* and start thinking about what I should read to Piyush. From the station I would take the bus to Malabar Hill and from there would walk another 15 minutes to the seafront complex where Mr. Mehta lived.

This was a different neighborhood than any I was used to, to say the least. Here I saw street sweepers cleaning streets, drivers washing cars, uniformed delivery men driving their vans, servants reporting to work and doormen guarding elegant bungalows with well-groomed grounds. There was also the famous Hanging Garden, a major tourist attraction atop the hill overlooking the sprawling city below. It was a glimpse into the lifestyle of Mumbai's rich and famous that I had seen only in Bollywood movies.

Mr. Mehta's apartment had a large living room, three bedrooms with attached bathrooms and balconies, a dining room, utility room and kitchen of the size of my one-room apartment! The apartment was elegantly furnished and had a magnificent view of the Arabian Sea. As I approached the complex, I passed servants washing cars. If one could afford a car in India, one certainly could afford to have people hand-wash it daily. At the complex, a doorman bowed and opened the door for me. The elevator operator also bowed and took me to Mr. Mehta's floor. At the apartment, a servant would open the door. Inside, as classical Indian music played on, another servant would bring me freshly brewed coffee as I began my tutoring session with the young man. There were other servants who attended to the needs of the four people who lived in this expansive apartment.

Every day I went from my one-room, shanty-town place to this opulent residence and marveled at how the rich lived in Mumbai. I was filled with great admiration and envy for their charmed life, but at the same time I would wonder: Might I ever have what they have? So far, my distressing experience in Mumbai had left me with a bitter feeling that I would never be able to afford anything like that. After the tutoring session, Mr. Mehta often asked me to stay for a cup of coffee to talk about Piyush. Mr. Mehta was a cultured man of many interests. He found in me an audience and also took an interest in me, which I appreciated. Sometimes he would ask his driver to drop me at the bus stop. I enjoyed the attention, but knew that as soon as our coffee session was over I was heading back to the brutal reality of Mumbai.

At lunchtime, like most office workers in Mumbai, I ate from the tiffin—a home-cooked meal delivered daily to hundreds of thousands of office workers for a pittance. In the evening, after a hard day's work, I would track back to the terminal to take the train home. Trains were always crowded, but particularly so in the evening. I rarely got a seat. Kandivali was about an hour away. I would be so bone tired that if I were not standing, I would be dozing away. I'd get home about 8 p.m., have a quick dinner and collapse in the bed, only to wake up at 5 the next morning and begin another day with the same routine. There was no such thing as quality time for Nalini and me.

Living in two worlds—Mr. Mehta's fairyland and the real world of shanty-town Mumbai—was splitting me apart. It also made me question: How was Mr. Mehta more qualified than I to have what he had? Why did he have so much and I so little? When we discussed issues of public policy or foreign affairs in our coffee sessions, I was his equal and could argue intelligently with him. We both had business degrees. I even had a law degree.

I surmised that what mattered was bloodline, not résumé—that he was rich and I was not because he had inherited substantial wealth and I hadn't. I didn't see him as any more intelligent or industrious than I, yet he lived a life of wealth and privilege while mine was a life of toil, travail and misery. While walking to catch the bus, I would rack my brain to understand the great inequity of our existences. How could I bridge the divide and live like Mr. Mehta? Invariably, I would come up empty.

Now that we had a relatively permanent place in Mumbai, Nalini was eager to start a family. Though I wanted to wait until I had a better job and perhaps a flat with more than one room, I relented. I wasn't going to deny her wishes. Nalini conceived, and we signed up for a local maternity home. It was not part of a hospital but rather a primitive facility that delivered babies. It was inexpensive and nearby. Most of our relatives lived in the far suburbs. Baa and Kaka were still in Savarkundla. We were basically on our own.

When Nalini's labor started I was at the office and had no way of knowing until the call came from the maternity home telling me that Nalini had delivered a boy! I rushed out of the office and went straight to the maternity home, to which Nalini had to make her way on her own. We were overjoyed about our newborn. Nalini was particularly happy that she had delivered a boy who would carry on the Gandhi name. With great pride and gusto, we named him Vikram, after the great Hindu emperor of ancient India, Vikramaditya, who was known for his generosity, courage and strength. Unfortunately, our baby was too weak to be taken home. In those days, we lived literally hand-to-mouth, and Nalini might not have gotten adequate nutritional and prenatal care. She stayed by our baby's side at the maternity home, but the baby got weaker. There was little medical care. A week after he was born, Vikram died. The loss of our child was devastating to both of us, but it was particularly hard on Nalini. In a life full of adversity, this was to have been her shining moment. She felt so defeated that she refused to come home during the daylight hours—she didn't want to be seen coming home empty-handed. I brought her home in the middle of the night.

For next few weeks, Nalini refused to have any visitors or to leave our little place. Because we had no running water, we had to go to a nearby outhouse to use the toilet. She would refrain from going there until it was dark and began to suffer from severe depression. I didn't know how to comfort her. I kept telling her that we would soon have another child, but she would have none of that. She thought she was cursed, that she would never have another child. I considered taking her out of town, but where would we go? She refused to go to Savarkundla. I couldn't afford to take her on a vacation. I had no money. And that would have required my taking a week off from work, an unlikely prospect since I had taken many days off to stay with Nalini after the birth. She was inconsolable.

———————

Even beyond the tragic loss of our baby, my family problems were mounting. I was unable to find a suitable mate for my sister or a job for my brother, who was still loafing around. Back in Savarkundla, the family business was a losing proposition. Kaka was suggesting that he might move to Mumbai with Baa and my remaining brothers. He thought that he could find a job there that would support the family. Given the difficulty I'd had finding a suitable job and place to live, I couldn't see Kaka succeeding in Mumbai. He was already in his mid-60s and had no formal education. He had dropped out of school to join the Independence Movement. Even if he found a job, how would he manage the hardships of Mumbai after a lifetime of relatively simple living in Savarkundla? Would he be able to put up with traveling in crowded trains? If I had a hard time making my way in my 20s, how could Kaka do it in his 60s?

But Kaka felt that he had no choice. Fortunately, he still had enough of Bapa's savings left to pay *pughree* for a two-room apartment in Borivali, a Mumbai suburb near Kandivali. So he relocated the rest of the family, including my mother and three other brothers. Kaka approached a distant relative who ran a prosperous trading firm about a job. The relative took pity on Kaka and hired him as an accounting clerk. So Kaka, in his mid-60s, started a new and more difficult phase of his life.

———————

My family's desperate move to Mumbai added to my sense of failure. If I'd been making money, this should have been my father's time to enjoy retirement. My failure to find a well-paying job or have a flourishing business was a continuing disappoint-ment for everyone, especially Kaka. True, now I did not have to look for a place to live every three months. And yes, I did have a job. But the more enmeshed I got in my daily routine, the more depressed I became. The crowded buses and trains, long walks to bus stops and train stations, the boring green-eyeshade bookkeeping job, tiffin lunches, working late on Saturdays—the boss would say, "What's the rush, tomorrow is Sunday"—amounted to a dreary existence. On Sundays and holidays, I holed up in our one-room home. We rarely ventured out to a movie or dinner. Where was the money? Though I had a job and a roof over my head, a wife and family nearby, I felt impris-oned. I often asked myself why I was failing in Mumbai, where many of my relatives and acquaintances were succeeding—some fabulously. I was jealous of the successful ones, so I stopped seeing them. If they came to see me, I shied away.

Once two college friends showed up unannounced at the office. I'd heard that one of them was getting ready to go to America and the other had an apprenticeship that would lead to a lucrative practice as a chartered accountant. When I saw them coming I rushed into the bathroom and asked a colleague to tell them that I was not in the office. When they were gone, the colleague knocked on the bathroom door and I came out. He was confused.

"Why did you hide?" he asked. "Do you owe them money? Were they here to collect?"

"No," I told him. But I didn't say that I was just too embarrassed and downhearted.

––––––––––

During those days of debilitating frustration, I often thought of two people who had faced greater hardships and frustrations in Mumbai yet were entirely at ease and carried on their daily lives with good cheer. One was Sharad Panchamia, a dear friend who was in a dead-end job at the Life Insurance Corporation. A man of medium height, with thick hair and thicker glasses, he always wore a shirt tucked into pants held up by a belt—he was too thin—and shoes. Though by Mumbai standards he had a good, secure job, it was clear that he would remain a clerk all his life. It wasn't that Sha-rad didn't want a promotion, but he lacked burning ambition. He was entirely serene and content with what he had. When we were together in law college, he'd seemed to be there for fun, while I was there to add the law degree to my résumé so I might secure a better job. I got my law degree, but it was not good for much. Teaching and learning in law school was as bookish as it was in business school. I got it without set-ting foot in a courtroom or visiting a law office. I was frustrated when my efforts to get a better job with my newly acquired degree didn't bear fruit. Sharad seemed unfazed. In time he married an equally content wife. They had two lovely daughters. They were all deeply devoted to him. After migrating to the U.S., I made sure to go and see him every time I visited India. I took him and his family to events where I was honored with some award. He seemed genuinely happy to see me being recognized for my success. As Sharad grew old he lost his eyesight, but I never heard him complain about it. The last time I saw him, he was walking energetically around in his living room. Without a hint of regret he said, "Now that I have lost my eyes, I am taking my walks at home!" That was the last I saw of him.

The other person whose equanimity amazed me was my maternal uncle whom I called Masa. He had struggled all his life, never succeeded but rarely complained. He had established a dry-food store in Karachi, then a Muslim city in British India. When India was partitioned, Karachi was claimed by Pakistan. Masa fled to India in the Hindu exodus from the city. Forced to leave everything that he had built in Karachi, he worked hard to establish his store in Mumbai, the only business he knew. At the end of a long day, he would close the shop and sleep in the open right outside the store. One night someone took away the cash bag that he had put under his head as a pillow. In a deep sleep after a long, hard day, Masa didn't notice that it was gone until daybreak.

Now Masa had to start all over again. He could no longer afford to run the store alone, so he entered into a partnership, becoming the junior partner and continuing to run the store. The senior partner took advantage of Masa's vulnerability and removed him from the partnership altogether, forcing him to become an employee in the store he had founded and built. He could not even go to lunch at his apartment a few blocks away. He had to eat out of tiffin in the store and work into the late evening. Despite the hardships and numerous setbacks, Masa never complained. He carried on with almost divine serenity. When I would get disheartened about my situation, I would often go to see Sharad or Masa and tell myself to learn from their stories. Why can't I be like them and take life with all its ups and downs? Why can't I be content with what I have and not continuously lament my misfortune? There were a large number of people living in Mumbai in worse condition than I was. What right did I have to complain?

The more I pondered my situation, the more I realized that I was suffering from an affliction of ambition. Ever since I could remember, I'd wanted to be different, successful and noteworthy, out of the ordinary—extraordinary even. For me, life in Mumbai was anything but that. There I was confined to ordinariness, even failure, and that was deeply frustrating.

––––––––––

Deep inside, I was still not giving up, determined not to be that "nothing man" unsparingly described in V.S. Naipaul's famous novel, A Bend in the River: "The world is what it is; men who are nothing, who allow themselves to become nothing, have no place in it." Similarly, my ambitious nature wouldn't let me reconcile with this "nothing" life. Yes, Masa and Sharad made peace with theirs, but that was not me. To accept a life like that would go against my grain. Something inside was telling me that I was meant to be different, that I was destined to be successful, relevant and important. Yet I didn't know how to reconcile the world of my dreams with the stark reality that surrounded me. In the midst of my mental anguish, it occurred to me that Mumbai might not be the right place for me to realize my destiny. Perhaps I should look elsewhere, maybe seek my fortune beyond Mumbai, even beyond India.

I had seen many openings for accountants and financial analysts in the Middle East. How about trying there? Maybe I should hitch my wagon to an oil-rich Arab sheik or work for an American company helping Arabs explore oil. What about Africa? Some of my relatives had gone there and become fabulously rich. I used to see them flaunting their wealth on their occasional forays back to Mumbai—staying at five-star hotels, dining at expensive restaurants, buying jewelry and fancy clothes.

But these alternatives would necessitate that I again leave Nalini behind until I got settled in a new place. And that would be risky, given her precarious condition after the loss of our child. While browsing through the *Times of India*, I saw several announcements of students going abroad, particularly to the U.S., mainly to get an MBA. Some of my fellow commerce graduates were there already. And some had returned. Armed with American MBAs, they were handsomely employed by American companies in senior positions that entitled them to Malabar Hill flats and cars with chauffeurs. Why not me?

I regularly read Walter Lippmann's syndicated column, "Today and Tomorrow," reprinted in the *Indian Express*. I had also read John Gunther's *Inside America*. I devoured newspapers in the American library in Mumbai. The U.S. presidential election of 1964 was in full swing and I made sure to know everything about it. I should be the one going there! Certainly, I thought that I was as deserving as any if not more than many Indians who went to America. What a waste, I thought. I knew so much about it. But they were rich and I was not. Only the rich in India could afford to go to the U.S. Airfare, college tuition and living expenses there would cost hundreds of thousands of rupees. All of this was way beyond my reach.

———

My only hope was my college pal, Navin Jarecha. When he went to the U.S. in 1960, I had hoped he would find a way to help me get there. In fact, when I went to Ballard Pier to see him off, I made my way to his ship's cabin and took him aside. "Please, Navin," I said, "do something, anything to help me get to the U.S. I would love to join you there." As my frustrations in Mumbai mounted, I kept sending Jarecha letters asking about chances, if any, of my going to the U.S. He always replied, usually in an aerogram bearing the American eagle logo on the top left corner. I would read each letter multiple times and cherish every word. If I didn't get a letter from Jarecha at least once a month, I was very disappointed. His letters chronicled his early American adventures—how he got off the ship at New York pier and took a Greyhound bus to Atlanta and then started working full-time in the bursar's office at Atlanta University, where he had studied.

I thought that now was the time to press him about my going there. It was the fall of 1962. "Would you please find a way to get me to America," I wrote, "and rescue me from my endless misery and misfortune?" I explained my Mumbai problems in detail. "You are my only hope." I waited for his reply for weeks and months, but no letter bearing that American eagle arrived.... I was heartbroken.

Yet the letter that finally came was worth waiting for. He wrote that he had arranged a college admission for me and I would soon get a letter from Atlanta University. He instructed me about the process: Take the form to the U.S. consulate to get a visa, then visit the Reserve Bank of India to get the required foreign exchange. I was thrilled. Nirvana! I was so excited that I couldn't keep the news to myself. As soon as I got home I told Nalini, "We are going to America!" She too was excited. She assumed that she would be going with me. I announced to relatives, friends and acquaintances that I was soon going to the U.S. I became a celebrity. Going to the U.S. for higher education was a big deal in those days. Dinner invitations poured in. Everyone in our little circle wanted to be near me. How had I managed such a feat? When would I be leaving? Nalini also enjoyed the attention. Her depression began to lift.

I received the requisite admission letter in a few weeks. I dreamed of a farewell party at which people talked glowingly about my hard work, initiative and skills, of being fêted with garlands at the airport, of my photo appearing in the newspaper announcing my departure to the U.S. for higher education. About this time, the U.S. consulate in Mumbai began showing *Circarama USA,* a documentary film of sights and sounds across the United States. A huge tent was put up in the middle of one of Mumbai's large downtown parks. The movie played continuously on the circular walls of the tent. This was no Hollywood movie, but the real America! Spectators stood in the middle of the tent and got the sensation of actually being in America. In about an hour, the video took viewers all around America, from the majesty of its natural wonders—great parks, lush gardens, the Grand Canyon, Niagara Falls—to the modern metropolises of L.A. and New York, to giant stadiums where athletes played baseball and football, to famous universities.

I was so captivated that I went to see the documentary a few more times, braving long lines and even longer waits, and still couldn't get enough of it. Standing in the middle of the tent, I felt lucky to be headed soon to this wonderful country. But the euphoria soon ebbed. In the fall of 1962 the Chinese invaded India on its northern border, mounting an aggressive military assault across the mountainous terrain of the

Himalayas. Tensions between the two countries during the '50s and early '60s concerned Tibet. The Chinese considered it part of China and occupied it, driving the Dalai Lama to exile in India in 1959. Overwhelmed, the Indian forces were in full retreat. The whole country was in a panic. An emergency was declared. All foreign travel was restricted. Foreign currency exchange was severely restricted. The Chinese unilaterally declared a ceasefire, but the emergency was not over. As a result, getting foreign exchange to study abroad was virtually impossible. But I had a bigger problem—I had no rupees to exchange for U.S. dollars even if they were available.

I needed hundreds of thousands of rupees to pay for passage and secure the dollars required to study in America. And what about Nalini? How would I provide for her while I was away? She was under the mistaken impression that she was going with me. I wrote to Jarecha about my urgent need for a large sum of money before I could hope to go to the U.S. "I am in no position to provide the necessary funds," he replied. "I have just started a new job." Jarecha had assumed that I could arrange the necessary funding myself. His letters stopped coming. Every day I looked expectantly at the mailman hoping for a letter from America. He would simply shake his head and I knew there was no letter for me.

Months went by. The semester for which I had been admitted had already begun. My disappointment was profound. I couldn't show my face to all the people whom I had triumphantly told that I was going to America, particularly those who had entertained me with dinners. Nalini saw this as part of a larger problem that had plagued us since we'd been married. "Nothing has worked and nothing will ever work for us," she said. "Face it, Natu, we are cursed! There is no hope for us!" I agreed and was crushed. I was also angry with myself. Why had I foolishly announced that I was going to the U.S. without making sure that all the necessary arrangements had been made? The only saving grace was that, in my euphoria, I had not resigned from my job. That would have been catastrophic.

After the brief period of excitement, I sunk into a deep depression. More than ever it seemed that I was condemned to a life of mediocrity and misery. I gave up looking for a better job, since I saw no prospects for getting it. Applying for jobs through want ads seemed pointless. Nor did I see myself going into business on my own. I had no seed money, no practical talent or expertise beyond the bookish knowledge that I had previously gotten from my studies. Seething inside with frustration, I resigned myself to a dismal existence. I had no choice. Nalini was in no better condition. We talked again of starting family, but she was hesitant. She didn't want to lose another child.

Kaka was gradually settling down in Mumbai, despite a tortuous routine. He saw my situation and pretty much gave up on me. He could see that I would never make enough money to help him and concluded that he would have to keep working for the foreseeable future to support the family. My brother was still without a job and simply loafing around. My other two brothers were enrolled in substandard public schools. And we still couldn't find a suitable spouse for my sister.

I carried on each day with the same routine—and a profound sense of helplessness. What right did I have to think that I was different, that I was meant for something better? I realized that I was just like the countless people I saw in the streets and trains, and no better. It was perhaps the darkest period of my life. I was just going through the motions. No hope, no excitement, nothing to cheer me up or look forward to. Sometimes I woke up in the middle of the night sweating profusely from a nightmare that I was in an endless dark tunnel.

I stopped going to Hollywood movies because they depressed me even more. I became cynical and bitter. When I heard about someone going to America, I would get insanely jealous and start hating the person for no reason other than he, and not I, was going to America. Fearing that I might be going insane, I constantly asked myself: "What is wrong with me? Why are others succeeding and I am failing? What am I not doing? Am I not trying hard enough?" But there was no answer.

Three years after foolishly announcing that I was going to America, I received a telegram from Jarecha. He said that he had again arranged for my admission to Atlanta University.

"Start packing," he wrote. "The fall semester is about to start."

"Sure," I mused. "You can't fool me again with that!"

This time I kept the news to myself. I had learned my lesson. I telegraphed Jarecha that my financial situation was still the same. I would need help to pay for everything—tuition, living expenses, the airline ticket and some additional money to send to Nalini. Jarecha replied immediately, saying that he had arranged for everything except the air travel, on which he was working with a foundation. He had arranged a scholarship, a part-time job in his office that would pay for my incidental expenses and the money I needed for Nalini.

He soon followed with another telegram saying the Herndon Foundation of Atlanta had agreed to pay for my airline ticket from Mumbai to Atlanta. The foundation was dedicated to educational and charitable purposes and did much to enhance the advancement of Atlanta's black colleges. It had been established by Alonzo Franklin Herndon, who was born into slavery but became one of Atlanta's first African American millionaires by selling life insurance, primarily to African Americans, and founded the Atlanta Life Insurance Company.

Since I was admitted to Atlanta University, a black college, Jarecha shrewdly thought the Herndon Foundation, with its history of supporting predominantly black colleges, might help. It worked. Having secured the ticket, Jarecha pushed for my quick departure, since the fall semester had started in September. It was now early October. I was in no hurry. Having been badly burned about going to America three years earlier, I wasn't inclined to do anything until all the 'i's were dotted and the 't's crossed. I kept quiet and told no one, including Nalini. I needed tangible evidence. One day a representative of Air India showed up at the office. I immediately asked him to wait outside, not wanting to arouse any suspicion in the office. When I went out to see him, he confirmed that a ticket had been purchased for me. "What date would you like to fly?" he asked. I said that I would get back in touch soon and asked him not to come to the office again. The poor man was puzzled as to why I was reluctant to have him come see me. Most people would welcome an Air India representative bringing such good news.

As soon as the documents arrived from the university, I approached Chandu, a friend who was a travel agent, and asked him to help me. Like many of my friends, he also wanted to go to the U.S. to study, and like most of them did not have resources of his own. Failing to get a good job in Mumbai's tight job market, he apprenticed with a travel agency and then ventured into the business on his own. A genial man with a quick tongue and sharp mind, he succeeded in building a prosperous travel agency. Chandu readily agreed to help me, but given what I had gone through the last time, he asked: "Natu, are you sure everything has been checked out? Are you going to America for sure?" He said he would help me get my passport, visa, foreign exchange and other items necessary to travel abroad.

Obtaining a passport is a major bureaucratic hurdle in India. One has to have a substantial sum of money in the bank to assure the Indian government that the applicant would not be a burden to the state if something bad happened to him while abroad. I didn't even have a bank account, much less any money in one. My meager salary was paid in cash and all of it was spent immediately. There were no savings. We operated entirely on a cash basis. I had to find someone with a large enough bank account to provide the guarantee for me.

I of course approached Ratibhai, my erstwhile benefactor, and told him about my plans to go to the United States. I explained that everything had been paid for and that this was a golden opportunity for me. But I would need a guarantee to obtain a passport, since I had no money of my own. Would he give me such a guarantee? I thought he would be thrilled to hear that I was going to America. Silly me! He refused.

Ratibhai said he was opposed to my going to the U.S. "You will go to America," he said, "but you will leave Nalini behind, right?"

"Yes," I replied. "I can't afford to take her there now. Once I finish my studies and get a job and get settled, I will send for her."

"What is the guarantee that you will send for her?" he asked. "I know a few young married men who went there and never called their wives. They abandoned them for American girls. If you were to do something like that, what would happen to poor Nalini? Who would take care for her? Her life would be ruined."

I couldn't believe what Ratibhai was saying. Despite my assurances that I would never do such a thing, he was adamant. "If this were to happen in your case," he said, "I would be blamed for facilitating your leaving for the U.S.!"

He wouldn't give me the needed guarantee. Case closed. He also told me that there was no need for me to go because I could do well in Mumbai without getting an MBA. "Just be patient and wait your turn," he said. But I had waited long enough for my turn—and I knew that it was never going to come to me in Mumbai, no matter how long I waited. I didn't ask Kaka to help me get a guarantee from the firm where he was working because I knew that he'd be opposed to my going to the U.S. for the same reasons. I couldn't believe that I wasn't going to be able to get a passport because of the lack of necessary guarantee. I explained my dilemma to the travel agent. "Nothing will move without a passport," he said.

Jarecha, meanwhile, was getting anxious about my coming to the U.S. In desperation, I blurted out my passport problem to Kanu Doshi, a long-standing friend. I'd met him in 1957, when I was living in a community hostel and his brother Anil was my roommate. Doshi would often come to see Anil. Though a statistician by training, he had a strong interest in literature. A man of sharp intellect and a fine sense of humor, he also had a keen understanding of politics. We quickly bonded, often going to movies together and sharing our frustrations about the difficulty of getting a good job in Mumbai.

Doshi was pleasantly surprised that I was planning to go to the U.S. He had long harbored hopes of going there himself for higher education. "Don't give up!" he said. "I'll ask my brother Anil to provide the guarantee." Anil knew me well from our days together in the community hostel and now was running his own business. He readily agreed. The travel agent bribed the appropriate officials at the passport agency to rush my passport through the system.

On to the next problem.

To secure a U.S. visa, one had to have a clean bill of health from a doctor officially approved by the U.S. consulate. I'd never had a physical examination—indeed, I'd never visited a doctor in my life. What if the consulate doctor found something wrong with me? One look at my photograph from those days confirms how undernourished I looked. I must have weighed around 120 pounds. Pizza Hut and Dunkin' Donuts had not made their way to India yet. Also, I walked everywhere.

The night before the examination, I couldn't sleep. At the appointed time I went to see the consulate-approved doctor. His office was in Breach Candy, one of Mumbai's most exclusive areas. It was beautifully decorated with pictures of American monuments such as the Lincoln Memorial. There was also a picture of President Lyndon B. Johnson that I instantly recognized. The doctor was very businesslike. After a thorough examination the likes which I had never experienced, the doctor asked me to wait in the reception area. My heart sank. Surely the doctor had found something wrong with me. Otherwise, why would he ask me to go out and wait? If I was all right, he would have given his approval right away. I almost had a panic attack. After what seemed an eternal wait—of perhaps 10 minutes—I was called in to see the doctor again. He saw the panic in my face. "Not to worry, Gandhi," he said with a smile. "You're in good health. Start packing."

Oh, what a relief! But it wasn't over. I still had things to do. First I went to the U.S. consulate for an interview with the visa official. Chandu briefed me about it, but I worried that I might not understand his questions or might answer them inadequately. My English was far from fluent. I also had problems understanding American accents. I often misunderstood dialogues in Hollywood movies. I recalled missing much of the story in Alfred Hitchcock's Vertigo. The travel agent had assured me that I would have no problems given what I knew of the United States already. And he was right. I was out in 15 minutes with a visa stamped on my passport!

There was hardly an issue concerning foreign currency exchange since I needed none. Still, I needed approval from the Reserve Bank of India. I went to the bank and showed the documents from the university. I told officials there that I needed no foreign exchange. The bank was giving only about $7 in foreign exchange anyway. I took that, but even if it were giving more, I had no rupees to buy it. Now, with the necessary documents in hand, I went to Chandu to book my ticket.

Out of the blue, an unexpected problem emerged. India and Pakistan, two neighbors, had been feuding ever since they'd become separate nations in 1947 when the British divided the Raj and left. There had been several skirmishes between them over the years, the issue always being the status of Jammu and Kashmir, a state at the northern tip of the subcontinent claimed by both.

A full-fledged war broke out in September of 1965, initiated by skirmishes that had taken place earlier in April. Casualties on both sides numbered in the thousands. The situation in Mumbai was tense. A blackout was in force for several days and air traffic was disrupted. Though a ceasefire was soon declared, there were rumors that hostilities might resume and a blackout could be imposed on major cities like Mumbai. If that happened, air traffic would be in jeopardy again. The Mumbai airport might be shut down.

I remembered what Nalini had said earlier about there being a curse on us. "Nothing works out for us," she'd said when I was planning to go to the U.S. in 1962, and the Chinese invasion roiled all foreign travel. I panicked and asked Chandu to book the first available flight for me. Luckily, he was able to find a seat for me on an Air India flight leaving Mumbai on October 10, 1965—just a few days away. Now I had a ticket in hand and could tell people that I was going to America for sure.

My first step was Nalini, of course. Elated, I went home and told her the good news. "I am going to the U.S. next week!" Until now, I hadn't told her. She thought my coming home late and meeting with the travel agent was office-related. She began to cry. Her rapid-fire questions overwhelmed me: Could she go with me? If not, when could she join me? What would happen to her while I was gone? How would she support herself? Would she have to go back to Savarkundla? Could she stay in Mumbai in our little room on her own, or would she have to live with Kaka and Baa? She told me emphatically that she did not want to put up with my brother Manu anymore. She detested him. Above all, she asked, what was the guarantee that I would not forget her and leave her for some American girl?

She raised all of the issues that had bothered Ratibhai. She knew that we would be separated again. Only God knew for how long. I patiently tried to explain what my plans were, that it would take at least a year before I could bring her there. At a minimum, I needed to graduate and get a job to be able to do so.

"Look, this is a great opportunity and we shouldn't pass it up," I said. "This is your opportunity to go to America, too. You'll be the first of our relatives to go abroad—to America.

"Just think... If you were to become a U.S. citizen, you could bring your brothers and sisters there as well. Wouldn't you rather raise our children in America, with all its advantages, than in Mumbai, where we are mired in misery and poverty?" I added, "Listen, if I stay here, our situation will not change. Is that what you want for us and our children?"

"I might not like it there," she responded. "Then what?"

"We can always come back," I said. "With an American MBA degree, I could get a good job at any American company in Mumbai that would provide us with a Malabar Hill flat, a chauffeur-driven American car and a big salary."

I seemed to be making headway with her. "How about that? I asked. "Aren't you tired of living hand-to-mouth in this hellhole? Going to America is the only way out for us. Thanks to Jarecha, we have this once-in-a-lifetime opportunity that we shouldn't miss."

Nalini knew that only the rich could afford to go to America. I reminded her that the only time we had gone to the airport was to bid farewell to lucky ones going to America. But now we could go to the airport and other people would come to see me off! "This is our chance, and I'm not going to let it pass," I said. "You know that both Ratibhai and Kaka would be opposed to my going, but for the sake of our future, let me go!" It was a long night, but I finally convinced her.

The next battle was with Kaka. Unfortunately, Baa had taken a fall the day before and had to be hospitalized. Since my departure was imminent, I went straight to the hospital and gave them the news. As expected, Kaka was opposed. He raised the same objections as Ratibhai. But I was not there to argue my case with him, only to inform him of my decision. He could see that I was determined to go. My mother was in too much pain to say anything. They had basically given up on me. Leaving the hospital, I couldn't help but think that most parents would be delighted to see their son going to America, arrange a big send-off ceremony, and publish an announcement in the newspaper with a photo. All I got from Kaka was a cold shoulder. From his perspective, I was once again shirking my responsibility and leaving him with the family burden. Even worse, I was adding to that burden by leaving Nalini behind in Mumbai.

A small group of friends gave me a surprise farewell party in a restaurant near Churchgate station. Unfortunately, they forgot to invite other friends who thought they should have been invited. Worse yet, they didn't invite Nalini! All of this created major problems for me during my last few days in Mumbai. I tried to salvage the situation by inviting all of the aggrieved people to the airport.

During my last few days before leaving for the U.S., I was so sick of the petty wrangling that I thought I should go off somewhere and just appear at the airport on the day of my departure. But I had a thousand things to do. I had to inform my office that I was leaving soon for the U.S. Reminding me of my earlier fiasco, some in the office joked, "I thought you'd already gone there!" But this time I had the ticket in hand. The joke was on them. People in the office and elsewhere couldn't believe my good fortune. They wanted to know how I had managed such a feat without many resources or support. My boss invited me to dine with him at his posh Malabar Hill residence and gave me money to buy a suit. I had never before worn a suit or put on a tie. He advised me to get a woolen suit and gave me a set of thermal underwear he had used during a trip to England. He said winter in America would be harsh and I would need extra protection. I rushed to have the new suit, tie and shoes made on an emergency basis. Ready-made clothes were not yet in vogue.

Late in the evening of October 10, 1965, I arrived at Mumbai's Santa Cruz Airport with a throng of people who had come to say goodbye to me. The old, small, one-terminal airport paled in comparison with today's shiny Chhatrapati Shivaji International Airport, India's second-busiest, which managed the comings and goings of some 45 million passengers annually. It was hot, humid, crowded and noisy. Among those who had come to say goodbye were old friends like Sharad and Doshi, several relatives, family members and assorted acquaintances—and above all, Nalini and my father. Baa was still in the hospital. Earlier in the day I went to see her. I touched her feet and she held me tightly. "Stay well, son," she said. "The goddess Kankai will protect you!" Ratibhai shied away, since he had refused to give me that guarantee I needed to obtain my passport. His efforts to persuade me not to go to America had failed.

The gathered friends and family fêted me with garlands around my neck and small gifts such as handkerchiefs, mufflers and gloves that they thought I might need in America. Some even brought snacks for my journey. It was in many ways the first triumphant moment in a life otherwise filled with failure and adversity. For one evening, at least, I was a celebrity. It was hard to bid Nalini goodbye in the midst of so many people. I took her to one side and gave her a gentle hug—kissing in public was taboo!—and whispered in her ear: "I will get you there as soon as possible!" Tears were rolling down her face. Earlier in the day we'd had a little prayer ceremony at home to gain the goddess's blessing. I also touched my father's feet, but no words were exchanged. Still, I could see a glimmer of pride in his eyes that his son was going to America.

Sharad came by to alert me that S.K. Patil, a powerful Mumbai politician, was on the same flight. "Maybe you should try to see him," he said. "This is your chance to tell him off!" In our numerous discussions over the years, I had been highly critical of the policies of the Nehru government, in which Patil was a senior Cabinet member. Promptly at the appointed time, we heard the announcement that the Air India flight to New York was ready and passengers should board. After one last look at all the people who had come to see me off, I headed for the gate.

In a letter I received weeks later, Sharad wrote that no one left the airport until the plane had taken off. As it did so, I felt immensely relieved.

Suddenly I was free—free of all my troubles, my worries, hurts and humiliations, and also free at last of all the heat, humidity, dirt, poverty, noise and suffocation. As I climbed the stairs to board the plane, I pondered my narrow escape. Determined never to return, I murmured a famous Khalil Gibran line: "Then we left that sea to seek the greater sea!"

Chapter 7

LOST IN BLACK AMERICA

That Air India flight from Mumbai to New York was my first plane ride ever. I was quite intimidated. Though with some idea from watching movies, I didn't really know what to expect. After the hustle and bustle of the airport, the plane seemed quiet, clean and well organized. An air hostess in a beautiful Indian sari—the Air India uniform—showed me where to sit. "Would you care for a drink?" she asked. I assumed she meant an alcoholic beverage, which I had never had in my life, so I asked for a Coca-Cola. She quickly came back with a Coke and saw me struggling with my seat belt. She helped me fasten it and then put my luggage in the overhead bin. I was perspiring heavily. The old Santa Cruz airport of Mumbai was not air conditioned, with the city quite warm even in October. Fearing cold weather in New York, I had put on thermal underwear given to me by my generous boss, and wore a woolen suit. She also asked if I wanted to remove my jacket, so I gave it to her. Air India was world-famous for its Maharaja—fit for a king—service in those days.

The last few days had been very hectic for me—a lot of coming and going and not much sleep. My eyelids were heavy, but before I gave in to sleep, a rush of emotion came over me. If in my hometown of Savarkundla I had dreamed of going to Mumbai, in Mumbai I had dreamed about going to America—the Promised Land. Now the dream was coming true. "Believe it or not, my friend," I said to myself, "you are on your way to America!" Having survived Mumbai, I knew that I could manage living anywhere in the world. Compared to Mumbai, I thought, America had to be a day at the beach. I smiled at the prospect. Then I collapsed in my seat and slept through the night.

When I awoke, the plane was about to land in Frankfurt. Because of the long layover there, I was able to deplane and explore the airport. It was quiet and clean. People were well behaved—the absence of shouting or shoving struck me, normal as it was for Frankfurt. Sunshine poured in through the waiting lounge's tall windows. I thought of Friedrich Nietzsche and the Frankfurt school of critical philosophy, and how he had thought of the concept of Superman and what pure human will might be. All of a sudden, I was filled with hope for a better life and a bright future. I felt immensely grateful to Navin Jarecha, who had made it all possible. I promised myself that I would never forget his kindness and friendship. Indeed, four decades later, when I published my first book of poems, *America, America*, I dedicated it to him. Back on the plane the stewardess served breakfast—cereal and milk, toast, butter and jelly. I had never eaten cereal in my life. But I watched how the person sitting next to me ate his and I ate my first bowl. My Americanization had begun.

———————

At New York's John F. Kennedy airport, I approached the immigration desk with some trepidation. Might there be some last-minute hiccup with my visa or passport? Might I be denied entry to the Magic Kingdom? Living in Mumbai had made me paranoid. Something would always go wrong at the last moment that would throw people back. The immigration officer looked up with a smile on his face and said, "Welcome to America!" Presto, I was in! October 10, 1965, the same day that I had left Mumbai. Next came the customs check. I had just one bag with several gifts from friends and a few clothes. My mischievous side wanted to play Oscar Wilde and proclaim, "I have nothing to declare but my genius!" But I did not play the wise guy, not wanting to complicate anything. Also, I needed to catch an Eastern Airlines flight to Atlanta. At the airline counter the receptionist ushered me to a booth so that I could phone Jarecha.

"I have arrived in New York!"

"Stop shouting," he said. "There's no need to shout." Unlike in India, where one had to literally shout in the telephone to be heard on the other side, the reception was good and clear. Jarecha said that he would meet me in about two hours at the Atlanta airport. After the call, the clerk directed me to the gate for the Eastern flight to Atlanta.

"Thank you," I said.

"You're welcome," she replied.

I thought that she was being hospitable and welcoming me to her country. So I said again, "Thank you!"

She again replied, "You're welcome!"

In India I was used to saying "Don't mention it" in response to a "Thank you." So I said again, "Thank you!" Before she said "You're welcome" again, she realized my confusion and concluded our exchange with "Never mind."

———————

Jarecha, accompanied by two lovely black women, was waiting for me at the Atlanta airport. He was smartly dressed in Western style—a suit with matching tie and shined shoes. Gone was the shabby Indian attire of *kafani lengha* and *chappals*. He seemed somewhat formal when he shook hands with me.

"Well, finally you are here!" he exclaimed. "How was the flight?" He introduced me to the young ladies accompanying him. "This is Gandhi, the friend I have been talking about. I have been waiting for quite some time for him to come to America." To me he said, "This is Felicia and this is Sandy, two of my best friends in Atlanta. They are students at the university."

He helped me to retrieve my luggage and deposited me in the back seat of his car with one of the young women, and we headed to Atlanta University. I was still excited about my trip and started talking about it as we settled into the car. Jarecha cut me short and told me that I was quite late arriving for the fall semester, but he had managed to convince university officials that I would be able to catch up with the missed coursework.

Jarecha was driving a Dodge Chrysler sedan effortlessly on a four-lane highway at what seemed to me a breathtakingly fast speed. Holding a cigarette in one hand and steering with the other, he talked incessantly. America had transformed him. He was completely at ease in this new environment. When I expressed my amazement at his driving, he said: "Don't worry, you could be doing the same in a year or two! And you will have your own car, too!"

That was hard for me to believe. I marveled at the orderly traffic, with each car staying in its lane. That seemed quite extraordinary to me. Traffic in Mumbai is chaotic at any time of the day—traffic signs and rules are routinely ignored. You take your life in your (or someone else's) hands when you drive. When I visit India now, I dare not drive in Mumbai. I'm afraid even to sit in the front seat when someone else is driving. In about an hour, we reached the Atlanta University dormitory where Jarecha had a one-bedroom flat. It was about three times the size of my Mumbai room—and had its own bathroom. I had never seen such a bathroom except in the movies. It had a shower, tub and basin, all with hot and cold water. It also had a toilet. I had never seen a shower or a toilet inside a bathroom. For me, taking a bath meant going to the river or washing myself with water brought from there in a bucket. And going to the toilet meant going out in the open or visiting an outhouse.

Jarecha showed me how to use the shower, toilet, and hot and cold-water faucets. I cannot express how much I enjoyed my first American shower! It is a wonder of the world—even if Americans take it for granted. Jarecha had reserved a dorm room for me next to his apartment. He gave me the key to his flat and said that I was welcome to his room at any time. He also suggested that I might use his bathroom, at least in the beginning, instead of going to the common bathroom down the hall.

After dinner, which was delivered to his flat, he took me to my room and told me to get a good night's sleep. "Tomorrow will be a big day—you will be very busy. Get some rest," he said, and left. Alone by myself for the first time in two days, I couldn't sleep. I kept wondering how my fortune had totally changed so quickly. About a month ago,

I was a thoroughly defeated man with no hope and nothing to look forward to. Now I was in America, a world full of possibilities, where even an ordinary person could enjoy the luxuries of life that are available only to the rich in India. Within three short years, Jarecha had a wonderful flat, a nice car, fancy clothes and much more. In due time, I thought, maybe I could have these things myself. No wonder people from all over the world flocked to America. I promised myself that I would not squander the wonderful opportunity that God and Jarecha had just given me.

———————

At around 6 in the morning, Jarecha knocked on my door. "Get ready," he said. "We have a big day ahead of us." Since I was late registering, Jarecha took me to various offices to get me registered. I could see how easily he was moving from place to place, how he was known wherever we went. As I accompanied him from office to office, all I encountered were black faces. In an entire day at the university, I did not see a single white person. At dinner, about a hundred students occupied the dining hall. All diners were black except for one white and a few Asians, including some Indians. It took me a little while to realize that I had come to a predominantly black college. In Mumbai I had seen some African students who attended Bombay University for undergraduate and graduate studies, but they were few and far between. They usually kept to themselves and rarely mixed with others. From my reading of books and newspapers, I was aware that blacks were an oppressed minority in the U.S. I had some familiarity with their plight and civil-rights struggle under the leadership of Martin Luther King, Jr., who followed the Gandhian method of nonviolent resistance. I was also aware of how slavery had brutalized them, and of the Civil War that emancipated them. Lincoln was a hero of mine even in India. Yet that was all academic. Atlanta University was my first face-to-face encounter with black people and it would take some time for me to adjust. My idea of America had been formed by Hollywood movies of the 1950s and early '60s that had mostly white people in them. I simply assumed that going to an American university meant that I would be surrounded mostly by white faces—of students, professors, administrators, staff and others. Now here I was, surrounded by blacks everywhere. I simply hadn't associated America with black people. I had a lot to learn.

The next day I researched my new home. Atlanta University had been founded primarily for black Americans, established in 1865—along with a few other colleges—to provide higher education to African Americans excluded from white colleges and universities. It is part of what is known as the HBCU (Historically Black Colleges and Universities) educational institutions. There were about 100 such predominantly black colleges, mostly in the southern states of Texas, Louisiana, Alabama, North Carolina, South Carolina, Arkansas, Georgia, Florida, Mississippi and Tennessee that had practiced racial discrimination on all fronts, including higher education, long after slavery had been abolished. Though HBCU colleges were open to people of all colors, the overwhelming majority of students were black. Systematic discrimination, especially in education, deprived blacks of the means of advancement. Schooling for blacks at all levels was substandard. Serious funding problems at some private black colleges forced them to merge with other black colleges or shut down altogether. For the rest, financial difficulties particularly prevented them from achieving any kind of academic excellence. State-supported black colleges were better off financially but only marginally. In general, black higher education was characterized as an "academic disaster area" by Christopher Jencks and David Riesman in a 1967 article in the *Harvard Educational Review.*

In the midst of this disappointing academic landscape stood some exceptional black colleges. Atlanta's Spelman College for black women had long been supported by the Rockefeller family. Xavier University of Louisiana regularly graduated black students specializing in science, technology, engineering and medicine. The Jencks-Riesman article immediately created uproar, particularly at the black colleges. Critics argued that the article ignored the fundamental fact that these colleges provide higher educational opportunities to blacks who were shut out by white colleges. Further, if the education at these colleges was so bad, how could they have produced outstanding lawyers, scientists, artists and performers? The critics cited numerous examples of distinguished alumni such as Thurgood Marshall, a prominent lawyer who later became a Supreme Court justice, Martin Luther King, Jr., and George Washington Carver, the famous African American scientist famous for his research into peanuts, soybeans and sweet potatoes associated with Tuskegee University. Long before and after the controversy, there have been legions of famous blacks who made important contributions in the arts, sciences and commerce as well as in nearly every field of inquiry.

Asian—particularly Indian—students at Atlanta University for the most part had no idea what they had gotten into. I certainly didn't. Jarecha, my benefactor, was a graduate of Atlanta University. I followed his lead. For us foreigners, admission to Atlanta University was easy and tuition was relatively cheap compared to an MBA program at a top-ranked university. The consultant in Mumbai who'd gotten Jarecha admitted to Atlanta University understood this dynamic and arranged for the admission of numerous Indian students there. He got his fees, and students got admitted to an American university. In due time they had their MBA degree. The bottom line was that they were going to America for a graduate degree, and they did not much care from what college they would receive it.

When these graduates returned to India, all that mattered was the label "America Returned" to establish one's value in the job market. With that, one could be assured of a good job in India, as well as a lovely bride from a good family. I'd heard the story of an Indian who received his degree from Howard University, a historically black college in Washington, DC, and passed himself off as having received it from Harvard University!

Like many of my fellow Indian students, I had some buyer's remorse based upon my understanding of the dynamics involved. But I reconciled myself to the situation and tried to make the most of it. Leaving Atlanta University for another college was not a practical idea. Besides, how could I say to Jarecha that the college where he had studied and was presently employed may not have been at the highest academic level and, therefore, I was leaving for another school? The best strategy for me was to work hard, finish the program and continue to learn about so many different aspects of which I had limited understanding or perception.

Given my vegetarian (not vegan) diet, Jarecha arranged for me to be served a grilled-cheese sandwich, milkshake and buttermilk. For the next several months, that was my daily fare. Salad bars were rare in those days. I was told that vegetables were for sissies— real men ate beef! The American students who sat next to me in the cafeteria availed themselves of my servings of beefsteak and other choice meats.

When I began using the common bathroom, I realized why Jarecha had suggested that I use the bathroom in his flat. Men in the common bathroom were mostly naked. This was shocking to my prudish Indian eye. In Mumbai hostels we took baths only with the doors closed. One was rarely naked, and then only by oneself. When bathing in the river, we were clad in our underwear.

––––––––––

Atlanta University had its advantages. One could get good grades without breaking much of a sweat. Since one didn't have to spend too much time studying, there was time left to take part-time jobs and earn money to defray tuition and other expenses. I found work in the bursar's office along with Jarecha and did other jobs in the library, kitchen and dormitory, all of which helped me to send money home to Nalini. Professors at Atlanta University were certainly better than the ones I'd had at Mumbai's Sydenham College. In Atlanta there was an attempt to link the classroom with the business world. Many professors had practical experience that they shared. Student teams were assigned projects that required them to go out and visit companies to understand business practices and procedures. Classes generally were made up of 20 to 30 students, who were encouraged to participate in class discussion. There were lively exchanges between professors and students both inside and outside the classroom.

––––––––––

When I arrived in Atlanta, the country was going through massive upheaval on two fronts: civil rights and the Vietnam War. Atlanta was a hub of the civil-rights movement centered around the Ebenezer Baptist Church, where Martin Luther King, Jr., and his father were pastors. Yet I rarely witnessed any public discussion of the issues, particularly the war. This was puzzling to me: Why such little interest in these burning issues? While major campuses around the country were erupting with protests against the Vietnam War, Atlanta colleges and universities were strangely quiet. I don't recall hearing about a single teach-in at any of the Atlanta campuses. Indian students, though perhaps academically smart, were among the most politically indifferent people I'd encountered. I forged no lasting friendships with any of them. Narrowly focused to a fault, they were there to get their MBAs and then get out as fast as they could. My association with black students and professors at Atlanta University prepared me for, and protected me from, the pervasive racism among whites in the South—and among many Indians, too. Later on, when I went to do my Ph.D. work at Louisiana State University in Baton Rouge, I would see that racism firsthand.

Working closely with black people at Atlanta University and then later at North Carolina A&T University, also a predominantly black college where I taught, I quickly came to see their goodness and strength. The more that I got to know and work with them, particularly in the District of Columbia government, the more I realized how intellectually sharp and sophisticated they were in economics, finance, accounting and budgeting. I could also see how their inner resources would have helped them persevere under the extreme circumstances of slavery and post-slavery discrimination. I was also impressed by their deep religiosity and instinct for survival. Few people in history have suffered as much as African-Americans in slavery while still emerging from the ordeal with their human dignity intact.

I was surprised to see how so many African Americans were dealing with the daily hurts and humiliations of discrimination. The adverse conditions did not make them morose—I saw many enjoying life more than other Americans. No matter where I was—in the classroom, restaurants, barbershops, grocery stores, bowling alleys, colleges, the dormitory kitchen—it was not at all unusual to see groups of blacks laughing; no matter what their station in life—janitor, cook, maid, professor, student, bank manager, university administrator—more often than not I found them jovial and full of laughter.

My academic burden was not too taxing, so I had extra time on my hands that I used to explore the city of Atlanta. It was the capital of Georgia and had a storied place in the Civil War as the site of one its major battles. General Sherman conducted a four-month siege of the city before his army burned it to the ground and marched to the sea. I had seen that calamity depicted in Gone with the Wind, the famous movie starring Clark Gable and Vivien Leigh, but I had no idea when I saw it in Mumbai's Metro theater that one day I would live in Atlanta. What impressed me most about the city in my early forays was its cleanliness. For such a large city, it seemed quite orderly. All of the things that I associated with Mumbai—the shoving and jostling, hustle and bustle, unruly crowds, haphazard traffic and ear-splitting noise—were absent. I enjoyed walking in Atlanta. Its tall buildings, broad sidewalks, clean streets, wide avenues, well-stocked department stores, restaurants serving Southern food (particularly pecan pie)—all of this fascinated me. Every chance I got, I would board a nearly empty bus for only a quarter and ride downtown.

Occasionally, I was invited to talk about India at a local public school. I found it impressive that even an ordinary school would have a library, gym, well-maintained playground, cafeteria and auditorium. Even more impressive was that schools were free for everyone. Libraries, swimming pools, parks and other public facilities were sprinkled throughout the city—free and available to all.

I was no longer in the cash-only economy. I got paid by check, no matter what or where my job was, and opened my first bank account. As soon as I started receiving regular paychecks, I applied for a credit card. I learned that once my credit was established, I could buy even bigger items, such as household appliances, clothes and the like. Big-ticket items such as cars and houses could be purchased on a long-term credit basis with only minimum down payments and paying the rest by monthly installments. I wished that we had such a credit apparatus available in India. That would have saved me so much strife and made my life immeasurably easier in Mumbai, where I was on a strictly cash basis.

I quickly discovered the American fascination with gadgets. Numerous appliances and devices such as pressure cookers, gas stoves, refrigerators, air conditioners, vacuum cleaners, dishwashers, washers and dryers, hair dryers, typewriters, lawn mowers, cars, telephones and much, much more could be found in virtually every household. Most of these gadgets made life easier, relieving people—particularly women but increasingly men—from the drudgery of housework. These labor-saving devices made it possible for women to get out of the home and work in offices. Through these gadgets, Americans have defined affluence worldwide. The rich and upper-middle classes in India proudly show off their latest gadget acquisition after trips to the United States. For many Americans, it was not enough to have these gadgets—they had to have the latest versions with all of the up-to-the-minute improvements. Every year, new models of cars, phones and appliances make their way into garages and kitchens and elsewhere in homes and offices. Inventors keep coming up regularly with new gadgets, and enough buyers scoop them up as soon as they appear in stores.

For people who take great pride in rugged individualism, personal freedom and liberty, I found Americans to be obedient regarding some of their collective obligations. Despite ample rhetoric and isolated protests about taxes, most Americans dutifully file their income-tax returns by April 15th. This level of voluntary tax compliance is exemplary by international standards and the envy of tax collectors worldwide. Similarly, I was impressed that the whole country voluntarily and simultaneously sets clocks forward an hour in the spring and backward an hour in the fall—and does so with little fanfare every year at the appointed time. Dictators only dream of such obedience, yet here in this individualistic society people often behave in lockstep, few questions asked.

Americans' obsession with cars had always fascinated me. Indians walk everywhere. In America everyone drives. It was quite a thrill for me to visit drive-in restaurants such as Hot Shoppes, not to mention drive-in movie theaters. In India, cars are luxuries that only a very few can afford. Here, it seemed, everybody had to have one. A car was necessary no matter what you wanted to do. And the easy availability of credit makes automobiles affordable even for common people. Widespread car ownership made it possible for people to move out of cities and live in far-flung suburbs. This led to heavy reliance on gas with profound political implications both domestically and internationally.

American grocery stores are another wonder of the world—a remarkable democratic phenomenon. On Saturday mornings, I would see hundreds of people loading up shopping carts with all kinds of food—bread, butter, dairy products, meat, fish and poultry, fruits, vegetables, soups and cereal. There was no shortage of anything. You asked for it and they would have it—and so inexpensive! It is a great tribute to American capitalism that the country has been able to provide life's basic necessities—food, clothing and shelter—to most people on such a massive scale, a reflection of democracy.

Soon after arriving in the U.S., I saw that American democracy had largely met that basic test. What good is the ability to vote if you can't feed your family? Yes, the ability to vote is important, but life's basic necessities should come first. The ability to vote should ideally lead to this goal, but that is not always the case. People in India have been voting freely for the last 70 years, but that has not led to India's becoming an economic democracy. Almost a third of its 1.2 billion people are still mired in abysmal poverty and deprived of life's basic necessities while India has the third-largest (111) population of billionaires in the world. A democracy that does not provide the basic necessities of life to common people or one that distributes them so unequally is a democracy in name only. That was the hard lesson I learned during my difficult years in Mumbai. Soon after arriving in the U.S., I saw that American democracy had largely met that basic test.

More than anywhere else, America's society and economy are geared toward the individual; the organizing principle, as it were, is to make life easy and more pleasurable for the common man. Hence the continuous invention of gadgets that help with household chores, and free and easy access to national parks, museums, monuments, schools and libraries to people at large.

When I visit the magnificent temples of India, I am awed by their distinctive architecture but appalled by the toilet facilities and their deplorable, unsanitary condition. From an Indian perspective, it was all right to spend huge fortunes to build great temples but looking after the needs of devotees and worshipers was secondary. In the United States I found that public spaces such as museums, monuments and parks were almost always equipped with appropriate facilities, including cafeterias and clean toilets.

Concern for the ordinary man is also extended to those who are disabled, particularly children. Special education is provided for children who have disabilities by providing them access to public schools and facilities. This helps these children explore their potential and become contributing citizens just like all others. Of course, the affluence of American society makes it possible to take care of those who cannot take care of themselves, but the guiding factor of such an enlightened policy is the basic American sense of fairness. Americans often take the nation's affluence and egalitarianism for granted. The rest of the world is in awe of this extraordinary accomplishment. At least I was—and still am. In addition to its stunning affluence, what impressed me were several surprising characteristics of Americans. For example, immediately upon arrival, I was struck by people's civility. Phrases such as "Thank you," "Please," "You're welcome" and "Excuse me"—so new to my Indian ear—were commonly used among people in all walks of life—superiors and subordinates, the elderly and children, the latter of which were taught proper manners at home and school.

The indignity and rude behavior that I had suffered in Mumbai would have been unthinkable in an American office. No one here would shout for a peon to bring him tea or coffee. There is generally a pot in the corner; anyone who wants coffee, including the manager, would simply get up and get a cup. If the coffee pot was empty, he would make another one—and usually wouldn't hesitate to take tea or coffee back to the secretary. I saw in this behavior an American emphasis on human dignity no matter how low or high the person's social status might be. Above all, I found Americans generally to be a generous and open people—open to new ideas, new people, new and different ways of doing things. The America of 2018 is a fundamentally different country than the one that I came to about 50 years ago. People come to America from all over the world and keep remaking the country as they remake their lives.

Another example of the American propensity to change can be found in the status of African Americans. When I came to the country in 1965, racism was quite prevalent all over the South and in many other parts of the country in various forms. It was highly improbable for blacks to get elected to any significant position nearly anywhere in the country. Since then there has been steady improvement in the condition of black Americans. Presently, they can be found holding high positions in practically every field including heading Fortune 500 companies. Today there are thousands of blacks elected to public office at all levels everywhere. Yet in the '60s, it was difficult even to imagine that an African American could get elected president of the United States, as Barack Obama had been elected twice—in 2008 and 2012. The American attitude toward women and gays has also changed fundamentally during my stay here.

To my Indian eyes, it was amazing to see how Americans changed their pattern of behavior so fundamentally. During the mid-'60s when I came, smoking was quite common everywhere. As late as 1976 when I joined the General Accounting Office in Washington, smoking was quite widespread, with TV commercials and billboards glorifying smoking quite prevalent. Today, smoking has been prohibited in most public spaces and shunned in private places as well.

I also found Americans to be generally pragmatic, optimistic and full of enthusiasm about life, with a guiding spirit that always seems to see the light at the end of the tunnel. Having come from India, where people are generally fatalistic, who seemed to have given up and submitted themselves to the vagaries of life ("What's the use?"), I found Americans full of a can-do attitude toward solving life's myriad problems. Rather than philosophizing about life, the attitude is more like "Get on with it!" If there is a problem, Americans generally follow up with, "How do we go about solving it?" Giving up is not an American trait. All of this was and remains quite refreshing to me.

Equally new was local initiative. Rather than waiting for Washington or state capitals to solve local problems, the emphasis was on doing things locally. Indeed, the general feeling was to stay away from Washington and keep things in local hands. Americans might also be among the hardest-working people in the world. They take fewer and shorter vacations than most Europeans; their workdays are generally longer and lunch hours shorter. As if this weren't enough, they take work home. They are also busy being handymen, fixing things when they come home. On weekends, I see them mowing lawns or fixing roofs, cleaning gutters, painting or adding a room. On weekends, American hardware stores are full of do-it-yourself "Harry Homeowners" looking for things they need to work on their projects or on hobbies such as furniture-making or running model trains. Many Americans do basic maintenance work around the house.

I also learned early on that most of my fellow students took on part-time work to help pay for tuition and incidental expenses. They didn't hesitate to do what Indians considered menial work like pumping gas, washing pots and pans in the dorm kitchen, shelving books in the library or waiting tables at restaurants. Even students from well-to-do families worked. Young people are encouraged to work from their high-school years. Mowing lawns and shoveling snow are quite common in most suburban neighborhoods. In summer it's not unusual to see lemonade stands put up by enterprising kids in middle-class neighborhoods.

Starting work early in life instills a work ethic and provides people with a sense of self-worth, discipline, responsibility and entrepreneurship. The workplaces I encountered here were quite different from those that I'd known in India. For example, the bank Jarecha took me to open an account was operated by several young women supervised by a manager; customers stood quietly in line waiting to see the cashier. At a similar bank in India, at least 20 adults, mostly men, would be working, as several peons ferried large account books from counter to counter while others ran errands for bank officials and brought them tea, coffee and snacks.

This is how America looked to me some 50 years ago. Interestingly, this is how I feel about it today, too. In fact, I regard America to be the most revolutionary society in the world.

A lot has changed in America since then and not all of it is necessarily for the better. Some of it is downright nasty, particularly the debasement of public squares and the toxic turn of its politics into hate-filled tribal warfare. Some of it is dispiriting, such as a gradual erosion of the middle class, the emergence of profound income inequality and the uncaring disintegration of its welfare state. Most disconcerting to me personally is anti-immigration hysteria, particularly when the country needs more—not fewer—immigrants to staff its firms, farms, factories, hospitals, homes and universities. If people would only step back, recognize how much the United States offers and provides, and not take for granted key aspects that many other countries do not so readily accept, the attitude toward immigrants may well be more welcoming. But the country has in the past suffered through such anti-immigrant phases targeting certain groups. For example, during the 1870s and '80s anti-Chinese feelings were so pronounced that the Chinese Exclusion Act of 1882 was passed. At other points in American history, other nationalities such as the Irish, Germans and Italians were scorned and subject to immigration quotas. Eastern-European Jews were also not welcome. Immigration quotas had been established for various nationalities. Despite it all, there has been a steady stream of immigrants who kept coming. In 1965 quotas had been eliminated and immigration was liberalized, of which I was a beneficiary.

During my 50-some years in America, I have lived through the turbulent times of the late 1960s and early '70s when the country seemed to be coming apart at the seams. I have lived through the assassinations of Robert Kennedy and Reverend Martin Luther King, Jr. In the aftermath of the King assassination I saw America's big cities burning. During the Vietnam War, I have seen its great universities erupting. I have seen students marching in the streets and gathering at the Pentagon chanting, "Hey, hey, LBJ, how many did you kill today?" I have seen the raised fists and heard the anguished cries of Black Power Now. I have also seen the American government put under severe stress during the Watergate era when a president flagrantly violated its constitutional norms and was nearly impeached. At each time, the American center did not appear to hold and the country seemed to be falling apart. But it did not. Given that America survived through these and other crises and still emerged triumphant gives me hope that it will do so again!

Chapter 8

SCHOOLED IN SOUTHERN CIVIL RIGHTS

Georgia was a hotbed of Southern racism and a flashpoint for protests during the late 1960s. The state's successive governors and legislatures were almost all segregationists. It kept sending racist congressmen and senators to Washington, the most prominent of whom was Richard Russell, who through his seniority and status in the U.S. Senate sabotaged most of the civil-rights legislation introduced there. While I was in Atlanta, it was at the heart of the civil-rights movement and gaining momentum in the mid-'60s. Martin Luther King, Jr., had his church there. Despite the state's avowed racism, Georgia's major newspaper, the *Atlanta Journal-Constitution*, was a voice of moderation. Its legendary editor Ralph McGill was a leading proponent of civil rights. He was also a supporter of the Vietnam War. How, I wondered, could a prominent journalist like McGill be for civil rights and not oppose the war in Vietnam? After all, both struggles were for liberation and self-determination. It seemed clear to me that the United States had misjudged the nature of the war in Vietnam. To the Vietnamese, it was a continuation of the war for national liberation they had fought against the French and decisively won at Dien Bien Phu in 1954. Now they were fighting Americans, who believed the struggle was against communist aggression from the North. Yes, North Vietnam's leader Ho Chi Minh was a communist, but he was a nationalist first. I believed that, despite their overwhelming superiority, American forces would meet the same fate as the French. That turned out to be the case, but before they left Vietnam, they brought havoc to a poverty-stricken Asian nation, killing hundreds of thousands of innocent people—and losing tens of thousands of young Americans as well.

Armed with these and other arguments, I wrote a letter to editor McGill asking for a meeting. To my great surprise, he promptly agreed, which immediately presented a problem: How would I get to his office? I was unfamiliar with the city's bus system, which ran mostly during the morning and evening rush hours. And I had no money for a taxi. So I asked Jarecha, "Please take me to Mr. McGill's office. This is a big deal for me!" He knew about the newspaper but not about Ralph McGill. He readily agreed. He wouldn't accompany me to the meeting, he said, but would run some errands and pick me up after about an hour. Jarecha must have been amused by my obsession with the Vietnam War. I showed up at McGill's office at the *Journal-Constitution* at the appointed time and a secretary took me inside. Piles of newspapers and books covered his desk. A stocky man with a head full of hair, he wore white shirt and tie. As we were about to sit down, his deputy, Eugene Patterson, came in.

I began by complimenting McGill for his leadership on civil-rights issues, telling him that I appreciated his courage and steadfastness in the face of the hostility he got from Southerners, especially his readers in Atlanta. Then I continued:

"Mr. McGill, I am at a loss to understand your support of the Vietnam War."

"But we must oppose the spread of communism," he said. "If we don't stop it in Vietnam, it would spread all over Asia, including your country!"

That was my signal; I went into my well-rehearsed arguments. "I am sure you know that Ho Chi Minh is more a nationalist than a communist. It is not a war of communist aggression but of national liberation. Besides, America has no business being there!"

I suggested that the concept of "Yellow Peril" was highly exaggerated, and the idea of the domino effect was an insult to the U.S. Pacific Fleet. I said that America could never win a jungle war in Indochina, which had been a graveyard for the French in the 1950s. In retrospect, this sounds like a mouthful coming from a young Indian student who had no training or experience in foreign policy. And to say it to an esteemed editor of the South's leading newspaper was clearly overreaching. I'm sure he had heard it all before, but he good-naturedly let me plough through these all-too-familiar arguments against the war. However, when I praised Senator J. William Fulbright—chairman of the Senate Foreign Relations Committee and an opponent of the war—for his courageous efforts to educate the country on the Vietnam War by holding committee hearings, it was too much for McGill. He held up his hand, clearly annoyed. "Young man," he said, "you should know that Fulbright is not all that courageous when it comes to civil rights for blacks in Arkansas!" This indeed was an electoral dilemma that Fulbright and other conscientious Southern politicians faced. They could not vote for legislation granting civil rights to blacks without risking white retribution at the ballot box. During the 40 or so minutes that the meeting lasted, Eugene Patterson—who later became a distinguished newspaper editor in his own right—said not a word. He must have been amused by the audacity of a young foreign visitor arguing with one of the most distinguished newspapermen in the U.S.

––––––––––

All of these extracurricular activities aside, my goal was to finish my studies and start working as soon as possible. Nalini wrote letters regularly—and passionately. How soon could she come? To get her to the U.S., I had to get a green card and to do that I had to have a job. Getting an MBA from Atlanta University was not difficult, but with that degree, getting a job was more difficult for a foreigner like me. Yes, the university had a placement bureau that helped graduates land good jobs with reputable companies. But it was of no use to foreign students. Companies like IBM and Xerox came to the campus to recruit freshly minted MBAs, but they mainly sought black graduates. There was tremendous pressure from civil-rights groups and the federal government to hire and promote blacks. Indian students applied, but few if any were called in for interviews, even those with superior academic records. I don't recall a single Indian student getting an offer from any major corporation that visited the university.

Here was the catch-22 for every foreign graduate at the time: You needed a green card to qualify for a job, but you had to have a job to get a green card! Only an employer could sponsor a foreigner for a green card. But how to find an employer? So, what next for me? There was only one way out. Black colleges needed faculty, particularly in science, math, engineering and business. White professors looking to enhance their academic career did not work at these colleges since very few had national reputations as research institutions. Qualified black professors were lured away by white colleges under pressure to hire black faculty. So there was a marriage of convenience among black colleges, which needed qualified faculty, and Asians, who needed sponsors for their green cards. That led to the hiring of a sizeable number of Asian professors at black colleges, including Indians. The predominantly black colleges desperately sought qualified professors to teach accounting, which my MBA qualified me to do. I applied to several places and was immediately called for interviews. I received job offers from every place to which I applied.

Private black colleges were facing severe financial stresses, yet state-supported black colleges were relatively better off. So I accepted a teaching position at North Carolina Agricultural and Technical University (A&T), a state-sponsored black college in Greensboro. I was disappointed that I couldn't get a job with a major American company, but was relieved that at least I had a job. Now I could apply for the all-important green card with sponsorship from A&T—of paramount importance. "Let's get that out of the way," I said to myself, "then we can think of other things." As soon as my exams were over—without waiting for the commencement ceremony—I headed to Greensboro to get started. My fellow students thought it odd that I would skip commencement. For them it was a big deal. Their families would show up and big parties would be thrown to celebrate the occasion.

My family was far away. Even if they were nearby, there would have been no parties. My family had never shown much interest in my education. Kaka had opposed my going to college to begin with, and also my going to the U.S. Despite all of the degrees I have earned—Bachelor of Commerce, Bachelor of Laws, Master of Business Administration and Doctor of Philosophy—I have never marched in a graduation ceremony or celebrated the occasion with family. In fact, my family had no idea what I was studying or why! So I paid my graduation fees and asked the registrar's office to mail me the diploma.

––––––––

In mid-August 1966, I took a Greyhound bus to Greensboro to start a new phase of my life. On the bus ride I pondered how chance plays a critical role in life. What would have happened to me if I had not met Jarecha on that fortuitous day at Sydenham College when I hesitantly approached him about putting my poems on the literary wall-paper that he edited? That encounter mushroomed into a friendship that ultimately brought me to America. During my time in Atlanta, I saw Jarecha almost daily. I went to the university with him. I worked part-time in his office. In practically everything I did—courses I took, places I stayed and visited, friends I made, people I met, shopping I did—I sought his help and advice. Indeed, he was helpful by nature and did not hesitate to help whoever needed it. But he was especially generous to me in his help and guidance, and in Greensboro I would miss him. There I was on my own.

Atlanta University played a pivotal role in educating me about black America, though only later did I come to understand the benefits of having been there. At the time, I'd felt somewhat cheated out of the mainstream American experience. During my initial years at predominantly black institutions, I thought that I'd been relegated to a small corner of American life. I was intrigued by the other America—the larger America—the one that I had seen in Hollywood movies. When I ventured occasionally beyond the campus to downtown Atlanta, with its high-class department stores and major universities such as Emory and Georgia Tech, I was overwhelmed and wondered what it would be like to be part of that America! Yet there again, my preconceptions were based on limited information and experience.

Years later, when I worked for the District of Columbia government, at the time an overwhelmingly black city, my early experience working mainly with black students, teachers and administrators proved most helpful. For some 16 years, I held senior positions in Washington, first as tax commissioner (1997-2000) and then as chief financial officer (2000-2013). In both positions I had a large staff of mostly African Americans. Though much in District government and politics was viewed through a racial prism, I never faced any issues of racial discrimination. Indeed, I was appointed to my positions by three successive mayors, all black. During my years in the District government, I had the pleasure of working with some of the finest civil servants I ever knew, almost all black and of exceptional ability and dedication.

––––––––

Greensboro, North Carolina, my new hometown, had a storied history in the civil-rights movement. In 1960, just a few years before I arrived, four A&T students went to Woolworth's department store downtown, sat at a "Whites Only" counter and asked to be served coffee. Following store practice, the waitress refused to serve them and asked them to move to the "Black" counter. The students refused, sitting at the "Whites Only" counter until closing time. The following day, 20 students appeared, sat at the same counter and waited to be served. They too were refused. This sit-in suddenly became a media event, and two days later 300 students protested in similar fashion.

The protest spread to other cities and expanded to include public facilities such as libraries, parks and swimming pools. The Greensboro sit-in was a crucial event in the history of the civil-rights movement that ultimately led to passage of the Civil Rights Act of 1964, under which public accommodations were desegregated throughout the South. In the aftermath of that, what would this historic city hold for an aspiring teacher?

There was no one to receive me at the bus station in Greensboro. I found my way to the college dormitory that I was to stay in temporarily. Inside, as across the college at large, I was among mostly black people. By now there was no novelty to it. With help of the college staff, I soon acquired room and board at the house of a Baptist minister. I still had no car so walked to and from the campus.

I was to teach my first class on Tuesday, August 23, 1966. The night before, I couldn't sleep. I'd never taught before nor spoken in a public forum, not even in my native tongue, Gujarati. Now I had to teach a class in English. I was afraid that I'd be struck with stage fright. I prepared my lecture and practiced in front of a mirror. Would the students understand my thick Indian accent? I still hadn't mastered the Southern accent or learned American idioms. What if they became noisy, unruly and made mischief in the class, as students do in Mumbai colleges when they didn't like a classroom teacher?

The appointed day came and I appeared before the class. The Graham Hall where I was to teach was rather drab. There was nothing except chairs and a blackboard. I had ironed my clothes the day before, and still had the same woolen suit and tie that I had brought from India. I was perspiring and it was quite hot in the classroom as there was no air-conditioning. The windows were open and the traffic could be heard whizzing by. One look at the students and I was intimidated. Here I was, an underweight Indian in an ill-fitting suit in front of 40 or so young men and women, each of whom appeared bigger than I. They looked at me expectantly. Like a beginning swimmer on a diving board, I jumped into my lecture. I couldn't tell how the first five or so minutes went, but the students were taking notes. I felt reassured. The rest of the class went quite well. There were no questions and I was relieved. Fortunately, I could repeat the same lecture in the next class; I began to relax.

As it turned out, I liked teaching. In short order I became a favorite professor whose classes were always fully subscribed. I was popular for several reasons: I was always well prepared and tried to make my lessons relevant by talking about what was going on in the wider business world. I started each class with a real-life, contemporaneous example related to the subject at hand. Also, my office door was always open. Students could walk in anytime they liked and ask me questions or discuss issues. I took personal interest in students both in and out of the classroom. I listened to them respectfully and was present in my office even on days when I had no classes to teach.

I also mingled with students socially. I wanted to get to know them and wanted them to know me. I needed their approval as much as I needed the approval of the accounting department head and school dean. I wanted my contract renewed and needed the college to sponsor me for a green card. I invited groups of 10 or 15 students at a time to my apartment, and would order snacks and soft drinks to serve. During one of my gatherings, a student sat down next to me. "Mr. Gandhi," he asked, "are you at all related to Mahatma Gandhi?" His name was Gordon and he was quite well read.

"No," I responded, "but I am a great admirer of the Mahatma." We talked about Gandhi's nonviolence movement and how it gained India its independence from the British."

"But that can't work here," Gordon said.

"Why not?" I asked. "Look at the 1960 lunch-counter protests right here in Greensboro. They were classically Gandhian and very effective, I believe."

Gordon countered, "Yes, but the whites did not have to give up much of anything. Wait till the question comes to jobs, privileges—the whites will not be so amenable. You don't understand America," he told me. "Your nonviolence thing does not work around here. This is a violent society. Wait and see."

He was clearly reading Malcolm X, the fiery black leader who had a sizeable following among young blacks. Malcolm X had openly questioned the efficacy of the nonviolent means advocated by Martin Luther King, Jr., who under the influence of Mahatma Gandhi had kept his protests peaceful and nonviolent. Gordon asked me to come to a public meeting at the university where Stokely Carmichael, the fiery activist and proponent of Black Power, was going to address the students. "Sure, I'll come," I said. "I've heard so much about him and want to hear what he has to say, of course."

Carmichael was mesmerizing. I had rarely heard such fighting eloquence. He was only in his 20s, yet showed the maturity of a veteran agitator. The students received him with a thunderous applause. I could see how he was a hero to young blacks who were impatient with the progress being made on civil rights under Dr. King's methods. Carmichael was also an outspoken opponent of the Vietnam War and asked blacks to refuse to go. He led an anti-war movement called "Hell No, We Won't Go." Disillusioned about the prospects of black people in the U.S., he later left the country and went to Guinea, joined the Pan-African movement, and changed his name to Kwame Toure to honor his African heroes Nkrumah and Toure. In the late 1990s, I saw Carmichael in Washington, DC, at a benefit event organized to defray his medical expenses;

he was suffering from cancer. It was difficult to reconcile his emaciated, cancer-afflicted body in a wheelchair with the firebrand revolutionary whom I had seen and heard 30 years ago in Greensboro.

On April 4, 1968, Dr. King was assassinated and the whole country exploded. Riots erupted in nearly all major cities, including Washington, DC. President Johnson had to call out the National Guard to protect the White House and Capitol. On our campus, the college president immediately declared a week-long holiday and asked students to go home. Had they remained on campus, riots no doubt would have erupted in Greensboro as well. Before going home, Gordon came by to see me, clearly agitated. We had a brief conversation about the death of Dr. King and what had followed. He was thinking about leaving school and joining the movement.

"Look Gordon," I said, "I understand your grief, but please do not leave the school. Get your degree and then do whatever it is that you want to do." When he didn't show up for my accounting classes over the next several days, I assumed that he was sick and would show up again when he got better. A few weeks passed and still no Gordon. I asked around, querying his friends, yet no one had any idea of what had happened to him. I never saw him again.

Chapter 9

ON THE ROAD

Shortly after settling in Greensboro, I boarded a Greyhound bus and traveled to New York to see the Statue of Liberty. It was a pilgrimage for me: I wanted to pay homage to Lady Liberty. I will never forget the experience as the ferry approached the mammoth statue of the "mighty woman with a torch." Walking through the grounds of Ellis Island and the refugee-processing center, I tried to visualize the millions of people—the huddled masses—who had come there to remake their lives in a new world. Emma Lazarus's immortal words rang in my ear:

Give me your tired, your poor,
Your huddled masses yearning to breathe free,
The wretched refuse of your teeming shore.

While still teaching at A&T, I tried to see if I could get a job at any of the local companies. I even applied to major corporations elsewhere. Unfortunately, nothing turned up. However, the National Urban League—the nation's oldest civil-rights organization—had a program that offered summer corporate jobs to the faculty of black colleges. As soon as I found out about it, I jumped at the first available opportunity. I got summer assignments at IBM and Jones & Laughlin Steel Company. It was my first experience working with white people, and also my first glimpse of a different America. In Atlanta and Greensboro, I had been lodged in a segregated corner of American society. Now I was able to see how the larger—and largely white—society in America worked.

Most of the white employees at these corporations appeared to be well-meaning, good-hearted people. They were very nice to me—an immigrant from India—and invited me to parties and other special occasions at their homes. It made me wonder how such nice people could be even tangentially part of the institutional racism that was widely prevalent in the U.S. at the time. Many of the blacks I met in Atlanta and Greensboro were angry about the injustice meted out to them, yet most of the white people I met at these companies and elsewhere were generally unaware of the suffering experienced by black people.

Blacks and whites seemed to live in separate universes. Even in Atlanta, a majority-black city long famous for being the "black Mecca," I met many whites who had only vague knowledge of Atlanta University and the existence of other black colleges there. Whites rarely, if ever, ventured into areas where black people lived and congregated. This was reminiscent of my days in Savarkundla: People from the upper classes never visited parts of town where the Dalits, or untouchables, lived. I had a vague idea of that part of town but never went there. I saw them only when they came to town to do their chores. We had a few Dalit children in our school, but they sat separately in a corner and I never exchanged words with them. Indian discrimination was based on a specific delineation by birthright. In America, however, skin color provided a clear distinction. In India, untouchables looked like any other Indians. For that reason, discrimination is far more pervasive and deeply rooted in villages where people know each other and can easily identify untouchables. Despite legal prohibition against untouchability, it still persists in rural India, where nearly 70 percent of India's 1.3 billion people live. It is more difficult to practice such discrimination in larger cities, where it is impossible to know and differentiate different castes, particularly the untouchables.

In Greensboro, my mobility was restricted because I didn't drive. To remedy the situation, I took driving lessons at the college. My teacher, Arnold—a young black student in my accounting class—was amused that his professor, at 26, didn't know how to drive. He enjoyed giving me driving lessons in his car. We got to be friends, and he would take me grocery shopping and help me run other errands. He eagerly took me to parties and other social events at the homes of his black friends. At those parties, girls would invariably want to know if I was married. Once they learned that I was, they would pepper me with questions:

"Was it an arranged marriage?"

"How did you pick your wife?"

"Is there dating in India?

"Had you met your wife before you got married?"

"Did you date? How long?"

"Is your wife here?"

"Can we meet her?"

"Do you plan to stay in this country or want to go back home?"

There were inevitable questions about roaming cows and the Taj Mahal, of course. When I got my driver's license, it was time to buy a car. The Ford Mustang was a hot car then, particularly among the young. Arnold insisted that I buy a Mustang and offered to help me. We made the rounds of car dealers and finally settled on one. Then Arnold took over. The salesman was annoyed that Arnold did all the talking for me. Nevertheless, I let Arnold negotiate a nice price. We went home with me in the driver's seat! It cost me $2,500. Nearly 10 years later, I sold it for just $500. Within an hour of the newspaper ad's appearance, I got a call. The prospective buyer came with cash in hand and, without any questions, put money in my hand and drove away with my much-battered Mustang filled with many memories. But the phone kept ringing for a few days and callers were willing to pay much more. I had not realized that the Mustang had achieved classic-car status.

Jarecha was right when he had told me that within a few years I would have my own car. I had my picture taken with the Mustang and immediately sent it to Nalini and my parents in India. With car keys in hand I felt liberated and started taking long, out-of-town trips. The very first trip I took was to Washington, before which I wrote letters to several prominent people and asked if I could come to see them. First among them was the great columnist Walter Lippmann, whose column "Today and Tomorrow" I used to read in India. An oracle of American opinion-making, Lippmann was one of the most sought-after newspapermen in Washington. Visiting heads of state, ambassadors, cabinet secretaries and others vied to meet him. Invariably, Lippmann was more important than the person with whom he was meeting. What I got from him was a form letter declining an interview. Later on, I had also written a similar letter to Edmund Wilson, the great American critic and another hero of mine. From him, I also got a tersely printed postcard saying that "Mr. Wilson does not give interviews." I should have saved such refusal postcards because they too had become collector's items!

Of several people whom I had asked to meet in Washington, only Richard L. Strout, a liberal columnist for the *New Republic*, agreed to see me. He took me to the National Press Club for lunch. I felt quite privileged—it was the first time that I dined at such an important venue. Nothing on the menu was truly vegetarian. Socializing with my students, particularly with Gordon and Arnold, I had begun to eat meat dishes such as hamburgers. So I ordered a cheeseburger. I was eager to see if there were any famous journalists dining at the Press Club whom I would recognize. I had started reading such columnists as Joseph Craft, James Reston, and Rowland Evans and Robert Novak. To my great surprise, I was able to recognize Evans there from his stamp-sized picture that used to appear along with Novak next to their newspaper column!

There was not much to argue about with Strout regarding Vietnam. Unlike Ralph McGill in Atlanta, he was quite sympathetic to my views. Nevertheless, I went through my well-rehearsed arguments against the war.

With great equanimity Strout told me: "Yes, but they all know this."

"And still they carry on the war?" I retorted. "How strange!"

"But I did not say they agree with your arguments," he replied. "They still see the war as communist aggression from the North and think we must go there to defend the South Vietnamese." Then he paused for a moment and said, "The real reason is that LBJ does not want to lose South Vietnam. He is determined not to be the first American president to lose a war, no matter how futile."

"Really?" I asked.

"Mr. Gandhi, you are too young to know, but we had a nasty 'Who lost China?' debate in this country. Johnson knows if he were to withdraw now and the communists were to take over the South, Republicans would crucify him, saying, 'You lost Vietnam!' He doesn't want that, so expect things to get worse before they get better."

With the new car at my disposal I started visiting Washington at every pretext. Each time I would stroll up and down Pennsylvania Avenue and could hardly have imagined then that one day I would have an office overlooking Freedom Plaza on that storied avenue. Of course, there was no Freedom Plaza then. City Hall—the Wilson Building, where I would have my office years later—was then surrounded by parking lots. There was no Ronald Reagan Building. The avenue itself was a disappointment, certainly no Champs-Élysées, nothing worthy of a great world capital. Walking eastward, on the right hand were drab government buildings, such as the IRS and Justice Department. On the left were old townhouses and a liquor store with a sign proclaiming "Apex Liquor." The imposing FBI building, the Navy Memorial, the Newseum, the Canadian Embassy and other buildings were not yet there. No one had thought of a highly imaginative Vietnam War Memorial yet.

Still, great monuments such as the Lincoln, Washington and Jefferson were all there in their grandeur. I was overwhelmed by the Lincoln Memorial. Looking out over the Mall from it, I visualized Martin Luther King, Jr., delivering his famous "I Have a Dream" speech. Climbing down the steps of the monument, King's prophetic words rang in my ears with all their Biblical force. During one of those visits, I went into the Capitol and attended a congressional hearing. It was not what I wanted to observe—a hearing of the Senate Foreign Relations Committee on Vietnam. But it was a revelation nevertheless. Again, I had no idea that two decades later I would testify there on numerous occasions about issues relating to federal taxation and the District of Columbia's finances.

In those days, I felt so strongly about the Vietnam War that I looked for important people with whom to discuss it. One such person was Professor Hans Morgenthau of the University of Chicago, an eminent political scientist who vehemently objected to the war. I wrote a letter saying that I would like to come and see him. I drove all the way to Chicago. His dimly lit office was underwhelming, with no pictures or decorative paintings on the walls. But there were books everywhere. As it turned out, he had been to India as a visiting professor at Jawaharlal Nehru University in New Delhi. He was also an admirer of Chanakya, generally regarded as the greatest Indian political philosopher of the ancient era, in the 4th century BC, and often considered the Indian Machiavelli.

Morgenthau discussed at length the futility of the Vietnam War. His objections were on practical grounds. "How stupid to think that America can win a guerrilla war in Indo-Chinese jungles," he said. "And for what?" Shaking his head, he announced in his thick German accent, "Mark what I say—they will have to leave those rice paddies just the way the French left, with their tail between their hind legs!"

Then he turned to me and asked what I was doing in the United States—and especially in the South.

"I am a professor of accounting," I said.

"Really? Where? Duke? Chapel Hill?"

"No sir—I am teaching at a small black college called North Carolina A&T in Greensboro."

All of a sudden, his tone and behavior changed. He said that he had other commitments and abruptly ended the interview. He seemed irritated that I was wasting his time talking about the great issues of the time. He must have assumed from my letter that I was a visiting professor of politics and international affairs of some distinction in India. Instead I turned out to be an accounting teacher at a small black college in North Carolina!

In taking a teaching job at A&T, my mission was clear. First, get a green card and then get Nalini to the United States. A&T promptly sponsored me and, in due time, I was called for an interview in Norfolk and was quickly granted the green card. Arnold offered to drive me to Norfolk in my Mustang. "Sure," I said, "if you want to come to Norfolk, that's fine!" In just a few weeks—August of 1967—my green card arrived in the mail. Yes, it was indeed green! I felt liberated; now I could do whatever and go wherever I wanted. Only an immigrant could comprehend what it meant to have a green card: the rare opportunity to remake one's life.

Finally, after two years apart, I sent for Nalini in late 1967. She had been patiently waiting to come to the U.S. and arranged to transfer our one-room flat to another renter at a price—*pughree*—that had doubled in the few years we had lived there. It took Nalini a few months to close down our household and obtain a passport and visa. My being in America and holding a valid green card made it immeasurably easy for her to get the needed documents and exchange clearance than it had been for me. My old friend Chandu was again a big help in obtaining the needed documents. When all was arranged, I sent Nalini an Air India ticket and she was on her way to America! Nalini reached New York on January 31, 1968. It also happened to be the day when North Vietnamese and Vietcong forces launched a major strike against South Vietnam known as the Tet Offensive. Though the North Vietnamese and Vietcong suffered heavy casualties, Tet marked a turning point in public perception in the U.S., destroying the myth that America was winning the war.

I drove to New York to meet Nalini. On the way there and back, I was glued to the car radio listening for the latest news from the war front. Arnold had again offered to drive me, but I politely declined his offer. I wanted to greet Nalini on my own, to make our first meeting in more than two years an intimate and strictly private affair. When I saw her emerging from the arrival lounge at Kennedy Airport, I rushed to greet her. We embraced but still did not kiss—the old Indian inhibition about a public kiss! I took hold of her luggage cart and we made our way to the parking lot.

As I was loading her bags into the car, I noticed that she was intently looking at it. "Yes," I said, "this is our car!"

"It is just like the pictures you sent me," she said. "It's beautiful!"

"Hop in. We have a long ride back home."

"How long?"

"About 10 hours!" I said cheerfully. "But we will take a break and stay overnight at a hotel."

After about five hours of driving, it was getting dark and I decided that it was time to take a break. We stopped by a roadside Howard Johnson's and ate a supper of grilled-cheese sandwiches, onion rings and milkshakes, then slept at the hotel. I was quite tired from driving. Nalini was also exhausted after her marathon flight and quickly went to bed. After a breakfast of pastries and tea, we got back on I-95 for another five hours of driving. Nalini was relaxed after a full night's sleep and kept glancing my way as I steered the car.

"Natu, look at you driving!" she exclaimed in Gujarati.

"In a few years," I replied, "you will be driving like this, too!"

We reached Greensboro late in the afternoon and unloaded Nalini's luggage in the furnished apartment that I had rented near the campus. As Nalini chattered away about various relatives in India, my mind wandered. More than the joy of uniting with Nalini, I felt relieved that she was here at last. I had failed her at nearly every step of the way in our marriage. From the beginning, we had to live apart for long periods. Doing so was a big blow for both of us. When she came to Mumbai, we'd lived a miserable, nomadic life. Now, at last, I could provide her with the kind of lifestyle that she could only have dreamed about in India. Most important, for the first time in our marriage, we would be living together with no one interfering in our privacy. When I had left her in Mumbai, I wasn't sure how things were going to work out. What if I couldn't bring her to America? What if I had to go back to India and settle in Mumbai? Those issues were now resolved, and we were charting a new life together as husband and wife.

In Greensboro, Nalini faced two immediate challenges—gaining conversational proficiency in English and learning to drive. I also enrolled her in a secretarial school in hopes that she could find a secretarial job once she was settled. This was an ill-advised move on my part, as it was quite a struggle given her lack of even basic English. The early days were difficult for Nalini. She found the winter weather very hard to bear and felt lonely. While I was teaching at the university during weekdays, she was left alone in the apartment with practically nothing to do. In Mumbai, she could walk out and greet neighbors, friends and family, socialize and go shopping. Not here. In Greensboro she had limited mobility and no social network. She was basically confined to the apartment until I got home.

There were a few Indian families in town, but visiting them required driving and we saw them mainly on weekends. During the week, Nalini was basically stuck in front of the TV; however, that daily television diet improved her conversational English and made her familiar with the American idiom. But her lack of proficiency in English still inhibited her. And her lack of a college education was a major hindrance in making her way in this new land.

Soon after she arrived, I enrolled her in a driving school, where also her lack of English was a real hurdle. She was embarrassed at her inability to communicate fluently and soon dropped out. Still, I wanted her to learn to drive so began giving her driving lessons myself. She was quite enthusiastic and did learn quickly; she had a hard time passing the written exam but easily passed the road test. Eventually, she got her driver's license and was a free bird. In preparation for coming to America, Nalini had taken some driving lessons in India at my request. But driving in Mumbai's chaotic traffic was very difficult and she gave it up after only a few lessons. In Greensboro she had to unlearn what she had absorbed in Mumbai—changing lanes often, cutting off other drivers, generally ignoring road signs and traffic lights, and, above all, driving aggressively—a necessity in Mumbai to get somewhere on time. Nalini also couldn't fathom why one drove on the right side in America and the driver's seat was on the left—exactly opposite of the way it is in India.

Despite her early difficulties, even her loneliness, Nalini never said that she wanted to go back to India. She was determined to make her way in this new world. Despite her difficulty reading English, she carefully perused the local newspaper for sales and coupons, then would drive miles to shop for the advertised goods. She also collected S&H stamps that brought her free household items. Now almost extinct, those trading stamps were quite popular in the '60s. Grocery stores, gas stations and other retail establishments used to entice customers by distributing these stamps that could later be redeemed for household goods and articles in special S&H stores, a rewards program run by Sperry & Hutchinson. Though slow in coming, Nalini's Americanization was underway in earnest. Her instant grasp and adoption of S&H stamps is but one example of how most Indians are so like Americans in their basic characteristics—material acquisitiveness and an emphasis on money and practicality that emphasizes what is here and now. Thus they generally feel at home in the U.S. despite the strangeness of the physical environment.

I enjoyed working part-time for IBM and Jones & Laughlin, and wondered how it would be to work full-time in such corporations. I wanted a job that would lead me to an executive position, yet despite numerous applications to various companies, I received no job offers of executive status. I surmised that to get an offer in the executive ranks from a big company, I needed an MBA from a reputable university. A master's degree from Atlanta University wouldn't do. But getting another degree from a major white university would require two more years of study, which I could not afford. So, I put aside the idea of joining the corporate world.

Moreover, the more I taught, the more I liked it. Perhaps I would like a career in teaching, which at the university gave me flexibility that a regular 9-to-5 job would not. I taught classes three days a week and then was free for the rest. Once I had prepared my lectures, teaching became progressively easier and I taught the same courses every semester. Moreover, students at A&T were not too demanding and the university's emphasis was on teaching. It couldn't afford to be a research university where the faculty would be under constant pressure to do research—"publish or perish."

But if I was going to stay in academia, I should be at a more challenging and prestigious university. To have an academic career at a major university, I would need a doctoral degree from a reputable university of national standing. But that would mean at least four more years of full-time study. Where was I to find the money to sustain my family that long? It had been more than a year since Nalini had come to America in January of 1968 and we felt relatively settled in Greensboro. Driving home from a kid's birthday party at a friend's house, we both wondered aloud how old our lost son, Vikram, would have been. Tears began streaming down Nalini's face. It was too much to bear. I told her that we should start a family.

She talked about the curse that had plagued us in Mumbai—that "nothing works for us. What are the odds that a newborn will survive?" she asked. "How can we know that it won't meet the same fate as our poor little Vikram?"

"This is America," I said, "with the best health facilities in the world. Let's at least go to the doctor and have him check you out." She agreed. We went to a gynecologist for a checkup and the doctor gave her clean bill of health. "There is nothing wrong with you," he declared. "You can have your baby!" With that, in the spring of 1969, we started preparing.

———————

To pursue a Ph.D., if I couldn't give up my A&T teaching position and become a full-time student, what about studying part-time? Luckily, the University of North Carolina (UNC), a major state university, was about an hour away in Chapel Hill. Its business school was nationally recognized in the field of accounting. What if I were to enroll on a part-time basis—say, just for two courses on days when I was not teaching? I knew that being a student and teacher simultaneously wouldn't be easy, but I was determined to start a doctoral program. I thought that if I did well and impressed the UNC faculty, I might get a fellowship that would let me pursue my doctorate full-time. So I enrolled in the UNC doctoral program and began commuting to Chapel Hill twice a week.

The other three days a week, I continued teaching at A&T. My teaching, commuting and studying left very little time for Nalini. Luckily, she was able to drive and so could go places. And she had made some Indian friends whom she could visit on her own. While studying at UNC, I discovered what it meant to be a graduate student at a major university. It was a lot of work. Compared to UNC, Atlanta University had been child's play. My UNC professors were very demanding, with fellow students well-prepared and highly competitive. I had a hard time keeping up with them. After a year of combined teaching, studying and commuting, I realized that it was more than what I had bargained for. No fellowship at UNC was forthcoming. I started applying to doctoral programs elsewhere, hoping to get a fellowship that would facilitate my full-time doctoral study.

———————

My persistence paid off. During the summer of 1969, I was admitted to the doctoral program at Louisiana State University in Baton Rouge. LSU gave me a teaching fellowship, which took care of my tuition, plus a stipend sufficient to sustain us if we lived frugally. Our car was paid off and we had no bills to speak of. We had stayed away from dentists and had no health problems. On top of that, I was assigned a two-bedroom apartment in the married-student housing complex near the university. The rent was negligible. Everything seemed manageable and I accepted LSU's offer. Baton Rouge's weather was more like Mumbai's—hot and humid—and we were at ease with it. By Mumbai standards, North Carolina was cold. So we put everything we had in the trunk of the Mustang and set out for Baton Rouge in the middle of August of 1969.

———————

What did I learn from my three years of teaching at A&T? First and foremost, I gained confidence in public speaking. Until teaching there, I had never spoken in front of a group of people, certainly not in English. Teaching gave me all the toastmaster training that I would need to make presentations decades later as a senior public official in Washington. My several Washington jobs required that I regularly address large and small professional groups, moderate group discussions, testify at congressional hearings and manage press conferences. I was generally at ease at those events.

My A&T experience also proved valuable in my teaching at LSU and other universities. Most important, it gave me great experience working with African Americans, which was quite useful when, decades later, I became a senior government official in the District of Columbia, which was overwhelmingly black. Being at A&T saved me from the stereotypical views that many whites and Asians, particularly Indians, hold of blacks.

At the same time, being associated mainly with black colleges right from the day I came to the U.S. gave me a somewhat jaundiced view of America. I saw it primarily from the perspective of black people. Only when I went to work at IBM and Jones & Laughlin, and enrolled in the UNC doctoral program, did I get a glimpse of what white America was all about and gain a broader perspective of how it worked, what its motivating economic factors were and how people related to each other. In some ways, by leaving Greensboro and A&T, I was leaving a part of America that had been held back. In going to Baton Rouge, I was headed for the America that I had known in the movies and magazines in India. How would the reality compare to the movies? Would I like the new world?

Chapter 10

SOUTHERN HOSPITALITY

In the early fall of 1969, we reached Baton Rouge, the home of Louisiana's principal institution of higher education, Louisiana State University (LSU), where I had a fellowship to pursue doctoral studies. The university was famous for its football team; so devoted was it to the LSU Tigers that it housed a live tiger, called Mike, on campus. I quickly learned that racism in Louisiana was as bad if not worse than in Georgia. During my early weeks on campus I came upon a contentious gathering in front of the student union. David Duke—the notorious Nazi sympathizer and leader of the White Knights of the Ku Klux Klan (KKK)—was giving a speech vehemently asserting the superiority of white people. A black student standing in the front of the crowd drew a knife.

"I will cut my vein to show that my blood is as red as David Duke's," he told the crowd, then turned toward Duke: "I challenge you to do the same and show the color of your blood. Let us see if your blood is as red as mine!" Campus police arrived quickly and escorted the student away. That was my introduction to Louisiana!

As if that were not enough, during the late 1960s a legislator proposed that the state keep two separate blood banks so as not to mix blood drawn from whites with that of blacks. If he needed a blood transfusion, the legislator said, he wanted it drawn only from the white blood bank. His forefathers had fought for the Confederacy in the Civil War, and he did not want his body adulterated with blood donated by blacks, using the N-word epithet for them.

I suppose that I should have been somewhat inured to institutional discrimination. After all, I was born and raised in a country with a caste system intended to separate classes of people based on birth and designed to keep them in their lanes—from lower-class untouchables to upper-class intellectuals. But this firsthand experience of such raw racism was jarring. I could see how damaging it was—for African Americans and the entire nation.

When we arrived in Baton Rouge, we had no trouble finding the university. With its sprawling campus, hundreds of buildings and tens of thousands of students, LSU met my image of an American university. When I went to register for my teaching fellowship, I saw mostly white faces. My previous teaching experience at A&T came in handy. I had no stage fright when I stood before my first class at LSU. I knew my stuff. After all, it was Accounting 101 and, as luck would have it, I'd used the same textbook at A&T. Nearly all of my students were white, as were the professors. The black people whom I came across on campus were mostly engaged in menial service jobs.

Baton Rouge is located on the eastern bank of the Mississippi River. During the late '60s, petrochemical and other industries along the river filled the evening air with pungent odors. The city's main preoccupation, however, was politics. It is the state capital and thus a hub of political activity. I soon realized that in Louisiana, politics is blood sport. The state has, over the years, sent to Washington some of its craftiest politicians, who, with their political longevity and seniority, became some of the most powerful congressional committee chairmen such as Allen Joseph Ellender, Russell Long and Majority Leader Hale Boggs.

LSU is home to a great literary journal, *The Southern Review*. When established in 1935, it was lavishly funded by Governor Huey Long as a part of his goal of making LSU a nationally prominent university. Its founding editors were the famed poet and novelist Robert Penn Warren and the distinguished critic Cleanth Brooks. Its first five years were hailed by literary critic John Crowe Ransom as "close to the best thing in the history of American letters." Yet this great literary achievement did not rub off on the university's business school, where the only thing that excited people was sports, particularly football. My fellow Ph.D. students and professors were thoroughly intelligent and street-smart in their own ways. Yet their discussion of current issues was sometimes pedestrian and reflected prevailing prejudices. I never saw anyone reading or discussing any of the intellectual journals of the day. At the student union and occasional parties, conversations revolved around fishing, football and food, particularly the latest dining excursion to New Orleans, a haven for foodies. None of that interested me. I'd rather talk about the latest op-ed piece in the Sunday *New York Times*—about which they couldn't have cared less. After a while, I gave up and tried to join the conversations about sports, mainly LSU football.

Every Monday, as soon as I sat down with the graduate students who were my regular lunch companions, talk turned to the previous Saturday's game. Don Chesterfield, whom I first met during registration, usually took the lead. "Did you see what Buddy Lee did on Saturday?" he might ask. "Do you believe it?" Lee was the LSU quarterback who would later be drafted by the Chicago Bears. Sometimes the conversation would get heated. Having been shut out of a major bowl game in 1969, LSU badly wanted to go to a major bowl in 1970. To do so, it had to beat Tulane and Ole Miss in the final two weeks of the season, which it did. After each of the games, Don went through a play-by-play analysis. When I didn't go to the LSU-Ole Miss game, which was played to a national TV audience and some 70,000 spectators in Baton Rouge, he reprimanded me: "Boy, you missed a big one!" The Monday-morning quarterbacking of the weekend's game would continue until the following Monday, when there would be a new game to analyze.

I was a sought-after lunch companion because I would rarely use my student-allocated tickets that they wanted to have. The games were sold out months in advance, thus any available ticket was a great catch. When football season was over, the conversation turned to basketball, often revolving around "Pistol Pete," the legendary LSU player Pete Maravich. My LSU colleagues avidly followed his professional career with the Atlanta Hawks. During coffee breaks and around the water cooler, students and faculty also talked about the size of the fish they'd caught during that weekend's fishing expedition or the New Orleans restaurants they'd visited. None of this interested me since I never went fishing and couldn't afford New Orleans restaurants anyway.

Atlanta University had introduced me to a sort of discrimination when I began looking for a job. Its placement bureau focused solely on black students; no amount of academic excellence would get a foreign student an interview with a visiting corporate recruiter, much less a job. LSU's placement bureau was no different. I would get an appointment with a potential employer, but when I showed up for an interview was told that my name had been removed. I once signed up to interview for a teaching position at a Georgia college that interested me at the time. I sent my résumé and other material to the potential employer, whose representative replied that he was interested in meeting me and would try to arrange for me to visit the campus. His eagerness seemed to reflect the school's need to hire accounting Ph.D.s, who were in short supply. Excited by the prospect, I had my only suit pressed at a cleaner's—the same suit that I had brought from India.

I prepared for the interview by rehearsing answers to questions that I might be asked. But when I arrived at the placement bureau, I was told that I was no longer on the list of interviewees. All of the slots had been taken. I went home puzzled. Had someone impersonating me called the bureau and asked that my name be removed? I strongly protested, telling the placement bureau that in the future my name should not be removed unless I showed up at the office and did so personally.

Fortunately, there was such a shortage of accounting Ph.D.s that I could apply on my own and meet with recruiters at annual gatherings of the American Accounting Association. However, that required me to attend the association's annual gatherings at various places around the country, which I couldn't always afford to do.

If many of my fellow students were racially insensitive, faculty members were no better. The attitude of many toward Asian students was patronizing, though not malign. In conversations, they set about explaining to me how the U.S. system of government worked, how a president is elected through the electoral college, and what roles the state and federal governments play in the American political system. The discussion was often at such an elementary level that I had to humor them and resist smirking. They tried to educate me on the evils of communism and how the Vietnam War was worth the sacrifice of American blood and treasure. Not wanting to waste emotional energy on the issue anymore, I wouldn't argue. Besides, there was no Hans Morgenthau or Ralph McGill among them.

Despite my attitude, which I look back on and now see as arrogant, I found people in Louisiana—including my fellow LSU graduate students and faculty—generally warm, gregarious and easy to talk to. At my first registration, a graduate student saw that I was confused about where to go next. "Looks like you're lost," he said. "Need any help? I'm Don." His name was Don Chesterfield, who shepherded me through registration. When he learned that I was a fellow Ph.D. student in the business school, he said, "Let's have lunch at the Student Union. I'll introduce you to other graduate students."

Nalini had conceived in the spring of 1969 before we left Greensboro for Baton Rouge. We celebrated the event but with a dose of anxiety. The last thing I wanted was for her to suffer again the way she had when we lost our first child. Our joy was mixed with concern. As it happened, Don's wife Holly was also expecting a baby. Shortly after we met, they came by our apartment and invited Nalini to go shopping with them for baby things on sale that day at a department store. As we got to know them better, they often came to our place to enjoy Indian food and occasionally invited us to join them at LSU football games.

The only lasting friendship that I developed during my time at LSU was with Louis Corsini, an academic refugee from Boston who needed a Ph.D. to get tenure at Boston College. Lou and his sophisticated wife Marilyn were kindred souls, generous in spirit and true Bostonians. To them, Boston was the hub of American civilization. They could hardly wait to get back. Lou, a skilled pianist who veered into accounting, disliked Baton Rouge but visited New Orleans often to try out its various restaurants. Marilyn was a kind-hearted liberal who taught in a Baton Rouge public school and tried to help students in any way she could. Later she also ran the city's welfare program designed to help abused women get back into the workforce. When he found me, Lou was looking for someone he could talk to at LSU. We quickly bonded. He was surprised at how much I knew about contemporary American politics and current affairs. After some 40 years, we still get together almost every year and reminisce about our salad days in Baton Rouge.

At the other end of the political spectrum, I was befriended by Dan Devine, a shrewd Mississippian who disliked Northerners he thought were hypocrites when it came to race relations. From him I heard stories of the South's gloried past and how it had been maligned by the North. Dan and I also got along well. He and his lovely wife Jo, a true Southern belle, would invite us to their apartment for special occasions such as Thanksgiving, bestowing on us their gracious Southern hospitality.

———————

I committed myself to ensuring that Nalini received the best prenatal care. That was not a problem in Greensboro, where I was fully employed. She visited the doctor regularly to get updates on her pregnancy. As a teaching assistant in Baton Rouge, however, my paycheck was drastically reduced. After all sorts of deductions, my monthly take-home pay was a meager $333. I had used up my Greensboro savings to buy a car and some essential furniture. Most of my fellow graduate students had working wives who basically supported their husbands' education and maintained the household. Nalini was still unemployable, given her lack of English proficiency. So we limited our monthly expenditures to the amount of my paycheck. We were about to find out how poor we were. One evening, as we sat down to dinner, there was a knock at the door. The visitor was an official from the Louisiana State Welfare Department. My first reaction was, "What did I do wrong?" She told us that my low income made us eligible for a welfare subsidy. "May I check your home and identities before the state starts sending checks?" she asked.

I was surprised by the visit and, I confess, somewhat offended that we were being deemed "poor." I politely refused the offer. "I believe we can manage on the stipend money, thank you very much," I said. Now it was her turn to be surprised. She said that in all her visits she had never come across anyone who had refused a welfare check. How was I to explain to her that I didn't want to be branded a welfare recipient? Besides, we were doing far better with my paltry stipend than how we lived with my full salary in Mumbai.

———————

Our next-door neighbor, Eleanor Porter, was thrilled when she realized that Nalini was about to have a baby, especially after she learned about the loss of our first one. She comforted Nalini and accompanied her to the doctor's office and elsewhere. A mother of three, Eleanor basically became an elder sister to Nalini. We knew that in the event of an emergency we could count on Eleanor and her husband Mark. We became good friends. Nalini would babysit their kids when they went out on the town. She also showed Eleanor how to cook Indian food and put on an Indian saree. They loved Indian food, so our families dined together often. After learning that we had no family in the U.S., they invited us to their home in Biloxi, Mississippi, for Thanksgiving dinner. It was our first Thanksgiving and our first out-of-town trip since our arrival in Baton Rouge. Biloxi was about 130 miles away. It took us a little more than two hours to get there. Though in November, it was not very cold and we even visited the beach near their family home. When Mark's mother learned that we were vegetarians, she cooked some spicy vegetarian dishes for us with Nalini's help. It was a fun event for all, especially after all the ladies said they wanted to be dressed in a saree! Nalini clearly enjoyed the attention accorded her as a special guest. We were overwhelmed by their generous hospitality. On our drive back to Baton Rouge, Nalini could not stop talking about them. Shortly thereafter, during our first Christmas in Baton Rouge, they surprised us with gifts.

———

We fell into an easy routine in the Louisiana capital. I would leave our apartment around 8 a.m. in the morning, take my lunch—basically a BLT sandwich without bacon, plus a Coke and a cookie—spend the day at the university, go home for dinner and return to the library to study. When I got home late at night, Nalini would be waiting for me with a warm glass of milk. We would tell each other about our day, and then our talk would turn invariably about the baby—how long it might be before it arrived and whether it would be a boy or girl. We wanted the baby's gender to be a surprise.

According to Indian tradition, the baby's aunt—the father's sister—has the right to name a baby. Since I hadn't received any suggestions from Hansa, my youngest sister, naming the baby was up to us. Each of us had strong preferences, so some arguments ensued. After one such argument, we reached a compromise: If it were a boy, I would be the one to name him; if a girl, Nalini had the privilege of naming her.

With all of my studying and teaching, I had little time to spend with Nalini during the week. On weekends we would go out together to shop for groceries and other items and occasionally for a Mexican dinner, since there were no Indian restaurants—and it was the cheapest fare in town. We made no trips to New Orleans to try any of its renowned restaurants. Initially, life in Baton Rouge was hard for Nalini since we had no Indian friends there. We later got to know a few Indian families in the area. Soon after arriving in Baton Rouge, we both got Louisiana driver's licenses, and Nalini started driving all over town, shopping for baby things. As she was busy preparing for the baby, I was busy studying for my Ph.D.

———

Because my fellowship was at the business school, all of my courses were business-related. I couldn't escape accounting. I was still following the career path that Ratibhai had charted for me in Mumbai, and for the same reason: Even in America, accounting was where the jobs were. The idea of enrolling in LSU's famed English department was very tempting, but my dream of specializing in literature had to be postponed yet again. I had to think ahead about getting a faculty appointment at a major university. Not surprisingly, it would be far easier with a Ph.D. in accounting than one in English. While being a student at Atlanta University had been a cakewalk, it was much more difficult at LSU. The sheer volume of required academic reading was daunting. I also found much of it arcane and boring. In addition, my fellowship required me to teach two accounting courses, for which I had to do a great deal of preparation; though the material was familiar, students were far more demanding. This was no A&T.

On January 23, 1970, I was teaching my 9 a.m. class when Nalini called the university. I always preferred to do my teaching early in the day—preferably the first thing in morning. The business-school secretary appeared at the classroom door and motioned for me to come out. "Nat, your wife just called—she's about to deliver the baby. Go home. I'll tell the class what's happening." We lived only 10 minutes from the university. When I got home, I learned that Eleanor already had taken Nalini to the hospital. So I drove to Our Lady of the Lake Hospital, which was another 10 minutes away. At 10:07 that morning, Nalini delivered a healthy boy weighing six-and-a-half pounds. The doctor came out of the delivery room and extended his hand. "Congratulations, Mr. Gandhi. It's a boy!"

I thanked him and asked, "Is the boy all right? How about the mother? Are they both all right?"

"Yes, they're fine," the doctor said. "There's nothing to worry. Come inside and have a look at them."

I went inside and saw our son. Nalini and I looked at each other. I could see the satisfaction on her face. "Thank God," I said. "How lucky we are!" In addition to joy, I felt an immense sense of relief that nothing untoward had happened. Since it was a boy, naming him was up to me. My preference was Apoorva—meaning unique, one of a kind. Back in Mumbai, I'd been fascinated by a hero of the same name in the film trilogy directed by the famed Indian director Satyajit Ray. The movie was based on a well-known Bengali novel, also a favorite of mine, called *Pather Panchali*, by Bibhutibhushan Bandopadhyay, that narrated the hero's life from early childhood to adulthood. Nalini had no problem with the name. All she cared about at the moment was that the boy was healthy and she would be able to take him home, which we did. As we left the hospital with Apoorva, tears were rolling down Nalini's face.

"Why is your wife crying?" the nurse asked me.

"These are tears of joy," I replied. "We lost our first child, a son, soon after he was born in India."

"You have nothing to worry about," the nurse said. "This is a healthy baby, a lovely baby indeed! Besides, this is America, not India—we wouldn't let that happen here."

When we got home, there was no family to greet the proud parents. I immediately sent a telegram to my parents telling them that Nalini had delivered a baby boy, and both mother and newborn were doing fine. I also booked a call to Mumbai. There were no cellphones yet. It took several hours to get my parents on the phone. They had to go to a neighbor's place to receive the call. My mother was crying when she got on the line; she wondered how soon she'd be able to see her first grandson who would carry the family name forward. Then she said, "Your sister will have to go to America to name the boy. Or you all could come home so she can name him! Until then the boy should remain nameless. That is our tradition."

I told her, "Baa, that is not possible. I had to give the hospital a name before they would let us bring him home. So, we had to name him."

"What is it?"

"Apoorva!"

"Well, no one in our family has a name like that. Why couldn't you name him something simple?"

I didn't want to get involved in explaining why we chose that particular name. I told her, "Baa, it is done. The hospital has the name and our son is home."

She wasn't happy about the name but asked, "When can I see my grandson?" I told her that I would soon send pictures of the baby, but it would be a while before she laid eyes on her grandson. Indeed, it was another five years before we were able to go to India for my parents to see Apoorva and his sister, who would be born nearly four years later. As soon as the good news reached my mother, she distributed sweets among family and friends to celebrate the arrival of a grandson, even though he was oceans away.

Despite my bravado with the officer from the welfare department, the truth was that we needed more money, especially now that there was an infant at home. I wanted to make sure that he was properly fed and well taken care of. We took him to the doctor regularly and religiously followed his instructions regarding raising the infant. I was still haunted by the early demise of our first son, Vikram. But how could a poor graduate student make ends meet? Then, at a party with fellow graduate students, I heard someone joking about the easy availability of "NDEA loans." Everyone was laughing about how they were taking advantage of these low-interest loans and using the money to take vacations and visit New Orleans to wine and dine. What was this NDEA loan, I wondered. I did some research. Following the 1957 launch of Sputnik, there had been an outcry in Congress that the U.S. was lagging behind the Soviet Union in science and technology. To remedy the situation, in 1958 Congress passed the National Defense Education Act (NDEA), providing substantial funds to universities. The purported purpose of the act was to encourage scientific education at all lev-els, and it provided low-interest loans to graduate students. Repayment wasn't required until students were fully employed. Best of all, every graduate student qualified for it, no questions asked.

"Can a foreign student qualify for such a loan?" I asked a fellow graduate student. "It looks like a great bargain!"

"Why don't you check it out?" he asked.

I rushed to the Office of Graduate Studies and inquired about my eligibility. "Why not?" the clerk said. "Everyone gets it. So you get it too!"

I couldn't believe it. Since I was at the office, I filled out an application right then and there. Soon enough, a check arrived in the mail, to be followed by other checks every semester.

What a country! I thought. *First, it gives me an opportunity to go to graduate school free of tuition, then it gives me an almost rent-free apartment coupled with a monthly stipend, and now it gives me a low-interest loan that I didn't have to repay until I would be fully employed!* When I put it all together, I was making more money as a student than I'd made working full-time in Mumbai. What a country indeed!

The more I studied academic accounting, the more disillusioned I became. Most of it was highly specialized, with a stiflingly narrow focus. Flipping through academic accounting journals, I found articles on such issues as how inventory valuation affect-ed the movement of stock prices. Entire dissertations were written on such subjects. Now I would be expected to write a dissertation on such a topic. I was not enthralled. I wanted to study and write a thesis on some larger issue, such as the future of capi-talism or the changing nature of work and how it would reshape accounting. During the 1960s, the distinguished Harvard sociologist Daniel Bell explored the concept of a service-oriented, post-industrial society. I thought it would be interesting to write a dissertation on what role accounting should play in such a service-oriented society. I examined the subject and concluded that accounting should move beyond profit and loss as measured in dollars and cents. No more balance sheets and income statements with dollar signs only—accountants should measure corporate performance in other than simple monetary terms.

I approached my faculty advisor, James Pattillo, and told him of my desire to do research on a broad subject rather than a narrow, specialized one. Pattillo was relatively young and had written his dissertation on the unlikely subject of fairness in account-ing. He was receptive to my idea but cautioned me: "You know, Nat, this is risky. No one does this kind of research anymore. You are moving into an uncharted territory. If you don't want to work on some specialized issue, that's your choice, but please remember, whatever you do, make sure you can collect a lot of data and rigorously test a hypothesis using quantitative methods. Above all, have a lot of numbers and equations in your thesis. Without that, the dissertation committee will not approve your thesis. Worse yet, you won't be able to publish it in academic journals."

"I understand, sir!" I said. But I didn't. It was a prescient warning, but I didn't truly grasp its meaning until much later. At the time, I nodded and moved ahead with my project.

It usually takes about two years to finish Ph.D. coursework and a year or more to complete a dissertation. However, a capricious and arbitrary faculty advisor could ruin that timetable by not approving a student's dissertation research. At LSU, I knew graduate students who'd had to stay in town far longer than the usual three years. Most graduate students tended to finish their course work as fast as they could, settle on a dissertation topic and then leave for an academic appointment elsewhere. The expectation was that the student would finish research, write a dissertation in absentia and come back to the university to defend it. There is some risk in leaving campus before finishing a thesis. Some students don't finish their dissertation and so join the ranks of failed Ph.D. candidates known as ABDs— "all but dissertation." The longer one spends on a dissertation, the harder it is to finish it. Some faculty advisors lose interest in students unless they are in their face. Out of sight, out of mind.

I finished my coursework in two and half years, after which I was eager to leave Baton Rouge and get on with life. I also wanted leave the South. I'd had enough of its focus on sports in Atlanta, North Carolina and Louisiana. So I began applying for teaching jobs at colleges and universities in the North. Coming out of LSU, I knew that my chances with any of the elite northeastern schools were minimal. Yet I thought that I might reasonably find a place at a mid-range school.

To be on the safe side, I also applied to several schools in far-flung states. One interview in particular stands out after some 45 years. A college in Omaha, Nebraska, was seeking professors in accounting, so I applied and was interviewed there. To demonstrate familiarity with the local scene, I inquired about Father Flanagan's Boys Town. I had seen the movie *Boys Town* (1938)—starring Spencer Tracy and Mickey Rooney—in Mumbai. The college quickly arranged for me to visit and wanted to hire me as desperately as I wanted the job. The faculty and dean wined and dined me for two days, and I met various college dignitaries. The first evening I was taken to a fancy steak restaurant where the dean had preordered my meal. When the entrée arrived, it was a big steak.... I didn't want my hosts to think that I was some sort of strange vegetarian who would shun the state's staple food, so I began cutting the steak—with little success as I was using the wrong knife! I had never eaten steak in my life. This was my first and last one. Steak or no steak, I was offered the job yet did not take it.

After a few more applications and interviews, I took a job as lecturer at the University of Pittsburgh to teach accounting in its Graduate School of Business. However, when I went to Pitt for my interview, I was warned about the research demands that would be placed on me if I joined the faculty. I knew my limitations as an academic researcher, yet decided to go to Pitt because it was my ticket out of the South. Once there, I thought that I'd be able to figure out how to succeed. That proved to be a major misjudgment.

––––––––––

Nalini was too busy raising our young son to bother with the minutiae of my job search, and she had little understanding of my academic ambition beyond the salary associated with a full-time faculty position. It did not matter at which particular university I would take the job or how prestigious it was; all she knew was that once I had a faculty position, we'd be able to live a much better life—and would be able to visit India soon and often. She wanted to live in a big house and throw parties like our Indian friends. But when I mentioned that we were going to Pittsburgh, she balked. We'd lived there in the summer of 1968 during my short stint at Jones & Laughlin Steel Company. She remembered its narrow winding streets and steep hills. "Don't worry," I told her. "You won't have to drive in the city streets. We'll live in the suburbs where you can have your big house, backyard and two-car garage. And you can throw as many parties as you want since we will have a big basement too!" Because we had lived in Pittsburgh in the summer, Nalini had no idea of its harsh winter. My LSU colleagues knew better, however. When they learned that I was planning to join the Pitt business school, they were aghast. Why would anyone want to live in a city notorious for its dirty air, bitter winter and endless snow? And why would I seek the punishment of attending a research-oriented "publish or perish" school over an easygoing one that valued teaching over research? In retrospect, I realized they were right: I didn't know what I was getting into. But my mind was made up.

––––––––––

My experience at LSU gave me confidence that I could work in white America. I was able to shed the inferiority that had unconsciously developed at A&T. When I'd come to the U.S. in 1965, I'd brought with me a sense of insecurity that many Indians suffer, wondering whether we would be able to make it in a white world. This was the legacy of hundreds of years of a British Raj that assigned inferior status to its Indian subjects. That insecurity had deepened during my early years in the mostly black worlds of Atlanta and Greensboro. Now, with three years at LSU under my belt, I felt that I could handle the white world with ease and grace. The LSU experience facilitated my entry into the world of Pitt (and later of the General Accounting Office in Washington, DC). Nalini and I packed our few belongings into a small U-Haul, attached it to our battered Mustang, and headed north toward Pittsburgh with our 3-year-old son, Apoorva.

Chapter 11

PUBLISH OR PERISH

When we arrived in Pittsburgh in December of 1972, it was snowing. We had seen snow in North Carolina, but nothing like this heavy and unrelenting downfall. Snow became a metaphor for our new life in this difficult—hilly and cold—city. Baton Rouge, with all of its warmth, looked better and better through our rearview mirror. Pittsburgh was a big industrial city located at the confluence of three rivers: the Ohio, the Allegheny and the Monongahela. It had all the hustle and bustle of a large urban center, and was also the site of my first big-city driving experience in winter. With its hilly terrain, tunnels, rivers and narrowly winding streets, it was difficult to get around. Pittsburgh's weather was cold, of course, but we didn't expect to find its people to be generally cold as well. We had found Baton Rouge to be warm, welcoming and congenial. It was easy to strike up a conversation with strangers or drop in at a neighbor's place without notice. In Pittsburgh, we had no idea for a long time who our next-door neighbors were. When we finally encountered them, our relationship amounted only to an initial introduction and nothing more. In elevators there was no chit-chat even about the weather—only silence or averted eyes. We missed the southern hospitality of Baton Rouge; here in Pittsburgh, at most we would get a cold hello in the hallway and sometimes a nod.

Though I went to Pittsburgh as faculty, I was hardly noticed by senior faculty members. Most came to the campus only on the days they taught, when they would teach their classes and be gone. They didn't hang around the faculty club to socialize with other members. It was difficult to get to know—much less befriend—them.

My initial months at Pitt teaching graduate courses were also difficult for me academically. Students, particularly those in the evening classes, were mature and many had both business experience and worked full-time. Some had held senior positions in companies such as U.S. Steel, Westinghouse and Alcoa. In fact, these students had more business experience than most faculty members, including their new professor from India. They didn't hesitate to question a professor and argue about an issue that they would have dealt with differently in their working lives. For example, during one of my evening lectures I suggested that accounting measures such as EPS (earnings per share) calculations should be downplayed in favor of other measures. A student sitting in the back of the room raised his hand.

"Really?" he asked. "Like what?"

"Well," I responded, "like employee morale or some such thing."

"Rubbish!" he shot back. "In my world, what I hear all day is nothing but EPS and how it helps the price of our stock in the market. No one gives a hoot about employee morale!"

I'd never had such an encounter in my undergraduate classes at LSU or A&T. I realized that I had to prepare more strenuously for classes to avoid such embarrassing situations.

———

The more time I devoted to preparing for my classes, the less was available to finish the dissertation, without which I was going nowhere. Fear that I might not be able to finish it haunted me. Without the dissertation, I would be considered a failure, joining the ranks of the ABDs ("all but dissertation"). Unfortunately, I brought all of this stress home. Nalini had no innate idea of what I was going through at the university. She had her own issues. After being at home all day with our young son, she needed some relief and quality time herself. We needed to make some Gujarati friends with whom Nalini could socialize.

Pittsburgh was a major urban center with hospitals, universities and headquarters of numerous Fortune 500 companies, so a natural home for Indian professionals. As a result, the area's Indian population was about 10,000 in the early 1970s. Some 30 percent of those were Gujaratis—people who spoke our language. There was also a Gujarati *Samaj,* an association that arranged social gatherings to celebrate Indian festivals, summer picnics and an annual dinner. This would be a social-networking bonanza for Nalini where she wouldn't have to worry about her limited English-language proficiency. It was not at all uncommon in those days for a Gujarati newcomer to look in the telephone directory for common Gujarati last names such as Patel or Shah and place a call, and tell the person who answered that he or she was new to the city and needed some guidance. More often than not the recipient of the call would invite him or her to dinner and make introductions to their friends and relatives. Bonds would soon be formed and the newcomer would become part of a social group of kindred souls.

That is what we did. In the phone directory we found a Patel family—Puran and Pratima—not far from where we were living. One evening I called them. Pratima answered the phone and quickly gave it to Puran.

"Puran*bhai*," I said, "my name is Gandhi, and we are new to the area. May we come by and talk with you and seek your guidance about schools, shopping and other things?" (Indians always attach the word "*bhai*," meaning brother, to a man's name, and "*bahen*," meaning sister, to a woman's as a gesture of respect and family intimacy.) After a few pleasantries about where in Gujarat we were from and where we had lived in the U.S., Puran invited us to their house.

"Yes, of course," he said, "please do come. How about this weekend? Would Saturday work for you? How about 7 p.m.? Have dinner with us—nothing special, just a simple get-together. We will also invite some friends so you can meet them, too. Please do bring the family, and come a little early so we have a chance to talk, okay?"

I reported to Nalini, "We have our first friends in Pittsburgh! We are going to their place for dinner this Saturday."

On the appointed day, Nalini, Apoorva and I went to the Patel home, which was about 40 minutes away in Allison Park, a northern suburb. I learned that Puran was an engineer at a steel company, and he discovered that I had worked at Jones & Laughlin Steel for three months in the summer of 1968. We found some common acquaintances and shared a few stories. Pratima was a housewife taking care of a large extended family. In addition to their own three children, Puran's parents were living with them, along with his younger brother who had just come from India for studies in the U.S. Puran also owned three motels in partnership with other Patels. The motels were located some 150 miles away in Breezewood, known as the "town of motels" at the cross-section of the Pennsylvania Turnpike and I-270. He would go there every other Sunday to check on them. "Come along some time," he invited. "It is a nice ride. Who knows, you might want to join our partnership!" He also asked my help in getting his brother admitted to Pitt, which I readily agreed to do.

The Patel community is known for its solidarity, family values and entrepreneurial skills. Indeed, they presently own many motels in practically every corner of America. Puran and Pratima exhibited all of the characteristics of the Patel community, particularly the hospitality. It is, after all, an Indian custom to treat an uninvited guest as someone quite special. The Patels seemed the very embodiment of that tradition.

Other guests arrived about 8 p.m. They all came with their families, including children. Some even brought their older parents. After initial introductions and greetings, the men, women and kids segregated into different parts of the Patels' large house. I took Apoorva to the family room, where kids were playing games while a big TV was on. Nalini joined other women in the kitchen to help Pratima. One of the ladies said to her, "It is all made at home." Gujaratis, particularly Patels, rarely would have their food catered no matter how many people were coming to dinner. They must have invited at least 50 people that day. Puran took me to the basement to meet the other men. "This is Gandhi," he said. "He is a professor at Pitt's business school. They are new to Pittsburgh."

The men gathered around and peppered me with questions about stock prices, which were showing all the signs of a bear market. This was on the heels of 1972, which was a good year for stocks. Soon after the January issue of *Time* magazine predicted a "gilt-edged" year in 1973, the market crashed.

"Tell us, Gandhibhai, you are a business professor—you would know where the market is going. Should we get out now or ride out the storm?" I was hesitant to give advice on the stock market, a dangerous thing to do. Though a professor of business, I had little entrepreneurial inclinations or desire to play or talk about the market. Then the conversation turned, thankfully for me, to football and the Steelers, even though about which I knew very little. The men tried to educate me about what was likely to happen in the 1973 season. They were happy that the Steelers had posted an 11–3 record in 1972 and won their first-ever AFC Central Division title. They fondly recounted the famous game in which the Steelers beat the Oakland Raiders when Franco Harris, the Steelers' MVP, scored a last-second touchdown known as the "immaculate reception." They also talked about the recent Super Bowl in which the Dallas Cowboys defeated the Miami Dolphins, 24–3.

Both before and after dinner, the men also talked about politics, particularly how the corrupt politicians in India were ruining the country. They praised Richard Nixon—how smart he was and how he defeated George McGovern in the landslide election of 1972. No alcohol was served at the dinner. Gujaratis generally do not drink or smoke. A few outliers retreated to a corner or the deck to do their smoking. When dinner was announced, men ate first, then kids and ladies. After dinner, adults gathered in the basement, where singing—mostly of Bollywood songs—went on until the wee hours of the night. Most people stayed till the end. As we were leaving the party, Nalini commented on how lucky we were to have found the Patels, simply by flipping the telephone directory and looking for a common Indian name!

––––––––

Nalini and Pratima quickly bonded. Pratima had made special sweets that day for us. "Please take this home in celebration of your first day at our home," she said. Then she invited Nalini to go shopping with her during the week. She also invited her to a *bhajan* group that met every Sunday morning to pray and sing devotional songs called *bhajans*. "You will meet many Gujarati families there!" she exclaimed.

We were now part of a wide circle of friends who socialized regularly. Afterward, no weekend was without some kind of social gathering with them. Going out to weekend parties was Nalini's only break from household chores and raising our son. It was the only way most Indian immigrants, particularly women, relaxed and tried to counter their social isolation from the larger American society. It is also where they could show off their latest acquisition of new sarees or jewelry from India. Nalini enjoyed these parties immensely. It was her time to socialize and form networks with other Gujarati women going through the same transition. She would insist on going early to parties and leaving late, wanting to attend every party even if it meant going to three successively on Friday, Saturday and Sunday. Sometimes a pared-down party took place midweek for playing cards. I found those parties a waste of a time. Usually I would be bored stiff and with my boredom written all over my face. Nor did I sing or play an instrument or cards. The parties were formulaic—the same people talking about the same things, same food, same songs—and they went late into the night, spoiling the following day for me. I had things to do: prepare for classes, grade papers and, above all, research and write a dissertation. Most of the men attending parties had regular 9-to-5 jobs. Once they were home, they didn't have to worry about the office until the next day when they showed up for work. With my negative attitude and disinclination to participate enthusiastically in conversations, I was spoiling Nalini's fun. After each party, she invariably would complain about my behavior, fearing that it would lead to fewer invitations and perhaps ostracism.

Because we were living in an apartment to be near the university, our parties were very small compared to those of our friends, many of whom lived in big suburban houses. Nalini had hoped that, because I was employed full-time now, we would buy a house as soon as we arrived in Pittsburgh. That desire grew after a few months of being cooped up in the apartment. She wanted to have a basement so she could give big parties. Our apartment living was curtailing her social activities and, as a result, her social status. "So, when are you going to buy a house?" her friends would ask. After years of nomadic living in cramped quarters in Mumbai, she naturally wanted to have a spacious and stable place where she could raise our son. However, I was reluctant to buy a house until I finished my dissertation and was assured of a tenure-track faculty position.

"When will that be?" she asked. "How long before you finish the dissertation? Why can't you do it sooner?" She had little grasp of what it took to do research and write a thesis. After all, her limited education did not prepare her for the lifestyle uncertainties of a struggling junior academic. Nor did I often share with her what I was going through at the university.

My first six months in Pittsburgh were spent acclimatizing myself to the university. That left little time to work on my dissertation. I started worrying that I might not finish it and would wind up having to go back to Baton Rouge to complete it. Jerry Zoffer, who as dean had national aspirations for Pitt's business school, would periodically call me into his office. Also, he understood the problems and difficulties of younger faculty members. He would often gently ask me, "Nat, how are you doing? Anything I should do for you?" And then he would inquire, "How's that dissertation progressing?" He would invariably end our meetings with a cautionary note: "Don't worry too much about teaching. Just worry about finishing that dissertation. You need that union card, remember?" Zoffer had seen junior faculty members let go because they couldn't finish their dissertation and he did not want that to happen to me. I also received occasional calls from James Pattillo inquiring about the progress I was making on my dissertation.

I needed no reminders. I was aware of the consequences and determined not to fall into the ABD trap. I had special reasons for concern. Unlike others who had fallen into that trap, I didn't have a working wife, accumulated savings or other income to support the family. There was also the matter of pride. I'd never seen an Indian Ph.D. student who couldn't finish his thesis. I wasn't going to be the first Indian ABD and got to work. I put together nearly 300 pages regurgitating arguments that Daniel Bell and others had made about the emergence of the post-industrial economy. At the end of it all, what I had was little more than the assertion that accounting should change without saying how! In retrospect, the whole exercise seemed preposterous. Still, I had a finished dissertation and went to Baton Rouge to defend it. I appeared before a committee composed of five senior business-school faculty members, including James Pattillo. I'd put together a powerful defense saying that the accounting profession should look forward and experiment with new measures of corporate performance. There was general grumbling about the lack of a justifiable hypothesis and quantitative analysis in my thesis, followed by sharp questioning from members of the committee. Pattillo, however, came to my defense. Since he had approved the thesis, he had a stake in the outcome. "Nat has picked the subject that cannot be tested," Pattillo said. "He is right in saying that the profession should look forward and experiment with new things. That is the only way we can make progress." The discussion went on for about 30 minutes. Then I was excused from the room so the committee could vote. That took another 15 minutes. I dreaded every one of those minutes. The longer it took, the more I feared the committee's disapproval.

I was particularly afraid of one member of the committee who had been a visiting professor in South Asia. I had tried to befriend him, once sharing with him a September 1970 *New Yorker* article, "The Greening of America" by Charles Reich. It was highly critical of contemporary America. The professor didn't like the article and assumed that I was being ungrateful to my host country. Our relationship soured. From then on, he would start a conversation by saying, "You know, when I was in your part of the world..." and always ended with something critical about his experience about whichever Asian country he was talking. I feared that he was out to get me, that I might have to come back to Baton Rouge and do more work on the thesis. A nightmare indeed!

Then the committee door opened and Pattillo came out. "Nat, come in," he said. I dreaded the worst. I thought the jig was up and saw the edifice of my new American life crumbling. I felt that academic life was not for me, that I'd better find a normal 9-to-5 job and enjoy Indian parties.

"Congratulations, Nat," Pattillo said. "The committee has approved your dissertation! We will let the Pitt people know you have successfully defended your dissertation. Good luck—and keep in touch!" With that he escorted me out and invited another Ph.D. candidate in who was nervously waiting to appear before the committee. I immediately called Nalini and let her know that everything was fine—that now we would be buying a house in Pittsburgh.

"I knew you were going to make it, Natu," she said. "You were unnecessarily worried. Make sure to drop by and see our old friends there."

I called Dean Zoffer and told him that I had successfully defended the thesis and that Jim Pattillo would be calling him to confirm the results. "Great, Nat, congratulations!" he said. "I look forward to getting a call from LSU."

I stopped by the following day to thank Pattillo before leaving for Pittsburgh. "I am just curious: How did I do in my defense yesterday?" I asked. "Why did the committee take so long?"

"Well, Nat, you did just fine," he replied. "But there was no guarantee that you were going to make it. Let's just say it was a narrow escape. But hey—all that ends well...."

Though I was able to sell my thesis to the LSU faculty, selling it to a larger academic establishment would be another matter. At least for now I had my union card. I breathed a sigh of relief. Now I could chart my future in academia—but I would soon discover that it was not going to be smooth sailing.

———————

Now that I had my Ph.D. and a tenure-track faculty position, we started looking for a house. Nalini wanted one with a large basement (for Indian parties), a backyard and garage, so we had to look in distant suburbs. We looked first in Allison Park, where several of our friends, including Puran and Pratima Patel, lived. We'd been there several times and liked the area. Its schools had a good reputation. Allison Park was about 15 miles away from the Pitt campus. During rush hour the one-way commute took 45 minutes to an hour, but I didn't have to go to school every day and could vary the time of my commute. So we bought a house there. With my dissertation done and a nice, big house of our own, our future seemed bright.

Now that Nalini had the house of her dreams and was getting involved in local Indian social life, with its parties and picnics and other get-togethers, she developed new friends. Our son Apoorva was about 4. He also liked going to parties and playing with other kids. When we returned from those gatherings, he often commented about being lonely at home. We decided that it might be a good idea to have another child so both children could grow up together. After Apoorva's birth without complications and his normal growth, Nalini felt comfortable with the idea of having another child. With her life settled in Pittsburgh, she thought the "curse" that haunted us in Mumbai had been lifted and now we were on to good times.

Our daughter Sona—a healthy, beautiful baby girl—was born on November 24, 1973. Nalini felt that God was smiling on us. We sent a telegram to my parents in India informing them that Apoorva now had a sister and quickly followed up with a phone call. They were pleased that we'd been blessed by *Lakshmi*, the Indian goddess of money and wealth. Daughters, particularly the first ones, are viewed as forerunners of good fortune.

"See," Nalini told me, "the curse is lifted. Goddess Kankai is smiling upon us. Good days are ahead."

———

The good days turned out to be scattered among some tense ones. Nalini had no idea what an academic position at a major university required. She assumed that it was just another 9-to-5 job like the ones that most of our friends had. She didn't realize that even on the weekends, I had to go to the library to do my research and writing. I was under great pressure to publish. After all, Pitt was a "publish-or-perish" school. One weekend morning while the kids were still sleeping, as I was about to leave for the university, she asked, "Can't you stay home at least during the weekends?"

I lost my cool. "Look here," I snapped, "you are married to a university professor. Yes, I have to go to the library even on Saturdays because I have to do research and write these damn articles. If I don't, I will lose this job and we will all have to go back to India. Is that what you want?"

She was taken aback at my sharp reply and broke into tears. At that, I relented and stayed home. I tried to explain to her how precarious my situation was at the university and the stress that I was going through. I'm not sure she understood. I sensed that the differences in our intellectual makeup that had been overshadowed by our struggle for survival in Mumbai were now coming to the fore. Now that America had given us a chance to remake our lives, I could see that the two of us wanted different things. She thought it was time for us to enjoy the good life—Bollywood movies, parties, a big house, a fancy car, trips to India to shop for sarees and jewelry. I wasn't interested in those things. I thought it was time to make something of ourselves by cultivating our intellectual lives—reading books, attending literary events, going to plays and classical-music concerts. Nalini wasn't interested in those things—if forced to go to them, she'd be bored.

I did see the stress that she underwent managing the household and raising our children. I tried to ease the tension between us and lighten her load by taking our son out, particularly on weekends. I took him regularly to swimming lessons, which he very much enjoyed. As a result, he became a good swimmer. After swimming, we'd go to Dunkin' Donuts and McDonald's, which he enjoyed even more. To get him into the habit of reading early, I took him to the library every weekend and brought home books, which I religiously read with him at bedtime. I also limited his TV viewing and regulated the shows that he could watch. This raised some tension with Nalini, but I stood firm. I often took him to Pittsburgh's Schenley Park, a natural wonder filled with playgrounds and nature trails, blissfully situated in the Oakland neighborhood where we had once lived. Occasionally I took Apoorva to a Penguins hockey game, which he enjoyed so much that he developed a lifelong love of hockey. Now in his late 40s, he still plays it recreationally. He also avidly followed the Pittsburgh Steelers and Penguins, though that allegiance has now been transferred to the Washington Redskins and Washington Capitals.

With my degree in hand, I was on tenure track. The university offered two three-year contracts to new faculty. If I proved capable of publishing regularly in academic journals, I would be granted tenure—meaning that I would be in for life. Once an academic institution grants tenure, it is nearly impossible to remove a faculty member. However, if by the end of the sixth year I hadn't established a publishing track record, I would be shown the door. The clock had started ticking on me. At universities like Pitt, academic journals are where the proverbial rubber meets the road. So how would I start getting published in them? I carved up my dissertation into a few publishable journal articles and sent them to academic journals such as the *Accounting Review*, the house organ of the American Accounting Association. If I got an article or two published there, I was home free.

Alas, my papers were rejected by all of the established academic journals, including the *Accounting Review*. This wasn't entirely unexpected. I had been amply warned by Jim Pattillo, my academic advisor at LSU. "Nat, you need numbers and equations in your writing," he'd told me. I had virtually none of that. My dissertation addressed the grandiose theme of the function of accounting in a post-industrial society—a premise that couldn't really be tested. Moreover, such global issues were not in vogue in contemporary academic research. Among the multitude of issues that accounting academicians read, wrote and researched, the nature of accounting in a changing society was nowhere to be found. The clock continued to tick.

A colleague who'd joined the Pitt faculty at about the same time I had was refused the second three-year contract. Two additional colleagues, who had received their degrees from top-ranked graduate schools (Penn and Yale), had been refused tenure even after they'd had their second three-year contract. I panicked. If these well-trained and well-connected colleagues had been shown the door, what hope did I have? I finally came to the grudging realization that I was not a good academic researcher. I was unlikely to do what Pitt required of me—publish in highly regarded academic journals. I considered leaving Pitt for an undergraduate business school that was not heavily research oriented but emphasized classroom teaching. After all, I was a good teacher and popular among students, even at Pitt. After much soul-searching, I decided to leave Pitt.

———————

My inability to get anything academically substantial published ruined my dream of making a start at a major American university. I'd been warned about Pitt by my fellow Ph.D. students at LSU, but thought that I'd be able to make it. Leaving Pitt would be a major setback for me, but I knew that it wouldn't grant me tenure for my excellent teaching, and I didn't want to do the kind of academic research it required. The choice for me was to leave voluntarily or be shown the door at the end of six years. Seeking a less stressful academic environment, I quietly began searching for a position at an average college in the South. Given my LSU degree, I thought that I'd have a better chance there. I limited my search to state colleges and universities that emphasized teaching and weren't focused on research and publications. (Unless they were amply endowed, private colleges were perennially plagued by financial issues.) But fortunately, there was always a shortage of accounting Ph.D.s because, as I was often told in graduate school, only fools or foreigners do Ph.D.s in accounting! I quickly received several offers and selected East Carolina University in Greenville, North Carolina, a state university. I told Nalini that we were moving back to North Carolina.

"Why?" she asked. "I thought we were doing fine here. We have a house and good friends, and the kids like it here, too. They seem happy and have friends." Despite the cold weather and snow, she liked Pittsburgh. For the first time, she felt settled in the U.S. She had a beautiful house that she'd decorated herself. Now she'd have to leave it. Even worse, she'd have to say goodbye to her friends. I tried to explain my difficulties in getting published and securing tenure. When I informed her about the Greenville offer, her first question was whether there were Gujarati families there and, if so, how many?

"I don't know," I said. "We'll find out, but there won't be as many as there are in Pittsburgh." She wasn't at all happy about leaving and had no understanding of my academic dilemma, but she reluctantly agreed. In truth, I gave her no choice. Armed with a job offer from East Carolina University, I went to say goodbye to Dean Zoffer. He was surprised that I would leave Pitt for some small Southern college. "I'm disappointed," he said. "Why so soon, Nat? You just came to Pitt."

I explained to him my academic dilemma. "I'm having trouble publishing in academic journals," I said. "My research interests are of a different kind and not in harmony with the prevailing academic trends. I don't think I can produce anything that will see the light of day anytime soon. Meanwhile, as you know, the clock is ticking on my contract."

"Nat," he responded, "have you thought about working with others on the faculty? Maybe you should work with some of your senior colleagues and publish something collaboratively. You should also explore publishing in second-tier journals. It might not be that difficult and would put you on the board. It would show that you are serious about publishing."

Then he pleaded: "Nat, stay put for a year or two. Look, you are a very good teacher. We need good teachers like you. Everyone on the faculty likes you. I have heard nothing but good things about you. Listen, I am going to raise your pay by $10,000!"

Well, how could I say no to such a generous gesture? It certainly would be worthwhile to wait for a year and see if I could make progress on the publishing front. With an appropriate apology, I informed East Carolina University that I wouldn't be coming after all. The school offered me more money, thinking that perhaps its offer had been inadequate for me to make a move. I explained that money was not the issue, and that if I were to make a move in the future, East Carolina would be the first place on my mind.

After my meeting with Dean Zoffer, I approached Jacob Birnberg, a distinguished academic renowned for his research in behavioral accounting. He had come to Pitt from the University of Chicago where he had worked with top-tier researchers. I thought that if I got something published with him that would be like getting an academic Good Housekeeping seal of approval. I approached him with some hesitation and sought his collaboration. "Nat, why don't you work on something and bring it over to me, and I will look at it?" he asked. I quickly put together two articles that emphasized the need to expand the role of accounting in social-program evaluation. Though this was not the kind of stuff that would get me into a first-tier accounting journal, it was the best I could do. My articles still had no numbers or equations, no statistical analyses—just an argument. Professor Birnberg looked them over, made a few changes and sent them off to respectable social-policy journals. To my amazement, both were accepted for publication. I also sent two articles from my dissertation to second-tier journals and got them published as well. Maybe I had a future at Pitt after all!

———

Unbeknownst to me, Nalini had told a few of her friends that we might be leaving Pittsburgh because I was having difficulties at the university. They were quite surprised. Pratima in particular asked her if her husband, Puran, could do anything to convince me to stay. She thought he might help us buy a motel in Breezewood or somewhere. Buying and selling motels goes on in the Patel community all the time, and it wouldn't have been difficult to acquire a small motel. At a party shortly thereafter, Puran cornered me. "Gandhi," he said, "I hear you are having some trouble at the university and looks like you might have to move to North Carolina. I would love to help you. We always need good, reliable people to manage our motels." I was offended by the idea of working as a motel manager after having earned a Ph.D. Those jobs were for barely educated immigrants. I laughed and said, "Oh, no, there's no trouble. A college in North Carolina is offering me more money, but I haven't made up my mind yet."

But I was beside myself. As soon as we got home, I had a bitter row with Nalini, our first major quarrel since coming to the U.S. "Why did you have to blabber our troubles to others? Why did you tell all our stuff to Pratima?" I asked.

"I don't want to leave Pittsburgh," she said. "Maybe Puranbhai could help. They have several motels, and you could easily fit in there. What is wrong with telling them? They are our good friends. They can help us, you know!"

That made me even angrier. She saw no difference between running a motel and being a professor. How could she? She was only minimally educated. She had barely finished high school. Her eldest brother and sister-in-law had treated her more like a helper and babysitter of their children. They did not care whether she finished her schooling. It was unreasonable of me to expect from her what was simply beyond her understanding. To her, both jobs were the same as long as each brought enough money home to run the household.

I told her to stay out of my job problems. "I can manage them myself, thank you!"

"Well, I am your wife," she said. "I have to know. Your problems affect me and the kids!"

Things got worse. "I will decide where I work," I said. "If you don't like it, too bad. You can always go back to India. I didn't get all this education to run a motel in the middle of nowhere!"

At that, she started crying. Unfortunately, this drama played out in front of the kids, who understood nothing except that their daddy was a nasty, angry man. After the altercation, we barely spoke for days. A cold war ensued between us, presaging troubles in the months and years to come.

I got a few articles published, but my future at the University of Pittsburgh still seemed uncertain. As I thought further about my academic prospects there, I came to the uneasy realization that the ivory tower was no place for me. I loved teaching and was deemed an outstanding teacher wherever I taught. But academic research was my Achilles heel. My heart was not in it. I was turned off by much of what I saw in academic journals. Most of it was arcane and profoundly boring. Life was too precious to be wasted doing that kind of work. All of this left me in a deep quandary. I was 36. At that age, it would be difficult for me to make a fresh start in the business world. I felt stuck in academia, where I was a misfit. I yearned to leave the academic environment but did not know just how.

Then I saw an announcement inviting business-school professors to apply for yearlong fellowships at federal agencies in Washington, DC. Under this arrangement, a faculty member would spend a year seeing how government worked. Ever since I had come to America, I'd been fascinated by Washington. I saw this not only as an opportunity to work and live in Washington, but also as a possible escape route from academia.

I applied immediately and was invited to visit several agencies. The Department of Agriculture and the General Accounting Office (GAO—now the Government Accountability Office) each offered me a yearlong fellowship. Though the GAO was a much smaller agency, it was considered important because Congress relied on it. The Agriculture Department, once an important federal bureaucracy when the country was mostly rural, now appeared irrelevant. With the emergence of manufacturing and services as the nation's principal economic activities, agriculture was gradually declining in importance. Since my ultimate aim was to find a way out of academia, I thought that my Ph.D. in accounting might give me a leg up in getting a long-term position at GAO than I'd have elsewhere.

It was time to move again.

Nalini opposed the move, of course. Settled into Pittsburgh with two children, she felt that another move would be too upsetting.

"I don't see any long-term future for me at Pitt," I told her. "I have to find a job someplace where I can have a stress-free life." I explained again the whole 'publish-or-perish' situation.

She wasn't convinced. "You're smart," she said. "You can manage it. Everyone likes you. Some of your faculty colleagues have been to our house. They will surely give you tenure!"

"Here's what we'll do," I said. "You stay here and I'll go to Washington. It's only for a year. I'll come visit you and the kids once or twice a month. How is that?" She didn't like the idea of being separated again. I tried to mollify her. "There will be many Indians there, even Gujaratis! Our old friend Doshi and his wife, Shaku, are there. We're not selling our house. We're coming back!"

Doshi had followed me to Atlanta University. Shaku and Nalini had developed a friendship in Mumbai while their husbands were in the U.S. They used to get together often and exchange notes and news. Both wanted to come to the U.S. as soon as their husbands could send for them. After graduating from Atlanta University, Doshi took the same path that I had taken. He got a job at South Carolina State College in Orangeburg, a predominantly black college, then moved on to Howard University in Washington, DC, another black institution. He'd then sent for Shaku as well as his parents and brother. They all lived together in an apartment in Hyattsville, Maryland, a Washington suburb.

Nalini liked the idea that she'd be reunited with Shaku and wouldn't be without friends in Washington. Seeing that I was determined to go, she relented and started packing our things.

Still, I had to be cautious. I would leave Pitt and go to Washington only for a year. I didn't want to lose the bird in hand. I approached Dean Zoffer again, told him that I was going to Washington for a year and suggested that my doing so would enhance the school's reputation. I didn't have to explain the advantages of my going to Washington. In fact, he liked the idea that a Pitt professor was headed there. It was quite common for professors from elite universities such as Harvard and Yale to go to Washington on sabbatical and then come back. He readily agreed but cautioned that I had to return to keep my tenure-track position.

"Dean," I said, "I am keeping my house here." We rented out the house for a year, piled up the necessary stuff in a U-Haul truck and headed to Washington. I drove the truck and Nalini followed in our old beaten-up Mustang that was still with us. It was a risky adventure—this was Nalini's first time driving on an interstate highway, and she had our son and his sister Sona with her. We stopped at rest areas every few hours and checked on each other. Finally, we made it to Washington and unloaded our stuff into an apartment that we had rented near where the Doshis lived.

I wouldn't call it an auspicious start of our new life in the nation's capital, but we were there.

Chapter 12

SEVEN-BILLION-DOLLAR MAN

Late afternoon on June 22, 1982, as I was getting ready to meet my carpool in the basement of the GAO, I got a call from the chief of staff of a powerful congressional committee.

"The chairman wants a briefing from you now," he said. "Come over—we are waiting!"

Chairman Dan Rostenkowski, the legendary Democrat from Illinois, presided over the House Ways and Means Committee, which had jurisdiction over more than half of the nation's budget. Rostenkowski was considered a god in the world of federal taxation.

I ran downstairs to tell my carpool to go on without me.

"Why? What's the matter? How will you get home?"

"I have to go to the Hill to brief Chairman Rostenkowski," I said. "Please go ahead. I'll find my way home somehow."

I wasn't going to miss an opportunity to brief one of the most influential tax legislators on the Hill. As chairman of the House and Ways Means Committee, he always had the first word on taxes in Congress. Back in my office, the messages grew more insistent: "The chairman is waiting!"

Why would one of the most powerful men in Congress need to see a mid-level bureaucrat in the GAO, a federal agency of "bean counters" that monitored federal spending? The one-word answer is insurance. Money talks, and a GAO team that I headed had discovered a way to bring $7 billion into the federal treasury by way of a change in the rules for taxing insurance companies. In the eyes of the chief government bean counters, that made me the "seven-billion-dollar man."

Ever since coming to America in 1965, when I watched President Lyndon Johnson's Secretary of State Dean Rusk on TV testifying before Congress, I'd dreamed of being a player in Washington's public-policy arena. I was glued to television coverage of the Vietnam War hearings before the Senate Foreign Relations Committee chaired by Arkansas Democrat J. William Fulbright. What a scene! A standing-room-only crowd in the hearing room, a phalanx of TV cameras, a swarm of reporters sitting behind the witness table furiously writing every word the secretary was saying, and angry senators demanding an early end to a quagmire war in the distant paddies of Southeast Asia where hundreds of young men were killed every week. Then there was the Buddha-like Secretary of State Rusk, a Kent cigarette dangling from his lips, patiently plodding through his foreboding analysis of the domino theory, according to which, if the U.S. did not stop the "red menace" in Vietnam, Hawaii and California would be afflicted by the yellow peril.

I was transfixed by the scene. How I wanted to be there! Even in India, when America was only a dream, Washington had fascinated me. In my perennial search for a good job in Mumbai, I had gone to see an acquaintance who had just returned from the U.S. with an MBA. He was handsomely employed by the Indian branch of Dorr Oliver, a leading engineering solutions-provider company. I thought that he might find me a job there. When I went to see him, I saw a huge map of the United States in his office and noticed that Washington was in the distant northwest corner.

"How strange it is to have the nation's capital pushed out in a distant corner of a vast continent," I blurted.

"That's Washington state, not Washington, DC," he corrected.

He then pointed out the latter on the map and told me that it had been established in 1790, when it was indeed in the middle of 13 colonies that originally comprised the United States. That was my introduction to Washington, DC. He explained that it was a federal territory and not a state. Little did I know at the time that one day I would be its chief financial officer. Nor did I have any idea then how a federal territory was different from a state, or that eventually I would have to wrestle with the economic consequences of that crucial difference.

––––––––

Given my fascination with Washington, I was thrilled to have an opportunity to work there. As soon as Dean Zoffer approved my one-year assignment in July of 1976, we paid it a short visit. It was America's bicentennial year and there was a big celebration on the National Mall. We took our two kids to the Mall, of course, joining the million-plus celebrants, and did other touristy things like visiting monuments and museums. But my mind was elsewhere. I wanted to make sure that we'd have a good place to live in the DC area. After a brief search, we settled on a two-bedroom apartment in the nearby Maryland suburb of Greenbelt. It was within a reasonable commuting distance of the city and had many kid-friendly amenities, such as swimming pools, a kindergarten facility and a good elementary school.

I also wanted to make sure that we would be near our old friends, the Doshis. There were numerous Gujarati families in the area as well who would give Nalini company while I was at the office and the kids were at school. One other thing I sought was a part-time teaching assignment at a local university. I wanted to keep my hand in teaching. My ultimate motive was to get a suitable job in the federal government, but if that were not to work out, perhaps I could land an academic appointment at a local university that was not hung up on research. There were several universities and all of them offered me positions. Again, this is the wonder of a Ph.D. in accounting! I selected American University, where I thought that I might find a congenial academic home if I did not want to return to Pittsburgh.

I was excited that I would be working at the GAO. Often referred to as the "congressional watchdog," it regularly conducted audits and investigations of federal agencies on behalf of Congress. Over the years, the GAO had conducted investigations and issued reports that were frowned upon by agencies and occasionally by individual members of Congress, as well as by presidents. Every time a GAO audit was announced, agency officials would become defensive. They knew that a critical GAO report would generate negative press, harm their reputations and spark congressional hearings in which they would be grilled by skeptical legislators.

A GAO report could lead to changes in policy, budget cuts and even the occasional resignation of an agency head. Congressional hearings often became tools for educating the public on complex issues of policy and governance. When I joined the GAO in the fall of 1976, it was undergoing a transformation. Since its founding in 1921, it had primarily concentrated on financial audits of federal agencies—determining whether they spent more than what was appropriated and in accordance with the law. When Elmer Staats became comptroller general in 1966, he wanted to change its focus from financial audits to performance audits—to see whether the federal agencies accomplished what they had set out to do. Congressional committees, particularly the tax-writing ones, needed nonpartisan, objective analysis and guidance to make their way through the maze of conflicting arguments about the nation's tax policy. Various industries complained about heavy tax burdens that hurt their international competitiveness; they vigorously lobbied the committees to preserve their favored interests.

Among the most vociferous of these was the life-insurance industry. It was also in the midst of an intra-industry squabble between publicly traded stock companies that were owned by shareholders and mutual companies that were owned by policyholders. The insurance industry was also eager to enter the larger arena of financial intermediation and compete with banks, which also had designs of their own to sell insurance. In a rapidly evolving financial world, the lines among various types of financial companies such as banks, savings-and-loan associations, cooperative banks, money-market funds and insurance companies were getting blurred. The GAO team studying the insurance industry needed a highly skilled accountant to understand the industry's accounting and taxation. Since I had Ph.D. in accounting and had taught at the college level, that person turned out to be me.

When Rostenkowski's office summoned me that day in the summer of 1982, I took the message to my superiors, who had to be informed of all important congressional contacts. Meeting Rostenkowski was as heavy duty as it got in Washington's tax arena. "Nat," my supervisor told me, "you can't go there by yourself. You are too junior. I'll accompany you to the meeting." Then he spelled out a series of bureaucratic steps that had to be taken before I was cleared to meet with the congressman. More GAO officials might want to join me. This was getting complicated. It was ultimately decided that three people would accompany me to the meeting. They also wanted to be briefed about the substance of the meeting before we marched to the Hill. They had very little idea, if any, of the subject matter.

I called Rostenkowski's office. Before I could say anything, the staffer on the other end shouted, "I told you the chairman is waiting. He has a flight to catch. What's taking you so long? The GAO is only a 10-minute cab ride away!" I explained my bureaucratic dilemma and told him that three other people would be accompanying me—after I briefed them!

"Why are they coming?" he yelled. "What do they know about the subject? Come now, or I will call the CG's office. Do you hear me?" The CG—comptroller general—is one of the few agency heads who do not change with each new administration. Each CG has a non-renewable, 15-year appointment. I told my superiors about the urgency of the meeting. They relented. But I still couldn't go by myself. Mort Meyers, the division director, would accompany me. "You brief Mr. Myers in the car on your way to the Hill," his assistant said. We rushed down to the GAO basement, where a government car was waiting take both of us to the Longworth House Office Building where Rostenkowski had his office. When we arrived, the staffer was fuming.

"Thank God you're here, Nat!" he said. "The chairman is waiting. You have just 15 minutes with him. Come with me." He took us to the chairman's thickly carpeted conference room. At one end of a long oval conference table sat Congressman Dan Rostenkowski with a scowl on his face and a few staffers sitting at a respectful distance from him at the table. Rostenkowski was an imposing presence—a tall, well-built man in his mid-50s with a head full of dark, curly hair and not much of a neck. He exuded power in everything he did. His legislative skills were legendary. In Capitol Hill par-lance, "He knew how to count." One Washington newspaper article put it this way: "Rostenkowski strode the halls of Capitol Hill as powerful and influential domestical-ly, it could be persuasively argued, as the president himself."

"Mr. Chairman," the staffer who'd arranged the meeting said, "this is Nat Gandhi of the GAO. He's done a lot of work on insurance taxation. He'll brief you on what we can do to raise some significant revenue from the insurance industry."

Rostenkowski looked at me with a touch of disdain. "Okay," he said, "let's get on with it. Just give me the highlights."

The next 15 or so minutes were the most important moments of my professional life. Here I was, briefing the powerful chairman of the House Ways and Means Com-mittee, and he was listening carefully to what I had to say. I was excited but not intim-idated. I knew my stuff well—I'd been living it for the past few years. I explained how insurance companies were using particular tax-code provisions to substantially reduce their tax liabilities. Minor changes in these provisions could close the loopholes.

"How much money would that raise?" the chairman asked.

"Looking at the past numbers, sir, I would say about $7 billion over the next 10 years."

The chairman sat up straight. "Say what? Did you say $7 *billion?*"

"Yes, Mr. Chairman," I responded. "That's a rough calculation. The JCT [Joint Committee on Taxation] would have to score it, of course."

Rostenkowski looked at the staffer in disbelief. "Okay," he said, "we'll do it." Then, pointing at me, he said, "Make sure you invite him to the markup," and walked out of the room. These markups are an opportunity for negotiation and horse-trading among congressmen representing competing interests. Our meeting lasted 15 min-utes at most. In the whole time, the chairman did not so much as look at Myers. As I missed the day's carpool, the taxi to my suburban Maryland home that evening cost me an arm and a leg, but it was worth it. I had accomplished something that I'd always wanted to do—be influential in Washington and play a role in public policy. At last, my dream had come true.

After we were settled in the nation's capital, I would take our Indian visitors to monuments and other special places in Washington. I loved showing them the White House and emphasizing its relatively small size as a reflection of the democratic nature of the U.S., a huge contrast with Rashtrapati Bhavan, formerly the grand residence of the British viceroy in New Delhi. That vast mansion, designed by British architect Edwin Landseer Lutyens and now occupied by the president of India, is unique among residences of heads of state for its size, magnificence and gardens. In those days, one could roam the Capitol building unhindered and casually encounter prominent senators or congressmen usually seen only on the news. Before 9/11 ended such visits to the Capitol, one could easily walk to the upper deck of the Western portico, where Ronald Reagan and every president who followed him took the oath of office, and get a panoramic view of the magnificent Mall that extended all the way to the Lincoln Memorial. The view from there of museums, monuments and a vast urban vista is unmatched anywhere in the United States. I would stroll with our visitors along Pennsylvania Avenue from Capitol Hill to the White House, not realizing that one day I would have an office in City Hall overlooking Freedom Plaza, where I would hold parties on Inauguration Day for friends and acquaintances to watch the parade. Of several inauguration parades, one sticks in my memory. On a very cold January 20, 2001, from my office window in City Hall, I could see a noisy demonstration on Freedom Plaza with handwritten placards reflecting the Florida vote count inscribed with slogans like "Fraud W. Bush" and "Hail to the Thief" as the parade passed them by. I saw American democracy in action.

I had no idea how convoluted taxing insurance companies could be until I went to Winston-Salem, North Carolina, to attend a one-week course on the subject. It was run by Booke, a company that conducts seminars in federal tax accounting and reporting for insurance-industry professionals. In my life as an accountant, I had seen many complex and boring things, but insurance taxation took the cake! I came back from Winston Salem thoroughly disheartened by the prospect of spending the next year studying and analyzing this supremely arcane subject. But I wanted to make a good impression on senior GAO officials; my ulterior motive was to get a full-time position there. I did not want to go back to Pitt.

So I threw myself into the project with enthusiasm, studying insurance-industry economics, meeting with senior industry executives and lobbyists, and briefing Hill staffers on the progress of our work. As soon as industry officials learned what we were doing, they sought us out. They wanted to make sure their case was given a proper hearing and was reflected in the report. For them, an adverse GAO recommendation could result in hundreds of millions of dollars of additional taxes. For the first time, I was doing something consequential in my professional life, and it was viewed as such by industry executives as well as people on the Hill. This was a far cry from working on a research project on obscure accounting issues at Pitt, where no one would take note of what I was doing. Here I was a key government official sought after by insurance-company executives, who came to Washington to see me and my team. I was also invited to their headquarters, where I met with senior executives, including CEOs and company presidents. I was asked to make presentations about the project before trade associations and at professional gatherings.

Within months I had become the face of the GAO's insurance work. Many years later, as I was entering an elevator in Washington, a stranger coming out of it saw me and blurted: "Section 809, right?" He was referring to a crucial section of the code relating to insurance taxation that we had studied for our report. Odd as it might seem, an Indian from an impoverished Indian village had become the GAO's insurance man. Though I got a lion's share of credit for much of the work since I was heading insurance tax-related projects, it should be noted that much of the GAO's work is done by a team of specialists. I have been very lucky to have on my teams some exceptionally talented people. The late Bill Simpson was an actuary with decades of experience in the insurance industry and gave our work a great amount of credibility. I worked very closely with Bill and we became family friends. Two exceptional economists, Thomas McCool and Steve Swaim, have been especially crucial to my success in the GAO. Steve in particular has been very helpful to me in my professional development in Washington. In fact, he brought me to Washington in the first place and then worked with me when I moved to the DC government.

I took the lead in briefing staff and legislators on the Hill, including Chairman Rostenkowski and other members of the House Ways and Means Committee. During 1981–82, I also worked closely with the Senate Finance Committee and its chairman, Senator Bob Dole (R-Kansas) on insurance taxation. I advised key Hill staffers in the committee's markup sessions, where the legislation was hammered out. I was thrilled to be on the Hill briefing staffers and legislators, participating in their deliberations and testifying in public hearings in the glare of TV cameras.

With hundreds of industry lobbyists swarming the cavernous hearing room of the House Ways and Means Committee in the Longworth Building, the environment was almost circus-like. To get into the room, one had to get in a long line early in the day. Industry lobbyists came at the hearing time and replaced assistants who'd been standing in line for them. Since hearings were focused on the GAO report, our team became lead witnesses. Business reporters and industry executives took notes, and paid close attention to our testimony and answers to the questions they'd fed to their favorite legislators. C-Span televised the hearings, usually on a time-delayed basis. Given that insurance-industry taxation didn't generate a great deal of public interest, our hearings usually were televised at odd hours—though it might have been prime time in Guam! If public interest in the subject was high and nothing newsworthy was going on elsewhere on the Hill, hearings were sometimes televised live. When I testified before Senator Alan Simpson (R-Wyoming) on June 13, 1995 about taxation of the American Association of Retired Persons (AARP)—certainly a hot topic among the elderly—my testimony was televised live. *The Washington Times*, a conservative-leaning daily, carried my picture the next day—my first-ever photo in an American newspaper! All of this was heady stuff for a college professor who would usually toil in obscurity. I couldn't contain my enthusiasm for what I was now doing. Given the critical nature of the job and my central role, I was soon offered a permanent position at the GAO. My strategy had worked.

————

I broke the news to Nalini. "The GAO has offered me a job here. I want to take it." This time she didn't resist. Washington's weather was warmer and much less snowy. And the suburban Washington area was easier to drive in than hilly Pittsburgh. We were renting near a large Gujarati community where Nalini had made many new friends. Our old friends Kanu and Shaku Doshi were already there. Then she asked, "What about the house?" "We will sell the house in Pittsburgh and buy a bigger one here," I said. "The same deal—four bedrooms, yard in front and back, and a two-car garage. You can decorate it any way you want. And we'll have a furnished basement where you can give as many parties as you want!" Nalini agreed. I quickly accepted the GAO's offer and resigned my position at the University of Pittsburgh.

————

As eager as I was to appear on Capitol Hill, it was easy to find congressional staff equally eager to initiate and manage hearings. So I cultivated congressional staff on the Hill who regularly kept sending requests to the GAO to initiate investigations or studies that I suggested to them. I was also asked to testify before the legislatures of states such as New Jersey, Oregon and Hawaii. They also wanted to rein in insurance companies. State legislators felt that they had scored a big deal by getting a GAO representative to come to their state capital to testify from Washington. Since several of the GAO reports prepared under my leadership recommended changes in tax laws that raised billions of dollars, our team got credit for the additional revenue. I received several agency awards and, more importantly, was promoted to Senior Executive Service (SES) rank. My success sparked some jealousy. Once when I joined colleagues—some of whom reacted against all of the attention that I was getting—for lunch in the GAO cafeteria, one of them blurted out derisively, "All rise, here comes the seven-billion-dollar man!" Senior GAO officials annually tallied how much they saved as well as raised through our recommendations that were adopted by Congress.

————

When I arrived in 1976, the GAO was a lily-white organization—minorities and women were rarely visible. In fact, in the senior ranks there was one black, one woman and one Asian. Senior positions were filled mostly by white men, many of whom had come to the GAO from western Pennsylvania and West Virginia with undergraduate degrees in accounting—and stayed. It was the only job that many of them had ever held and they intended to stay there until retirement. These old-line GAO auditors tended to hire and promote their own kind. I didn't fit the profile of a GAO auditor whom they considered worthy of promotion to senior managerial positions. For some of them I was a "foreigner." Worse yet, I was viewed as a "professor" who had lucked into success on the Hill. My higher academic credentials and subject-area expertise meant nothing to them. I was just a Johnny-come-lately who should wait his turn for any promotion, and never to the senior ranks. Their not-so-subtle racial bias was evident when I sat with them at lunchtime in the GAO cafeteria and was ignored in conversation. Sometimes they would not invite me to meetings that would have impact on projects that I was working on. Even in carpool, some fellow riders would talk past me and ignore any comments that I would make. When I saw this as a pattern, I dropped out of carpool and drove myself, incurring considerable cost in fuel and parking.

In work-related visits to the agency's West Coast offices—where there were numerous Asian Americans on the staff—I asked around whether they felt discriminated against, particularly regarding project assignments and promotions. Despite their large numbers, not a single Asian auditor held a senior position in any of the western offices. Even those with seniority and expertise were confined to staff-level positions and never put in managerial roles. Whenever a vacancy would open for the head position in a regional office, a white male auditor would be brought in from headquarters or elsewhere. Other minorities faced similar discrimination, particularly African Americans. Though they were there in large numbers, nearly all of them were concentrated in lower-level jobs in the mailroom, print shop or elsewhere, or worked as janitors or housekeeping staff. A few held clerical positions but only one was in senior management. Angered by the systematic discrimination, black employees held a protest demonstration outside GAO headquarters. Also, two class-action lawsuits were filed against the GAO. In October of 1984, the Equal Employment Opportunity Commission (EEOC) determined that blacks had indeed been discriminated against in seeking promotions at the GAO. In July of 1985, it settled both cases and agreed to pay $3.5 million to 300 present and past black employees. Finally, blacks were promoted to senior staff positions and a few were groomed for management jobs. Seeing the success of African American employees, I thought that it would be good to organize an Asian American caucus and let management know of our discontent with the prevailing discrimination. Asians were nowhere near the blacks in numbers; however, they were well educated and highly skilled—in most cases more so than their white colleagues.

I arranged a meeting with the assistant comptroller general, apprised management of our grievances and asked for an action plan to correct the situation. I let it be known that I was in touch with lawyers at the EEOC about my particular case. A group of us South-Asian Americans also approached congressional staff about our predicament.

Congresswoman Connie Morella (R-Maryland), who represented Montgomery County where I lived, sent a letter inquiring about the glass ceiling faced by Asian Americans at the GAO. We also formed an Asian American Liaison Group to coordinate our concerns, and issued a data-based report suggesting the existence of a glass ceiling at the GAO and asked for a plan for the systematic promotion of deserving Asian Americans to management positions. We further requested that senior management regularly meet with us to resolve issues underlying our grievances. Senior GAO officials were worried that the agency might face another class-action lawsuit like the one it had faced from African Americans. They readily agreed to open a dialog with us and take corrective actions. Within a few short years, Asian Americans were being promoted to management positions, particularly in the West Coast offices.

Much in the GAO has changed since Charles Bowsher became comptroller general in 1981. He was a visionary leader with broad public- and private-sector experience. For decades, he was a senior partner with the accounting firm of Arthur Andersen. From 1967 to 1971 he was comptroller and assistant secretary of the Navy. A highly respected figure in Washington's fiscal arena, he quickly but deliberately moved to diversify the agency, particularly its senior ranks. Many able women and minorities were promoted and given opportunities to testify before Congress. I was among those promoted at Bowsher's prodding. He had heard of my successes on the Hill and wondered aloud why I wasn't in the senior ranks. Still, I was bypassed when an opening occurred to head the GAO's tax area and its large staff. I contemplated challenging the agency in court, but thought that legal action would be protracted and counterproductive. It would have labeled me as a troublemaker, which might have foreclosed possibilities for career advancement elsewhere in Washington. I decided that if the GAO didn't want me, I didn't want the GAO. I also sensed that, after 20 years, my time at the GAO was coming to an end. I had hit my own glass ceiling and it was time to move on.

In October of 1997, I turned 57 and assessed my prospects. Yes, I was well-known in insurance-tax circles, but too old to be hired by an insurance company or consulting firm. Given my work on the Hill, any prospective corporate employer would want me to lobby to preserve the industry's narrow tax loopholes. Though it paid handsomely, I detested lobbying for what I saw as its lack of professional integrity. If I wasn't going to lobby in Washington, should I consider going back to academia? Or would that subject me to the vagaries of publish or perish yet again? I was in excellent health and not ready to retire. I decided to go back to academia but only with the understanding that I would not be subjected to a publish-or-perish regime. I would go only to a school that would hire me as a tenured professor—I wasn't going through the hassle of getting tenured again. I identified a few schools where teaching was the primary consideration for hiring and promotion, and where my Washington experience would be considered an asset. Because of my strong résumé, I was quickly called for interviews at colleges in New York and Philadelphia. Though those jobs would require moving from Washington, I still considered them. Even so, I was hardly enthusiastic about returning to a university. I also had reached out to acquaintances in other federal agencies and elsewhere, and informed them of my plans to leave the GAO.

An unexpected call came from my good friend Ira Goldstein. "How would you like to be the next tax commissioner for the District of Columbia?" he asked. Goldstein and I had worked together for years and bonded at the GAO. He'd been responsible for diversifying the agency's senior ranks under Comptroller General Bowsher. A former whiz kid who had worked with Defense Secretary Robert McNamara at the Pentagon, Goldstein was an enlightened public servant who had produced a highly informative how-to manual on presidential transitions. He had seen what I had done at the GAO and understood its value. He'd taken a personal interest in my advancement at the agency. When he learned that the District of Columbia needed a tax commissioner, he thought that, given my tax work at the GAO, I fit the bill and recommended me for the position. But what would that entail?

During the mid-1990s, the city of Washington, DC, was nearly bankrupt. Its annual local budget of $5 billion faced perennial shortfalls; the city ran yearly deficits. Its finances were a mess. Its fund balance, essentially a savings account, was some $500 million in the red and its municipal bonds were rated junk by Wall Street. Vendors weren't being paid on time for their services. In 1995 Congress, which has constitutional responsibility for the nation's capital, put the city government under receivership and established a Control Board to manage the District's finances. It took financial powers away from the mayor and other elected officials and established an Office of the Chief Financial Officer within the Control Board framework to manage the District's finances. The District's financial staff, nearly 1,200 strong, was put under the authority of the independent CFO. The new authority controlled the District's financial operations, including tax administration, revenue estimation, treasury, budgeting, comptrollership and even the city's lottery. Anything and everything financial and fiscal had to have the CFO's approval. This extraordinary concentration of powers was unique, yet Congress saw it as necessary to restore the city's fiscal health. The District CFO had a five-year term and could not be removed from office without cause, most importantly only with congressional approval. Armed with independence and extraordinary powers, the first CFO of the District, Anthony Williams, set out to fix the financial mess. His first order of business was to remake the District's tax office, which he saw as the source of the city's financial woes. The tax office was mostly broken—it didn't even carry out its primary function of collecting taxes. Worse yet, it was notoriously corrupt. The staff was thoroughly demoralized, suffering constant changes in management and lacking adequate technology and resources. The tax office needed aggressive and energetic management and fresh leadership to motivate and inspire its employees. It was quite a daunting challenge.

At Goldstein's urging, I met with CFO Williams and offered my services. He was impressed with my experience on tax issues, my familiarity with the IRS and its senior officers, including several past and the present commissioners, my credibility on the Hill and accounting background. He instantly offered me the job of running the District's tax office. But should I take it? I thought that I could handle the job despite its many challenges. Heading the District's tax office was the first major managerial position offered to me in the U.S. I would manage a diverse staff of some 600 people. I thought that if I did well, it might lead to other major opportunities. Who knew—it might even lead to being IRS commissioner if a future president were looking for an Asian to lead the nation's tax agency! I may never get another such offer, I thought, so I might as well grab it. Besides, I was bored after 20 years of doing basically the same thing at the GAO. I wanted new challenges and this job was full of them. I accepted the offer to head the District of Columbia's tax office.

When I told my GAO colleagues that I had accepted the job of DC's tax commissioner, they were aghast. Many of them had audited the District's operations and knew that it was a financial quagmire. They thought it unwise, if not downright foolish, for me to give up a secure senior position at a premier federal agency for such a risky venture. Before jumping ship, I made a point of going out to lunch with several GAO staff who had audited the DC government. They strongly advised against my taking the job.

"Nat, do you know what you're doing?" one asked. "You're giving up a tenured SES position at the GAO. And for what? The District of Columbia?"

I tried to laugh off their concerns. "How bad could it be? I'm from India and have seen worse."

"Well, this would be worse," one of them said. "You never faced racism in India. Here you will have to face that. Remember, you are not black. You will be discriminated against. Mark my words, you will be begging to come back to the GAO within six months. Besides, you will have to live in the city."

That shook me up. At the time, the District was still recovering from a drug epidemic that had plagued it since the 1980s, when it was labeled "the murder capital of the nation." Marion Barry, the disgraced mayor who had been jailed for drug possession, was now back in City Hall as mayor again. I went back to see CFO Williams and conveyed my concerns. He said that his office was completely independent of the mayor and would not tolerate any interference.

"Nat," he said, "I will put in writing that you will not have to live in the city. I understand your concerns." I went home and told Nalini that I was about to change jobs.

"What?" she asked. "Are we moving again?"

After being in our house for nearly 20 years, we were deeply invested in the neighborhood. Near our home was a newly built Hindu temple where we went regularly for religious prayers and festivals. We had a busy and fulfilling Gujarati social life. The children also enjoyed their Gujarati friends.

Nalini said emphatically, "I am not moving!"

"No, we are not moving!" I assured her. "There will be no change in our social life. My new office will be only a block away from the GAO."

With that she was mollified, and I took the District job. I had no idea what I had gotten myself into.

Chapter 13

DR. NO

On Monday morning, February 3, 1997, I showed up at City Hall to take charge of the District's tax office, located on 4th Street NW, just a block away from the GAO. My new workplace was a nondescript, poorly designed office building that was hardly worthy of being the City Hall for our nation's capital. Its long, dimly lit and cheaply carpeted corridors were lifeless. The windowless halls let in no sunshine. The old City Hall on Pennsylvania Avenue across from Freedom Plaza—a grand old building designed in the Beaux Arts style—had fallen into disrepair. While it was being renovated, the mayor and City Council had moved the District's headquarters temporarily to the 4th Street building. When I went up to the fourth floor, L'Aquila Shark, the tax-office receptionist, greeted me.

"How may I help you?" she inquired.

"I am Mr. Gandhi," I responded, "and I am here to take charge of the tax office."

She had not been aware of my impending arrival that day, but took me to an empty room nearby. "This will be your office," she said.

The scene was underwhelming. There was a desk, an old battered chair and a conference table surrounded by a few more chairs. The window shutters were broken and hung haphazardly. The walls badly needed painting; the green carpet was dirty. My heart sank. I asked the receptionist to set up a quick meeting of the senior staff. "But they are not here, Mr. Gandhi," she said. "They are on travel." That's when I learned that most of the senior staffers, instead of eagerly waiting for their new boss, were on a two-week junket, the ostensible purpose of which was to visit several tax departments around the country to look for ways to improve the District's tax operations. They didn't bother to wait for the man who would be in charge of improving those operations.

I soon discovered that the tax department was in serious disrepair. Many things in the office—telephones, Xerox machines, elevators, even the staff—didn't always work. Fire alarms frequently went off, causing the whole building to be evacuated. The staff was thoroughly demoralized and there was constant turnover among senior management. There were no computers or other modern tools of operation. The DC tax office might as well have been operating out of shoeboxes. There were no established policies and procedures. It took months to do basic things such as processing tax refunds. Its customer service was so poor that *The Washington Post* once labeled it the Department of Finance and Rigmarole, parodying its old name, the Department of Finance and Revenue. Effective management was nonexistent and the absence of any staff training left office workers essentially to fend for themselves. One day early on I opened a closed door and to my horror found a room full of bins piled from floor to ceiling—filled with thousands of unopened tax returns! I couldn't believe it: a tax office that would neglect its most fundamental document—a tax return—in such a manner. Returns were not processed or filed in a routine fashion, which meant there was no way for the office to know who owed how much. I quickly called the CFO's office and asked for an urgent meeting. Anthony Williams immediately got on the phone.

"What's the matter, Nat?"

"Tony," I said, "you're not going to believe what I just saw."

"What is it?"

"Come down and see for yourself."

"Okay, I'm coming down."

When he arrived at my office, I took him to the room filled with unopened tax returns.

"My God!" he exclaimed. "How did this happen?"

"Well, some people got tired of opening tax returns and tossed them aside," I replied. "And pretty soon you have a mountain of them."

"But some of them may have checks in them!"

"Yes, that is quite possible."

"Here's what we will do, Nat," he said. "Take pictures of this and show them around so people can see how bad things are around here. This is Exhibit A. No one would believe this! But you will have to fix it, Nat—that's why you are here!"

So we took pictures of the tax-office disarray and set to work.

Many District citizens, having gauged the dysfunction of the tax office, had stopped paying DC taxes while diligently paying their federal taxes to the IRS. They knew full well that the District would rarely, if ever, come after them for failing to pay. Those who overpaid their taxes through withholding were at the mercy of the tax department for receiving their refunds. It often took months, numerous calls, even office visits to get their refund checks.

There were immediate consequences of the tax-office dysfunction. The District's external auditor, the accounting firm KPMG, gave a "qualified" (unclean) audit opinion saying that its financial report (CAFR) was not reliable. KPMG couldn't verify the District's tax receivables. How could they, with what I saw in that room in the tax office used as a warehouse for unopened tax returns? There was no reliable accounting of who owed how much to the District.

The unclean audit opinion meant that Wall Street rating agencies such as Moody's and Standard & Poor's couldn't rely on the District's accounting. With that, the District lost its credibility on Wall Street and its bond rating tumbled to the junk category, making it difficult to borrow money at a reasonable rate. Higher interest rates led to greater borrowing costs, leaving less money for delivery of services. So the first priority of CFO Williams was to clean the accounts and books, and get the qualified opinion on the District's CAFR removed. As the head of the tax office whose dysfunction had caused the problem, fixing it fell to me: an overwhelming task. Upon learning of the adverse opinion from auditors, Williams vowed to have the problem corrected in one year—or he would resign! He was widely praised for taking responsibility, a rarity in the District, where fingers typically pointed in someone else's direction. When I heard of Williams' willingness to resign if the situation were not fixed in the next audit, I panicked—it would be my responsibility to clean up the tax department and our next audit was only six months away. Having just seen the horrific sight of that room filled with unopened tax returns, I knew that it would be nearly impossible to clean up tax receivables in that short a time. I also knew that if Williams were to go, I would quickly follow him. And I had been on the job only a few weeks. It suddenly seemed that my former GAO colleagues' warning that I wouldn't last more than six months in the District government might prove prescient! In fact, my departure could happen sooner.

I immediately gathered the senior tax staff and explained the predicament we faced: "We are in big trouble. As you know, the District did not receive a clean bill of health from our auditors. Until we get that clean audit opinion, we are doomed. We can't go to Wall Street and borrow money with reasonable rates. Mr. Williams just announced that if we don't get a clean audit opinion, he'll resign. If he goes, I go. And before I go, all of you will go, too!

"Williams can't fire us," one of the old-timers said. "We're DC government employees."

I shot back: "Yes, he can fire all of you, and me too—and everyone else around here. Remember, he just fired the whole real-property assessment staff."

Williams had done precisely that a short time earlier because of the District's shoddy assessment of residential properties. Congress had given the CFO absolute authority over personnel and procurement to help buttress his independence from the mayor and council.

The risk of losing one's job was a great motivator, but I also challenged the staff's professionalism. "How is it that our neighboring jurisdictions can keep their books but we can't?" I asked. "What's wrong with us?" There were murmurs about not having enough resources, not having any management support, low employee morale and more. "All that might be true," I said, "but none of that is going to change in a big way in the short term. Right now, the challenge facing us is to remove that adverse audit opinion or lose our jobs. We're all in the same boat." I could see heads nodding. They were getting my point. "This is not rocket science," I said. "All we do is to open those returns in that room, classify them properly and file them correctly so the auditors can find whatever returns they want to examine. It's elementary! If we can't solve such a rudimentary filing problem, then we all should be fired!"

I reached out to Wilma Matthias, an exceptionally able GAO auditor and former colleague, and coaxed her into joining District government. I put together a select team of tax staffers and put Matthias in charge of them in a war room where they all worked together tirelessly. I met with them regularly to offer words of encouragement. I also got CFO Williams to visit the room and see what we were doing. The people on the team understood what was riding on their efforts and were energized by the attention. Their hard work paid off. When KPMG began their audit, they were able to find the sample returns and agreed to remove the audit qualification. The District would get a clean audit opinion. We all breathed a big sigh of relief, especially Williams. Matthias and her war-room team had saved our jobs, including the CFO's.

The biggest problem I'd faced upon becoming DC's tax commissioner was a culture of apathy. Employees were thoroughly demoralized. There was no effective management at the top or in mid-management ranks. There was no continuity. Turnover at the top kept staffers guessing about what the next guy would do. The tendency among the rank and file was to wait out the new guy and carry on as usual. With no modern tools such as computers and databases, efficiency was predictably low. Worse yet, political interference disheartened the staff even more. The climate was ripe for corruption. My immediate task was to shore up management with experienced tax professionals. I did that by hiring a number of retired IRS staffers. I introduced modern technology and procured an integrated tax-management system, without which no modern tax department could operate efficiently. Above all, I let it be known that I was there to stay, and that from then on unethical behavior would not be tolerated. The word was out: "A new sheriff is in town and he isn't going nowhere!" All employees had to go through mandatory ethics training, and we established an internal-audit unit that had carte blanche to go anywhere to audit operations and report back to me. We caught a few employees crossing the line. I fired them.

Having removed the principal impediment—an unclean audit opinion—to the District's access to financial markets, I turned my attention to the thorny issue of tax collection. Nonpayment of taxes by many not only added to deficits but also was unfair to those who paid their taxes voluntarily. Aggressive but equitable enforcement of tax laws was necessary to establish the tax office's credibility. So I decided to take forceful steps on tax collection. While hiring experienced tax administrators from the

IRS, I made a point of including those with expertise in improving compliance and collection, and with experience in criminal prosecution for noncompliance. We let the media know of our intention to aggressively go after people who did not pay their taxes. To show our determination, we began prosecuting select cases of tax scofflaws and auctioning off properties owned by delinquent taxpayers. We obtained a list from the IRS of DC residents who paid their federal taxes but avoided paying District taxes. I established a telephone unit in the tax office that reached out to nonpayers and warned them about the consequences of nonpayment including criminal prosecution. We contacted long-term nonpayers and also offered general amnesty with a waiver of penalty if they paid their taxes; we even offered an installment option for those unable to pay in one lump sum. We posted on our website names of longtime tax evaders who had left the District in hopes of learning their whereabouts. I fired tax collectors who had been caught taking bribes. The entire staff was on notice: Corrupt practices would not be tolerated; any staff member caught indulging in corruption would be apprehended, fired and prosecuted. The results of these aggressive steps were quickly visible. After years of annual deficits, the District began showing surpluses year after year. For 1997 when I joined the District, its books showed a surplus for the first time in years. Annual deficits of earlier years, however, had created a negative fund balance (essentially a savings account) of $535 million in 1995. Now it turned net positive. The Wall Street rating agencies that had put the District's bonds in the junk category took a second look. With DC's extraordinary financial performance, CFO Williams was portrayed as the District's savior. In a front-page story, *The Washington Post* lionized Williams. The article started with the improvements we made in the tax office. This was the beginning of a "Draft Tony for Mayor" movement.

Given the majority black population, the District had elected only African American mayors. Most Council members were also African American. Of all the District mayors, Marion Barry had the most impact on District finances, development, politics and race relations. During his early mayoral years, the District went through a building boom, especially downtown. The District's image as a sleepy southern town slowly began to change. Further, Barry opened mid-level government jobs and lucrative contracts to African Americans who were previously shut out of both. This created a loyal following among blacks who thought they now had a voice in how their city should be run. Indeed, primarily because Barry opened such government opportunities, the city and nearby Prince George's County in Maryland became a Mecca for black professionals. Barry started his government career as president of the school board. Later he was elected to Council for the first time in 1975 and then mayor in 1978. He would go on to serve four terms as mayor, the last after he had served six months in jail in 1990 for cocaine possession in the infamous Vista Hotel sting operation. As a politician, Barry was shrewd, colorful, charismatic and effective at staying in power. He had a remarkable hold on the District's majority-black population, particularly the poorer citizens who lived east of the Anacostia River. It was especially with their support that he kept getting elected despite his personal failings and character flaws, including unabashed philandering that made news. By his own admission, Barry was a "night bird" and addicted to drugs and alcohol. In short, he flaunted his misbehavior as if normal rules did not apply to him.

However, there was no escaping from the rules and reality of finance. In 1995 the District faced a $722 million deficit for the year and was hurtling toward bankruptcy. President Clinton appointed five distinguished District citizens to the Control Board and named Andrew Brimmer as chairman. Under his leadership, the Control Board was a hard-charging, close-knit group that soon imposed its imprint on the city's finances. When Alice Rivlin succeeded Brimmer, she continued the financial vigilance with her detailed knowledge and unique understanding of the District's economy. Both Brimmer and Rivlin worked closely with Anthony Williams, the first independent chief financial officer. With the Control Board and CFO in place, Congress stripped Barry and the City Council of all financial powers regarding the city. Williams as CFO became city's financial czar.

As Marion Barry's fourth mayoral term was ending in 1998, the District was rife with speculation whether he would run for an unprecedented fifth term. And if so, could he get re-elected? In the largely white wards of northwestern DC and among the city's old-line black establishment, there was a concerted effort to convince CFO Williams to run for mayor irrespective of Barry's intentions. Barry had a good nose to gauge which way the electoral winds were blowing and decided not to run. Immediately, four sitting Council members jumped in the race to replace him. Now there was increased pressure on Williams to run for mayor. The city's business establishment also had enough of Barry and wanted Williams—with his financial acumen—to run for mayor; he soon jumped in to the highly contentious mayoral sweepstakes. His opponents ridiculed Williams as a mere bean counter not equipped to run the city. However, with the overwhelming support of the city's business community, the white establishment and *The Washington Post*, Williams was elected with a large majority. It was a new day in DC.

When Williams replaced "Mayor for Life" Marion Barry, the city's black establishment—which had controlled important positions in City Hall and enjoyed the lion's share of lucrative contracts—felt threatened. Its hold over the city appeared jeopardized. Williams started appointing qualified candidates regardless of race. He named Norman Dong, an Asian American, as city administrator. He was later replaced by a distinguished federal official, John Koskinen, a Washington fixture and go-to guy who had served the country in a variety of capacities. His skills as a problem solver were legendary and his integrity impeccable. He would approach any assignment that was given to him—be that the Penn Central bankruptcy, Y2K, Freddie Mac and even the IRS—and address it with great gusto and bottomless energy. Enticing Koskinen to join the city was a major coup for Mayor Williams. The appointment of non-blacks to senior city positions created concern in certain quarters and raised a question among some black politicians: Was Williams black enough? Williams also appointed younger, highly credentialed blacks with no DC government experience and thus no loyalty to the old black establishment. One of his chiefs of staff, for example, was an immigrant from Somalia, and another came from Florida with no connection to the city. An intense lobbying effort began to make sure the new CFO would be a black person with deep District roots. That clearly was not me.

Meanwhile, black women in the District started a campaign of their own, saying that Williams had not appointed enough of them to senior positions. Their efforts had resulted in a female chief of staff early in Williams' term, and now they wanted a black woman in the CFO chair. My name was also floated as a potential CFO. Because I had worked closely with Williams and gained his trust as tax commissioner, some people thought that I was a shoo-in for the position. Some counseled the mayor that, given the crucial nature of the CFO position, he should choose someone with a proven track record and expertise regardless of race, color or gender. With that in mind, they assumed that I would get the job. There were considerable odds against me. For starters, I was viewed as a foreigner and such an important position shouldn't be wasted on an immigrant. I was also seen as a strong person that the black establishment would not be able to control. More important, the Control Board wanted to make sure that the CFO was independent of the mayor and I was viewed as Williams' man.

The Control Board eventually prevailed upon Williams to appoint Valerie Holt, a black woman then serving on its staff. She had deep roots in city politics, having spent almost all of her professional life in District government. Her appointment in such an important position would also assuage the concerns of women's groups. Late in the evening of May 4, 1999, as I was about to go to bed, the phone rang. Nalini answered it.

"It is the mayor," she said, then added reflexively, "looks like you got the job!"

I took the call. "Good evening, Mr. Mayor."

"Nat, I do not have good news for you. I'm sorry I won't be able to offer you the CFO job. You understand political pressures in the city."

"Yes of course, Mr. Mayor. I understand."

"I want to thank you for all that you have done for the city. I hope you don't leave because of this. We still need you!"

Then he hung up. I told Nalini, "Don't get excited. I didn't get the job. We'll see what we do next." She started crying. "It is that curse again! It never leaves us alone.

You are so qualified, why would the mayor not appoint you? I thought he was your friend." I tried to console her but to no avail.

Mayor Williams' nomination of Valerie Holt as CFO encountered strong resistance from the City Council. Members who had been around for a while remembered her role as comptroller from 1990 to 1994. According to some members, she hadn't kept Council apprised of the city's dire financial straits at the time. Despite the Council's serious misgivings, Holt became DC's chief financial officer with Control Board support. I was clearly disappointed and knew that I was far more qualified than her, but also understood political realities and reluctantly accepted the Control Board's decision.

I began exploring other opportunities. As soon as the word was out, I was advised by friends and colleagues not to leave city government. I also received calls from Hill staffers urging me to stay with the city. They had seen Holt perform during the city's financial crisis and had no confidence in her. But more telling was the advice from my friend and former GAO colleague, Ted Barreaux, one of the shrewdest political operatives in Washington who enjoyed the game of politics. A lifelong Republican, he had worked in the White House as an aide to Presidents Nixon, Reagan and Bush Sr. He was a William Casey protégé and worked with him at the Securities and Exchange Commission. His physical appearance, personality and demeanor reminded one of Paul Girard, a presidential aide played by Martin Balsam in a political thriller, *Seven Days in May* (1964). Given his lifelong involvement in politics, Barreaux had a knack for knowing what works in Washington. He loved the city and could recite its history from block to block. His life revolved around three data points—Georgetown, where he lived in a fashionable condominium with his lovely wife Jean; the Metropolitan Club, where he regularly dined; and Bermuda, where he had been vacationing with the same group of international friends for decades. Barreaux and I worked together at the GAO under Comptroller General Bowsher. Though our politics were quite different, we bonded because we thought politics mattered and took serious interest in it. He was among the few at the GAO with whom I could share my frustrations about the agency, especially about its parochial and old-fashioned senior staff that was resistant to change. It was Barreaux who sponsored me for membership at the Metropolitan Club and introduced me to many distinguished Washingtonians, including Judge Stanley Sporkin, a legendary figure in the securities arena.

Over a drink at the Club, I told Barreaux that I was considering leaving the District because I was bypassed for the CFO job. He bluntly told me: "Nat, don't do it. Don't leave the city!" He said that Valerie Holt was chosen for all the wrong reasons and would most likely fail, and then added, "Williams would have to turn to you for the job. He said that given her public record as comptroller she would not be able to manage the CFO job that was far more complex and political in nature. Just wait and see." he said. Barreaux's advice proved prescient. Holt's lack of requisite managerial skills was overlooked as the year progressed, but her failure to get a timely, clean-audit opinion—the critical requirement for any CFO—was her undoing. It caused an uproar in DC financial circles and in the City Council, which refused to move forward on the next year's budget without the auditor-certified city financials. Capitol Hill also expressed concern. The sense among Wall Street ratings agencies was that the District's finances were backsliding and the progress made under Williams was in jeopardy. A chorus built up asking for Holt's resignation. The District was nearing the end of a four-year requirement to produce a balanced budget and clean audit every year to have the Control Board go in abeyance. If the District failed to fulfill that requirement, the Board would stick around for another four years. That was unacceptable to the mayor and Council. Moreover, without a clean audit, it would be difficult to go to Wall Street and raise funds at reasonable interest rates.

On the morning of May 2, 2000, I got a call from the mayor's office inviting me to have lunch with him that day. We talked about the importance of finishing the year with a balanced budget and clean audit opinion. "You know all this," Mayor Williams said. "And you know why I asked you to lunch today. I want you to be the next CFO. I will take it up with the Control Board." Williams urged the Board to let Holt go so the city could be assured of a clean audit the next year with a new CFO. Facing both internal and external pressures, Holt resigned three days later. Mayor Williams announced my appointment the same day and asked that I begin right away. I called Nalini with the good news. She was ecstatic and said, "We will throw a big party!"

My appointment was happily received not only in many parts of District government but also on Capitol Hill. The House Appropriations Committee noted in its report on the District that "the Committee is extremely pleased that a person of [Mr. Gandhi's] caliber has been appointed Chief Financial Officer." It was a moment of great satisfaction for me. At last, my talents, merits and professional skills had been recognized—and I realized my dream of landing a key Washington position in which I could make contribution. It was a eureka moment in a life that had experienced more than its share of adversities and setbacks.

While at the tax office my staff numbered around 600; now—as CFO—that number nearly doubled. In addition to the tax department I was now responsible for revenue estimation, economic analysis, budgeting, controllership, treasurer duties and even lottery operations. I didn't have much time and had to make sure that the fiscal year ending in September 2000 was balanced, and that on February 1, 2001, the District's annual report would receive a clean audit opinion from the external auditors. We had to have four consecutive years (this was the fourth) of a balanced budget to avoid having Control Board oversight for another four years. The first task was to balance the budget and get the annual report ready for audit. The school system, police and health departments, and public hospital were habitual overspenders; their budgets nearly always fell short of their extravagant spending. Because they provide critical public services, money had to be found elsewhere in the budget to make them whole. I called an emergency meeting of senior CFO officials in these departments and asked them to identify their "spending pressures," a euphemism for overspending. The result was bad news: At the end of the fiscal year, the District could face a deficit of about $200 million if spending were to continue at the current rate. There was no additional revenue in sight. The shortfall had to be covered by cutting from other departments, so that the District's total expenditures would stay within its appropriated limit. We made specific recommendations to the mayor and Council, who had no choice but to accept. The day of reckoning was fast approaching. On February 1, 2001, I would have to release the District's annual financial report with a balanced budget certified by external auditors. We were ready before the deadline. On Friday, January 26th, we got word from the auditors that the District would get a clean audit opinion certifying a $241 million surplus for the year. I briefed the mayor, council and Control Board, and scheduled a press conference for the following Monday to release the report.

While preparing over that weekend, I was preoccupied with news of a catastrophic event in India: A major earthquake had struck my home state of Gujarat that Friday, India's 51st Republic Day. Though it lasted only two minutes, it measured 6.9 on the Richter scale and caused some 14,000 deaths and enormous property damage. Throughout the weekend I tried frantically to get in touch with relatives and friends to see how they were doing. Fortunately, none had been affected. To get some relief from news about the earthquake and preparations for the press conference, on Sunday I turned on the TV and kept my eyes on Super Bowl XXXV, which was being played in Tampa, Florida. It helped for me to see the Baltimore Ravens beat the New York Giants, 34–7!

On Monday, January 28, 2001, we held our press conference at City Hall to announce the balanced budget and auditor's clean audit opinion—and the Control Board's impending dormancy. This was a big deal for the District. Numerous dignitaries attended the press conference, which I opened by summarizing the financial results—and heralding the return of home rule. The District, I noted, had successfully met all requirements necessary to put the Control Board in abeyance. "We are prepared to take the financial destiny of this great city into our own hands and never have the need for a Control Board to oversee our financial operations again," I said. The District's elected representative to Congress, Eleanor Holmes Norton, echoed the theme: "Our worst financial crisis in 100 years is over. The control period is over." The banner front-page headline in *The Washington Post* the next day read: "District Completes Its Fiscal Comeback, 2000 Surplus Marks Fourth Balanced Budget in Row, Spelling End to Control Board." I knew full well, of course, that this was just the first step in a long journey to stabilize the District's finances. There were profound issues plaguing DC's bureaucracy to which the CFO's staff was not immune. Chief among my concerns that I had to deal with were a culture of apathy and the lack of an ethical climate. Still, this day was a milestone not only in the District's checkered history, but also in my professional life. At last, I had found my calling.

While depriving the District of democratic home rule, the Control Board had provided much-needed fiscal discipline. Now that its mission was accomplished, with the Board essentially gone, what was next for the District? Who would keep its potentially extravagant spending habits in check? Who would make the difficult choices required to keep it financially viable? Above all, who would make sure that the requirements Congress had imposed to keep the Control Board at bay would be met? Each year the District had to meet its payroll, debt obligations and pension liabilities, among other things. Miss any of these primary cash obligations and the Control Board would be back! The District's congressional overseers were worried that with the Board now dormant, District politicians would revert to old habits that had put the city under financial stress in the first place. Also, without the Board, what would happen to the CFO who derived his authority from it? Would he again be under the mayor's control and, like any other agency head, have to do the mayor's bidding? Some in Congress objected to this and initiated steps to see that the CFO remained independent from the mayor and Council. District officials objected that such congressional action would compromise its home rule. What other state or municipality in the country would accept such an abridgement of its democracy? Black activists saw it as another racist measure on the part of Congress, since the District was a majority black jurisdiction. Council read the tea leaves and passed its own legislation largely mirroring the Hill's sentiments concerning the CFO position's independence. Congressional committees charged with District oversight would look primarily to the CFO to ensure that the city remained financially stable. Essentially, the CFO stood between the District and Control Board. He would have to impose measures, however unpleasant, to guard the city's finances and make sure that it never went anywhere near its pre-Control Board brush with insolvency. Thus, as CFO, I had the onerous task of denying the mayor and Council a variety of projects and programs in order to preserve the city's fiscal health. Little wonder that, in time, I became known as the District's Dr. No.

As CFO, I was at the center of the District's finances—an easy target. If anything went wrong anywhere in the city, I was often blamed. For example, when the city's only hospital east of the Anacostia River—a predominantly black area—faced financial problems, the CFO would be criticized for putting the city's finances ahead of the health and welfare of the poor, notwithstanding that the hospital habitually overspent its allocated budget and always asked for more money. Public-safety agencies, such as police and fire departments, always ran out of money and demanded more for the overtime they would pay to their personnel. They made clear that people's lives were at risk and would point to crime waves, rising murder rates and worse if more money was not provided. So it would be the CFO's duty to find money for them, with nearly all agency directors resenting that their individual chief financial officers reported not to them but to me. As one agency director bluntly put it, "Of the 10 people sitting in my senior staff meeting, there is one guy who does not report to me. How can I run an agency if I don't control its finances?" The public school system was a special case. It had among the highest per capita student spending in the country and still was among the worst and a perennial overspender. Successive school superintendents blamed me for poor school finances. Their attitude was that they were engaged in public service of the highest order and that the green-eyeshade CFO hindered their efforts to serve the District's vulnerable children. Balancing budgets, improving the city's credit ratings and other financial issues to them were picayune.

Given that the District is a city, school district and state all combined into one jurisdiction, it has had to borrow more money than any other city of similar size. It needs funds to build roads, libraries, recreation centers and other capital projects with an inadequate tax base. The city cannot tax suburban commuters. Federal properties comprising a large chunk of the city's commercial real estate are also tax exempt. Its per capita debt burden is among the highest in the country. However, the more the city borrows, the more it costs to service its debt, increasing pressure on an already hard-pressed budget. Thus I recommended a borrowing cap that was enacted in law. However, developers resented a limit on long-term borrowing since that would prevent them from building large projects such as sports stadiums, each of which would require the District to borrow hundreds of millions of dollars, adding greatly to the city's debt burden.

A spirited debate ensued when Mayor Williams promised to build a new stadium if Major League Baseball were to move the Montreal Expos to the District. The city once had a baseball team in the Washington Senators but no more. Sports enthusiasts wanted another team. Developers quickly took up the cause and pressure grew on the CFO to borrow more than half-a-billion dollars to build the stadium. Any doubts or questions about the project's finances were portrayed as harmful to the city's economic development. But I had the duty to make sure that any borrowing would not harm the city's fiscal stability. Representatives of Major League Baseball—led by Jerry M. Reinsdorf, an owner of the Chicago White Sox—were hard bargainers and were prepared to walk away. Yet I stood my ground and insisted that certain changes had to be made to the agreement between MLB and the District's Sports Commission before I would go and borrow the required money. Ultimately, changes relating to financial reserve requirements were made to ensure that the city's finances were not harmed. We borrowed the requisite amount of money and a shiny new stadium was built where the Nationals, the city's new baseball team, opened the 2008 MLB season against the Atlanta Braves on March 30th and won 3-2 with a leadoff home run from Ryan Zimmerman. After leaving the District some 33 years ago, baseball returned to DC.

Because of the CFO's unique position, I became embroiled in several issues that were not necessarily monetary but legal. One was the legality of married gay couples filing joint tax returns. Under tax law, the District as federal territory had to follow IRS rules and regulations, which did not recognize marriage among gay couples, though it was sanctioned under District law. This presented a dilemma for the CFO who is also an overseer of the District's tax system. Similarly, I was caught up in an effort by lobbyists from the gambling industry to bring Internet gambling to the District. Because the lottery fell under the CFO's supervision, proponents wanted me to sanction such gambling while the overwhelming sentiments in the Council and on the Hill were against it. In these and many other cases I had to live up to my moniker Dr. No and make unpopular decisions.

Despite our efforts to instill a culture of honesty and integrity in the District's financial operations, there were pockets of resistance within the tax office and elsewhere. By my insistence that each employee take ethics training and that we have a strong internal audit and investigation capacity, I was upsetting some employees who had been around for years and knew how to game the system. Take the case of a mid-level tax-office employee, Harriet Walters, whose arrest in November 2007 was, without a doubt, the worst day of my professional life. By using a manual routine used only in exceptional cases, Walters had circumvented a newly established system that processed refunds. By doing so, she created bogus real-property tax refunds. She had done this for nearly 20 years under several tax commissioners—including me. It was the largest financial scandal in the District government's history. The wonder was that Walters was not caught long before that horrible day when the news broke. She had financed her lavish lifestyle, including an account with Neiman Marcus, with the stolen money. When FBI agents raided her house, they found a treasure trove of designer clothes, jewelry and hundreds of pairs of shoes. From that day on, to me she was "Harriet of the shoes." Ultimately a vigilant bank employee alerted law-enforcement officials about the large number of District refund checks that Walters and her co-conspirators were cashing. She and 11 other people were caught, tried and convicted. Her 18-year maximum sentence was reduced by six months because she cooperated with city investigators. It had to have been obvious to her colleagues that she was living far beyond the resources of a mid-level city employee, but no one ever said anything about it. This underscored the culture of apathy within the DC tax office: See no evil, report no evil. Walters also bought off a few low-level officials by spreading her largesse among them.

On November 7, 2007, when the scandal was unveiled, and for months thereafter, I often recalled what my former GAO colleagues had said about the District's climate of corruption: "Nat, you just don't know what you're walking into!" It became the darkest chapter of my professional career. For months, I was an object of derision in the pages of *The Washington Post*, including an editorial-page cartoon, on TV channels, in hearings before the Council, on the Hill, in community meetings and at business gatherings. The Council asked a major Washington law firm, WilmerHale, to look into the scandal and report back with its findings and recommendations.

The *Washington Business Journal*, an unofficial voice of the business community, published an opinion poll about my future: 58 percent of the respondents thought I should resign, while 42 percent said I should stay. I met with Mayor Adrian Fenty and offered my resignation. He refused. "We still need you," he said. Months later, WilmerHale issued a report absolving me, saying that the long-running tax-embezzlement fraud had been perpetrated by lower-level employees and blamed it on a prevalent "culture of apathy and silence" in the District's tax office. Similarly, the feeling among business leaders and labor chieftains, as well as on the Hill and in Council, was that I should not resign. Most thought that I had worked hard to reform the near-dysfunctional tax office and done a lot to improve the city's finances. In due time, they believed, I would also fix the present mess. In short, the general consensus was that the District was better off with Gandhi than without him.

In short order I went to Wall Street and explained the whole affair to the credit-rating agencies and our financial advisors. They were relatively blasé about the whole thing, noting no impact on the District's credit rating or creditworthiness. Said Karl Jacob, the seasoned ratings official at Standard & Poor's: "Obviously, it's a little crack in the armor, but it is not enough of a structural problem to damage the ratings." They had seen such things happen elsewhere. In fact, the rating agencies emphasized the role I'd played in the District's financial turnaround. Said Richard Raphael, executive managing director of Fitch Ratings: "[Gandhi] has been very important to the District's turnaround, and if he left it would be a loss." Thank goodness. It seemed nothing short of a miracle that I had survived such a massive scandal—and would remain the District's CFO for six more years.

Whenever I got into a predicament, my approach has always been practical. Despite my best efforts, the scandal had happened; I should accept responsibility and work hard to fix the circumstances that allowed it to take place. I could have said, "To hell with it," thrown in the towel and left the District. But that would have been a cowardly thing to do. Yes, I had failed, but failure is part of life and one must learn to manage it. Once Mayor Fenty refused my offer of resignation, I threw myself into the battle of fixing the tax office—again. For that I needed an able staff and group of wise advisors.

For a person holding a senior position to succeed anywhere, he or she needs an able and devoted staff. I was especially blessed in this regard. None of my successes would have been possible without the professional staff that I had assembled. Above all, they were dedicated to the financial integrity and stability of the District. Among my senior staff, I was particularly grateful to have three remarkable chiefs of staff—Rick Hayes, Lucille Dickinson and Angell Jacobs—and my highly competent and eminently wise general counsel, David Tseng, as well as financial advisor Marcy Edwards, a Wall Street veteran who, with her nuanced advice, guided me through the complexities of bond-rating agencies where she had once worked. This group of talented and deeply loyal professionals collectively helped me navigate through the treacherous waters of District politics. Two of my executive assistants—Pam Madison and Lynnette Jones— jealously guarded my office with loyalty that saved me from many mishaps. Pam— with her mother-superior demeanor and army background—was particularly effective in managing the front-office staff, while Lynnette—with her quiet grace—efficiently managed all of my external relationships. She was particularly good at managing my ever-persistent Indian friends and acquaintances who would often call for favors, yet I obviously could not oblige them. It was amazing how she was able to sort out all of the various Patels and Shahs (common Indian last names).

While blessed with a dedicated and loyal staff, I was equally blessed with a stable of internal and external advisors who carefully followed my progress. They could see how hard I was trying to fix the broken financial infrastructure of the District and were eager to help me in that worthy enterprise. Many of them had been long-standing District residents who loved the city. They had seen how Barry and his political cronies had ruined the government and put obstacles in the path of improvement that the Control Board and CFO Williams had charted.

At the Control Board, I had the full support of its two distinguished chairmen, Andrew Brimmer and Alice Rivlin. Brimmer (1926-2012) was a no-nonsense economist who would not hesitate to take unpleasant decisions such as slashing the well-entrenched District bureaucracy. The first-ever African American member of the Federal Reserve System, he was a Harvard-trained economist who also taught there. He had experience in both the private and public sectors. When as the District's tax commissioner I would ask for additional funding to enhance tax compliance, he would readily agree because he realized the importance of a strong tax department that could effectively collect taxes as well as implement tax laws equitably.

Alice Rivlin also knew the importance of an effective tax agency. She followed Brimmer as chairman. Rivlin had a great reputation as a federal budgeteer. The only person to head both the Congressional Budget Office as well as the Office of Management and Budget, she was and still is an icon in Washington in all matters relating to the federal budget. A distinguished economist, she was the first female president of the

American Economic Association. She has been a longtime District resident who cares deeply for the city. In the midst of her myriad activities at the federal level, she always found time for the city. In 1990, she had studied the District's fiscal predicament and warned of the looming crisis. Despite her Washington eminence, she had no air about her, both down to earth and practical in her guidance. I sought her advice regularly over numerous breakfasts, meetings and calls, and she was always available.

Among other Control Board members, Constance Newman and Steve Harlan were particularly effective. I worked closely with Harlan, a major figure in the accounting profession who was always eager to help me. He facilitated funding of the Integrated Tax System that I needed to run an efficient and modern tax agency. He would also protect the tax department from ill-advised cuts foolishly proposed by District Council members who wanted to fund their ward-specific projects at the expense of the tax agency. Even after Harlan left the Control Board, I continued to meet with him and seek his wise counsel on a variety of District issues.

Linda Cropp, the highly capable and shrewd Council chairman during much of my District tenure, was always ready to help. Jack Evans, chairman of the Council's Committee on Finance and Revenue and a long-standing Council member, has seen the District through all of its ups and downs. Trained at Penn's Wharton Business School, he has an instinctive grasp of municipal finances and the importance of a city that is financially viable and fiscally stable. He has been an effective spokesman on behalf of the city on Wall Street. Vincent Gray, the Council chair who later became mayor, has an unusual grasp of the city's budget and understood the importance of fiscal prudence. At my urging, he initiated a cap on borrowing when the District's politicians, goaded by developers, wanted to go on a borrowing binge. His amazing ability to plod through the city's business while under intense criticism made him survive one of the worst prosecutorial indiscretions several weeks before the election that ruined his chance for a second term as mayor, yet he was elected as a Council member two years later and has since made important contributions to the city.

Phil Mendelson, once on the Council staff and now its chair, is a master of details and knows the whereabouts of every budget dollar. Mary Cheh, a law professor at George Washington University, is a highly civilized voice of reason on the Council when her colleagues would often say irresponsible things from the dais. She is a breath of fresh air while some of her colleagues nearly always have the cloud of unethical behavior over their head. Three members of the Council, including a chairman, had been removed from the office for stealing public funds and receiving bribes; two of them served time in jail.

The Control Board was supported by its able executive director, John Hill, a soft-spoken GAO accountant who had studied the District's finances in great detail and produced a seminal GAO report that led to congressional takeover of the District and establishment of the Control Board. Hill, an African American, was exactly the right choice to run the Control Board while Barry, playing his usual race card, was pursuing an aggressive campaign against it. Barry and his acolytes viewed Brimmer, Hill and CFO Williams as stooges of Congress who were trampling the District's democracy. Despite all the criticism, Hill stood his ground and ably managed the Control Board's relationship with the city and Congress. I often turned to him for guidance, and his support for me was a great source of strength throughout my District tenure. True to his dedication to public service, Hill spent five years as CFO of Detroit, where he was engaged once again in stabilizing another city in financial trouble.

I have written earlier about Ted Barreaux and how he advised me to stay with the District when—impulsively—I was about to leave following the selection of Valerie Holt as CFO over me. We often discussed District issues. In one of our meetings, he introduced me to Stanley Sporkin, the highly regarded federal judge and an SEC enforcement legend. After serving admirably in both the Securities and Exchange Commission and CIA under William Casey, Sporkin distinguished himself as a judge on the U.S. District Court for the District of Columbia. Judge Sporkin was a great help to me in the aftermath of the Walters tax scandal (see introduction). He brought the late Irvin Pollack, another SEC legend, to the CFO oversight committee that I had set up to help me navigate through the scandal. Judge Sporkin took personal interest in me and made sure that I kept on managing the city's finances as ably as before, during several ongoing inquiries following the tax scandal. When I was questioned by WilmerHale lawyers in their investigation of the tax-office scandal, he represented me and sat next to me all day, an extraordinary gesture. He would often check on me no matter where he would be, at home or abroad. Judge Sporkin has been a mentor and great source of inspiration with his wise counsel and guidance through my tenure in the District and afterward.

Another important source of guidance has been Comptroller General Charles Bowsher, with whom I stayed in touch even after we both left the GAO. He kept an eye on my post-GAO career and regularly advised me. He was particularly helpful both during and in the aftermath of the tax scandal. He advised me to set up an oversight committee and helped me to recruit its members, including the late Sheldon Cohen, a former IRS commissioner. Cohen, who had long experience in tax matters, was a go-to guy in Washington for all issues relating to tax administration.

Among all such people in Washington, few are more influential than Vernon Jordan, a legendary civil-rights leader and advisor to presidents, particularly Bill Clinton. He is a District resident and very much appreciative of what I had done financially for the city. I often used to visit him and seek his advice about various city issues. During the tax scandal, he was concerned about my future with the city. I clearly recall receiving a telephone call from him while waiting for the train back to DC in a bar at the

Madison Square Garden station in New York. I had just briefed the ratings agencies about the city's finances. It was a very brief call. He emphatically told me in his booming voice, "Don't resign, Nat, don't resign, do you hear me?!"

On the Hill, I had great support from many legislators including Representatives Tom Davis (R-VA) and Darrell Issa (R-CA), and Senators Kay Bailey Hutchison (R-TX) and Mary Landrieu (D-LA). They all distrusted District politicians and wanted the presence of an independent CFO as a restraining influence on the District's spendthrift habits. These legislators saw the CFO as a prerequisite to the District's emergence into a fiscally sound city. They always found time from their busy schedules to see me. In general, I found Republicans more supportive of the Control Board and CFO than Democrats, who viewed the Board more as an impingement on the District's democracy. Davis was an imaginative and shrewd politician who took a lead in the establishment of the Control Board and CFO position. He also made sure that the latter became a permanent feature in the District's governance. I recall visiting Davis in his Virginia office soon after the scandal. In all of that post-scandal storm, he told me to stay put and not overreact. "Look, Nat, you are an accountant. You understand debits and credits. This is a debit to your account; however, you have accumulated a great deal of credits. So just go back to your office and do your work!"

Among the congressional staff, none was more important and supportive than Americo (Migo) Miconi, who had extensive experience as staff director of the House Appropriations Subcommittee for DC. He stayed in that position for years through several Republican and Democratic chairmen of the committee. Because of his long tenure, he had substantial influence on District matters and was once dubbed "the unofficial mayor of Washington." Thoroughly disenchanted with District politicians, he saw hopes for the District's revitalization in the office of a strong and independent CFO, and zealously guarded the position from political encroachment. He also made sure that the CFO was paid at cabinet level, among the highest salary paid to federal officials. I knew him during my GAO days and sought him out soon after I joined the District in 1997. He was ready and eager to help me in whatever way that he could.

In City Hall, I had a collaborator in Gregory McCarthy. An avowed runner who had run marathons on all five continents, he is a good friend and supporter who educated me on the intricacies of District politics with his deep understanding. He was Mayor Williams' legislative liaison and we quickly bonded. Our regular lunches and breakfasts involved numerous city issues as well as national policy matters; he had varied interests including foreign policy that he had studied. We remain friends in my post-District life.

Among my fellow members at the Metropolitan Club, Edward Weidenfeld was most supportive. A distinguished District resident and lifelong member of the Republican Party, Weidenfeld was ready to help with his sage counsel and wide contacts in the Washington establishment. We also remain good friends. He wanted private-sector companies to use my municipal-finance expertise and worked hard to find me a post-District career. On the Democratic side, Judith Barnett, another District resident and an indefatigable fundraiser for various presidential candidates, always looked out for my interests. She lovingly considers me a part of her family and makes sure that I would be present at various Jewish festivities that she celebrates with gusto. Even now, Judith, Mary Cheh and I get together for a long dinner every other month to talk about various city issues.

Donald Graham, then the distinguished publisher of *The Washington Post*, took personal interest in the city. Soon after his graduation from Harvard University, he worked as a beat cop and got to know the city and its problems firsthand. Following his legendary mother Katharine Graham, he deeply cared for and worked hard to reform the city's struggling school system. I periodically met with Don Graham, also an aficionado of the celebrated novelist Anthony Trollope, over breakfast and sought his advice. Wet behind their ears, the younger and aggressive *Post* reporters assigned to City Hall gave me a hard time in their perpetual search for a Pulitzer. However, the *Post* was generally supportive of me, particularly on its editorial pages under the highly esteemed editorial-page editor, Fred Hiatt.

I worked for the District in two critical positions, first as tax commissioner (1997-2000) and then as independent CFO (2000-2013). During these 17 years, there have been dramatic changes in the District's finances. It became financially solvent and responsible. Although I am proud of playing a substantial role in the District's financial and fiscal transformation, as I have mentioned throughout this book and elsewhere a lion's share of the credit goes to the Control Board and the District's first independent CFO, Anthony Williams. During my long tenure as CFO, DC tax collection improved substantially to the extent that it enjoyed a healthy fund balance when I retired, in place of a huge deficit. This reversal of the District's financial fortunes began to be acknowledged. Recognition and awards from the press, community and professional associations came my way. Also, given my success as CFO, I was offered the CFO position at Amtrak. But I wanted to do something else with my life. After Nalini's death in 2009, I generally lost interest in work. Though I continued in my job for another four years, my heart wasn't in it anymore. By concentrating on my career, I had lost out a lot in life. I was not going to do that anymore.

Moreover, the District was in extraordinarily good financial condition. Its fund balance stood at a healthy $1.5 billion, and its bonds were rated AA and AAA. Leaving on such a high note seemed like a good idea. I recalled a wag saying, "One should retire when people would ask, 'Why?' rather than 'Why not?'" Besides, what more could I have done for the District? It was time to go. But I had been reappointed just a few months earlier to another five-year term. Would leaving the District so soon after renewal of my contract be considered a dereliction of my duties? When I joined the city in 1997, I'd had an ancient Athenian oath vaguely in my mind. It says in part: "We will ever strive for the ideals and sacred things of the city, both alone and with many.... We will transmit this city not only not less, but greater, better, and more beautiful than it was transmitted to us." This had been my creed—what I tried to do over the last 17 years in Washington, DC. I believed that I had kept that oath, and that it would be all right to leave the city now that it was greater and better, at least financially, than I had found it in 1997.

There was another, more significant reason for me to retire. Panna Naik, a distinguished Gujarati poet and her husband, Nikul, were longstanding family friends. They'd been patrons of Indian art, culture and literature for nearly 50 years in Philadelphia. Panna and I were part of a group of Indian American literati who established the Gujarati Literary Academy of North America. I became its organizing secretary/treasurer when Panna was president. Our families visited each other often and got together to collaborate on literary events. Nalini passed away in 2009 and Nikul in 2004. Each of us had a long-married life—Panna and Nikul were married for nearly 50 years while Nalini and I for 47. Through our respective losses, we kept in touch and tried to console each other. During a literary visit to India in 2011, we bonded and decided to live together.

As I write this, Panna and I have been life companions and partners for about seven years. These have been the happiest years of my life. At last, I have found a life partner who at once understands my emotional needs and with whom I communicate freely. Above all, I love her deeply. Living with each other has been a new reality for both of us. Each has new friends and relatives with whom we regularly socialize. We also have two homes—one in Philadelphia and the other in DC, and Panna maintains them both with the energy and enthusiasm of someone far younger than her age. She has lived in Philadelphia ever since she migrated to the U.S. in 1960. She put her roots there and built a network of friends and family who provided her social safety net. After spending a month or so in Washington, she yearns to go back to that city of brotherly love at least for a week or two. Panna personally selected and decorated our condominium in Washington, where we presently live.

While Panna is deeply attached to Philly, I am also invested in Washington where both Apoorva and Sona live with their families in nearby Maryland suburbs. After numerous moves in the U.S., I found Washington to be the most congenial place for me to spend the remaining years of my life. Presently, Washington is no longer the sleepy southern town that it once was. It has a vibrant cultural scene bubbling with literature, music, museums, monuments and theater. For all those who have interest in public policy and politics as I do, it's a Mecca. Also, I sit on the boards of Arena Stage, Shakespeare Theater and Gallaudet University, in each of whose activities I am involved. In Washington, I also belong to the Metropolitan Club, which has given me access to who's who in DC, which is my last station and I'm disinclined to leave it for Philly except for short visits. So Panna and I carry on our life divided between two cities, though we are together more often than not. She invariably joins me in all of my social activities in Washington, including theater events and special dinners at the Metropolitan Club, as I am with her in nearly all of her social activities in Philadelphia. We are also together when we visit friends and relatives at home and abroad, especially in India. It is a special joy taking vacations with her. Our retirement gives us many opportunities to take cruises that we love to interesting destinations around the world.

By 2013, I had been working, either part-time or full-time, for nearly 60 years. For practical reasons, I mainly had worked in accounting! For all of my life, my heart has been in literature. I'd wanted to specialize in Gujarati literature in Mumbai, but I'd given up such a "silly idea" at the suggestion of Ratibhai, my financial benefactor, and majored in accounting. I stayed with accounting ever since, including getting a Ph.D. in the field for one simple reason: That's where jobs were. Late in life, I did turn to literature and published three volumes of poetry in Gujarati. But that was all done on the fly, stealing time from my day job. Now I wanted to turn to it full-time. So, like a good accountant, I checked with my financial advisor—yes, I do have a financial advisor—and asked him whether I could live on my retirement savings without sacrificing too much of my living standard. I'd already sold the family house after Nalini's death and downsized myself—and my expenses—into a city condominium.

"Nat, you are in good shape," he told me. "You may retire if you want to without sacrificing much of anything."

"Really?"

"Yes, you have enough stashed away to carry on your life pretty much the way you've lived. You might even splurge on an occasional trip to India or elsewhere. So enjoy yourself!"

––––––––––

In a financial briefing with Mayor Vincent Gray on January 29, 2013, I informed him of the District's impressive performance for the fiscal year that ended September 30, 2012.

"Mr. Mayor," I said, "the District had a surplus of $417 million. You should be very proud of it." And then I handed him my letter of resignation. "Mr. Mayor, it is time for me to move on!"

It would be an understatement to say that he was shocked. "What?" he exclaimed. "Why? What happened?" He pointed out that I'd been overwhelmingly reconfirmed, 12 to 1, by the City Council just five months earlier. "Why do you want to leave *now?*"

This was a difficult time for the mayor. The U.S. attorney had opened a lengthy investigation into the funding of his mayoral campaign. Ultimately, he was not indicted, but it caused a major political upheaval and doomed his chances of reelection. It was not an opportune time for the mayor to lose a well-regarded CFO who provided a sense of financial stability in an otherwise politically volatile District. I assured him that my reasons were personal, telling him that I had a new love in my life and that I wanted to spend more of my time and life with her. I also told him what I later said in my resignation letter: "I feel comfortable retiring at this time because the city is in excellent financial condition, perhaps the best in its history. The fund balance is as high as it has ever been, revenues are rising, and at this time it appears they will continue to do so. Our bond issues are regularly oversubscribed and sell at historically low interest rates." I assured the mayor that I wouldn't just walk out the next day or week but would work out a mutually acceptable date for my departure. He asked that I help him find a successor and transition him or her to the office. I readily agreed—not realizing that it would take another 10 months! I resigned on February 1st and didn't leave until the following January. Though I wasn't leaving soon, I wanted to make the announcement so the search for the new CFO could start immediately.

On February 2nd, *The Washington Post* carried the news of my resignation on the front page, and three days later ran a laudatory editorial: "A bottom-line success, Natwar Gandhi's legacy is a District that can be proud of its finances." The editorial reminded readers that "when Natwar Gandhi was named chief financial officer in 2000... [DC's] fiscal health was wobbly at best. Data were unreliable, systems were faulty, and elected officials had to be restrained from a propensity to spend more than what the city took in. Mr. Gandhi changed much of that, playing an instrumental role in the District's fiscal turnaround that should not be forgotten or go unappreciated as he departs from the office.... The city is in good shape. It is as good a time as any to [leave], he told [in his resignation letter] ... what amounts to an understatement of the District's robust finances at a time many states and local governments are struggling."

After a long, hard search, the mayor nominated Jeff DeWitt to be my successor. DeWitt had a distinguished record as chief financial officer of Phoenix, Arizona, and was easily confirmed. At the 2013 Christmas party for senior staff, I introduced him and told the assembled crowd that I would now turn to writing poetry and not worry about submitting annual financial reports on time with a clean audit. I would also ease up on reading the Metro section of *The Washington Post*. That was now for Jeff DeWitt to do.

Not long afterward, Panna and I left for a long vacation in India.

Chapter 14

TIGER DAD

One day in late 1979, when I came home from work, Nalini greeted me with a look of concern.

"What's the matter?" I asked. "Is everything okay?"

"Apoorva is upset," she said. "He's in his room."

I went straight upstairs to see him.

"What happened, son? Are you alright?"

He started sobbing. I hugged him and kept asking what the matter was as he continued crying. At last he pulled away, wiped his eyes and looked me in the eye.

"You... you expect too much from me!"

"Really? Like what?"

"Like grades," he said. "You always want me get an A in everything. I can't do that. And you want me to join everything—everything! Touch football, swimming, ice hockey, piano, even silly tap dancing! Then you want me to write that stupid diary every day. No one I know keeps a diary. Why do I have to?"

He broke down again.

I stood there looking at my son. He was only 9—lanky, energetic, a gregarious guy with many friends both Indian and American. I was very proud of him. He was the best in the eyes of his mother. He wanted to please me, but was I too demanding? Yes, I wanted him to join everything. Yes, I demanded that he excel. True, I made him keep a daily journal. Why? I was haunted by the specter of my father, who neglected his children to the point of not caring whether they even went to school. I guess I was compensating for my father's lack of attention to me. But this was not what I was expecting after another rough day at the office.

———————

Apoorva lost it that day over one central demand. I'd gotten him a journal and required that he write a page a day chronicling his activities. I wanted him to get into the habit of writing every day in hopes that it would improve his writing skills. One day, looking for something in his room, I accidentally saw a whole page of Apoorva's diary that contained his true thoughts:

I hate writing this stupid diary.

I hate writing this stupid diary.

I hate writing this stupid diary.

When I confronted him about it, he said, "Yes, I think it is stupid to write a diary."

I didn't react well. "Well, I have news for you, young man. We do many stupid things in life. This is your stupid thing to do. So you'd better do it, okay? Case closed."

Apoorva had often complained about not getting an allowance. Most of his school friends got a few dollars from their parents that they could spend when they went to the shopping mall.

"Sure," I said, "I will give you an allowance, but only if you keep an account of where you spent it."

"Why? No one keeps an account—why do I have to?"

"That's my rule if you want an allowance from me."

Reluctantly he agreed. He wanted money.

Fast-forward some 30 years.

I made a similar proposition to his son, Gaurav, when he was about 12. I would give him an allowance if he would keep a diary. He agreed on one condition: It was to be private, and no one else would be allowed to read it.

"Fine," I said. "Let me know when you are done writing for the week and I will send you the allowance."

Every Friday or Saturday I would get a text message from Gaurav saying, "Diaries are done!" And I would send him the requisite allowance via PayPal.

Back on that day in 1979, however, when Apoorva complained that I was the problem because I expected too much of him, I didn't back down.

"You're damn right I expect too much from you," I said. "You are a son of an immigrant. Never forget that. You will have to work harder than all your friends if you want to get ahead in this country. Do you get that?"

By this time, Nalini had come upstairs to Apoorva's room. She intervened and asked me to leave the room, and closed the door to console our still-sobbing son.

———————

Decades later, when I recalled this episode on occasion with Apoorva, he would laugh. But tears rolled down my eyes. Why did I have to be so harsh with him? As our children were growing up, I'm afraid that I was a tiger parent. I expected them to excel in everything, especially at school. I enrolled them in all kinds of sports and extracurricular activities without ever bothering to inquire whether or what they liked. I created unnecessary stress for them, as well as for Nalini, whose chore it was to ferry them to these myriad activities, in addition to running a busy household. Apoorva, being our first child, had to bear the brunt of my dictatorial demands.

What's worse, while I imposed a strict regime on Apoorva, I failed to do my part, to perform the usual rituals expected of an American father, such as taking his children on fishing or hunting trips where some bonding might occur. I didn't even take my son regularly to baseball, football or hockey games. I showed little interest in my children's activities. Having been raised in India, these activities were alien to me. I made no effort to learn American sports, nor did I watch games on TV with him.

Apoorva grew up in Baton Rouge and Pittsburgh, places where football is king. Each town would go crazy when there were home games. But I was untouched by the hysteria. Even when I ferried Apoorva to a sporting event he was playing in, I didn't join other parents in cheering the team. When I took him to practice, instead of socializing with other parents, I would find a quiet place to read a book or newspaper. He surely must have been disappointed in my strange, un-American behavior. When I reminisce about all of this with Apoorva, he vigorously disputes my characterization and charitably points out the variety of ways in which I was involved in their lives. Good son!

———

By the time Sona was growing up, I had wised up a little. She wasn't required to do all of the extracurricular activities that I had imposed on Apoorva. Still, I didn't waver on my stricture about television viewing. While most of their friends were watching cartoons on Saturday morning, I would take the kids to our neighborhood library and load them up with books to read at home. I limited their TV viewing to one hour a week. Moreover, I decided what shows they could watch and sat with them to make sure they didn't change channels.

Nalini loved Bollywood movies, but I didn't allow my children to watch them. I now thought they were silly and devoid of genuine entertainment value. This created additional tension in the household. I regarded those movies as the worst manifestation of Indian society and culture. I didn't want our children to learn about India from such movies.

———

When Apoorva was old enough to drive, I bought a car for him. It was a true jalopy—a used Oldsmobile so big that he called it a tank. I wanted to make sure that if he were involved in an accident, he would be surrounded by all that steel. I would go for drives with him while he was in the driver's seat. I even made him do a trial run with me to the house where he was going to pick up his prom date.

When Sona was ready to drive, I got her a new Toyota Tercel. Why such a differ-ence? I guess that it was a course correction on my part. I didn't want to impose the same harsh restrictions on her that I'd visited upon Apoorva. Still, she felt my implied expectations and once complained that she was afraid she would disappoint me. Thus she got involved in several extracurricular activities. Joining the neighborhood swim team required her to go for practice at 5 a.m., and her ballet classes required attendance every evening after school. Yet she also had an independent streak and occasionally rebelled, while Apoorva generally abided by what was expected of him. For example, I once asked Sona to make a sandwich for me. Instead of doing so like a dutiful Indian daughter, she said, "Let me show you how to make a sandwich so you won't have to ask me or Mom to make one for you in the future. Then you can make a sandwich whenever you like!"

It was unthinkable in an Indian household that a daughter would refuse to make a sandwich for her father. So I asked her, "What will you do when your husband asks you to make a sandwich for him?"

Without missing a beat, she replied, "What makes you think he wouldn't make a sandwich for me?"

I was not happy. "If you don't make a sandwich for me, that's okay. I can do without it—but I pray for your husband!"

And I walked out in a huff. The sandwich was never made. I never got such a response from Apoorva, who often observes that Sona had a much easier time growing up than he did. He is right.

Apoorva graduated from the University of Maryland with a business degree. He currently holds a senior management position with the Marriott Corporation. He travels the country and the world representing Marriott as a highly regarded speaker and spokesperson for corporate diversity. When I see him make one of his presentations, I am filled with parental pride and joy, and so was Nalini. For her, Apoorva affirmed that she could do something right in a life filled with failures and adversities. To her, Apoorva was always "my beautiful son." She jealously guarded and took care of him day in and day out. After all, he was the only male child of our Gandhi clan to carry forward the family name.

Sona followed in her brother's footsteps and also obtained a University of Maryland business degree. After graduation she joined a consulting firm but soon decided that it was not for her. With a deep, instinctive spirit for public service, Sona turned out to be the do-good liberal in the family. She went to India and spent six months working at a rural university in Gujarat. She wanted to see how the poor in India lived and how she could help them. While in college, she'd served as an intern in the office of Maryland's governor, then later as an intern in the office of First Lady Hillary Clinton. She also worked for a short period as a staffer in charge of constituent services in the district office of a California congressman.

Sona later earned a master's degree from the Wharton School of Business at the University of Pennsylvania. She then landed a well-paying position at a Wall Street investment bank. Once again, her public-service bug led her to quit Wall Street and join FINCA International, an organization devoted to improving the lives of the poor worldwide through microfinance and social enterprises. Sona always wanted do something useful for the larger society beyond just making money. She reminds me that she got that bug from me!

Always in search of that "perfect" work, she does not hesitate to take risks. After a stint in Jordan for FINCA, she ran its operations in Guatemala before returning to Washington. Her emergence as a strong, principled and compassionate woman is a matter of great pride for me, as it was for Nalini. Yet we were often confused about her various moves, for example her decisions to leave lucrative positions with a safe future for opportunities that paid a fraction of the salary that she was making on Wall Street. We were bewildered at her choice for a FINCA position that took her away from the U.S. As immigrants who had struggled mightily to reach financial security in the land of our dreams, we felt that she was sacrificing what we had worked so hard to give her, yet we certainly respected her decision to work for FINCA.

––––––––––

Raising children in America is a matter of perennial concern for immigrant parents, particularly those of us from traditional societies. We come here with the expectations of our cultural heritage and emotional baggage that at times are too heavy to bear. Coming from a society that values family over the individual and in which elders are instinctively respected, lack of deference for elders in America is difficult to grasp. Immigrant parents also fear that they will lose control over their children if they are raised in the American way. We don't like America's libertine permissiveness and its lax sexual mores.

In a traditional society like India, parents are heavily involved in their children's lives, even when they grow up. In the small towns and villages of India, parents make all-important decisions for their children, especially regarding the selection of career and spouse. Indian parents typically decide what school or college their children will go to, what they will major in and thereby what careers they will pursue. In an extended Indian family, a grandfather or person of similar authority can even overrule parents about their children's important life decisions. In families with scarce resources, elders often decide which son among his brothers will be provided funds to advance his career.

A girl's future is often sacrificed in favor of her brother's. Such parental strictures, of course, are likely to be resisted by a child raised in America. I was determined to make sure that Sona got all the opportunities that her brother got and nothing less.

Call that my Americanization. The Americanization of Indian children begins as soon as they start watching Sesame Street. The process is further enhanced in school, on the playground and in the neighborhood. Indian socialization imposed at home only creates stress for the young.

Like sleepwalkers, many children of immigrants learn to tread in two different worlds, one at home and one in the world beyond. As they grow up, however, they develop their own identities, assert their independence and begin to resent parental encroachment in their lives. An immigrant Indian parent finds it hard to stomach teenage rebelliousness in America. Attempts to impose parental likes and dislikes on children usually backfire. The more rigid and insistent the parents are, the greater the chances of conflict.

Occasionally this results in tragic outcomes, particularly when it comes to marital choices. For example, in one sad case, I had heard about a young girl who committed suicide when her parents strongly disapproved of her marrying an American boy. They had already chosen an Indian boy whom they thought would be appropriate for her. In another case, a strict and traditional family took a young daughter to India, married her off to an Indian boy of their choice and brought both of them back to the U.S. Once here, the boy disappeared! Apparently he had a sweetheart who'd migrated to the U.S., leaving him behind in India. He viewed the marriage as an opportunity to get to America. As soon as he was here, he left his newlywed bride to reunite with his sweetheart.

Naturally, Indians worry about the marital choices of their adult children. They prefer that their children select spouses of their caste or sub caste residing in America. Failing that, they will settle for an Indian boy or girl over an American. If the son or daughter did marry an American, and if that person were African American, Hispanic or, worse yet, Muslim, panic would ensue in a Hindu household. I have seen cases in which parents and their adult children became estranged because of the latter's marital choices.

Indian social norms require that one stay in a marriage even if it is unhappy or difficult. Marriage is viewed as a lifelong bond that should not be broken. It has a social purpose, and thus individual likes and dislikes should not matter. For that reason, most marriages are long-lasting, and divorces are relatively rare. Indeed, divorces are socially frowned upon. Immigrants are aghast to see how common divorces are in America.

After all of our harrowing years in Mumbai, Nalini and I knew that we were not going back to India, determined as we were to make our new life in the U.S. We knew a few Indian families who had returned to India and nearly all of them—particularly their children—had found it hard to adjust to Indian realities. Most of them came back and resettled in the U.S. Nalini and I were not going back to India, so we made the conscious decision to let the kids be "American." Still, we had come to America with our own cultural baggage and thus preferred—like most of our Indian immigrant friends—that Apoorva and Sona choose Indian spouses. We knew, however, that as parents all we could do was to guide our children in their marital choices. Any pressure on them about their spousal choices would be counterproductive.

For all practical purposes, our children look Indian and have lovely Indian names, Apoorva and Sona. However, they are as American as any children in the neighborhood. America is their home—and the only country they know as their own. They have little emotional attachment to India or familiarity with Indian rites and rituals.

To alleviate the lack of Indian culture in their day-to-day living, many immigrants and their adult children try to preserve their cultural heritage in a variety of ways. They follow many Indian customs and religious rituals. They celebrate traditional Indian festivals such as Diwali, comparable in importance to Christmas for Christians. They learn to cook Indian food. Indian children make presentations about their cultural heritage at schools. Some even go to India to find their roots. They want to see firsthand what it was like for their parents and grandparents to live in India. Both Apoorva and Sona did many of these things. Sona even went to India and spent about six months at a rural university. She learned Gujarati and gained some level of proficiency, particularly in speaking the language.

––––––––––

Many of our Indian friends insisted that their children live at home and commute to college, fearing that campus life would draw them into the permissive American lifestyle. We on the other hand—determined not to be "helicopter parents"—encouraged our children to live on campus even though we were only a few miles away. We thought that would help them integrate better into the mainstream. They also needed to escape the parental shadow and learn to live independently. Further, it was there that they were likely to find their future spouses and make career choices. That worked. Both of them found spouses at the University of Maryland. As we got to know them, we felt that they had made the right choice. In any event, the choice was theirs and not in any way pressed by us.

On one weekend break from classes, Apoorva came home with a smile that he could not hide.

"Mom, Dad, I have news for you!" he said. "You should know that I have met someone. Her name is Ruchi and I want you to meet to her."

"Who is Ruchi?" I asked.

"Who are her parents? How soon we might meet her?" Nalini asked.

"How long have you been going out with her?" I inquired.

Nalini peppered him with more questions. He told us that Ruchi was the daughter of Viren and Rekha Sharma, immigrants from India, just like us. They had come to the U.S. at just about the same time we had and lived in Salisbury, a small town about 125 miles from Washington. Viren was an engineer and successful entrepreneur who ran his own business. Rekha was a literate, sophisticated woman who'd raised Ruchi and her brother, Vidhu.

"I met Ruchi at Delta Sigma Pi," Apoorva said, a professional business fraternity that they both belonged to (and which Sona also joined). "You will like her!" he assured us. "I like her very much." Apoorva suggested that we meet Ruchi.

So we arranged to meet over dinner at a restaurant. At the last moment, however, Nalini changed her mind and said that I should go there with Sona. She'd prefer to meet Ruchi at our house. She also wanted my opinion of Ruchi before she got together with her. Sona and I went to dinner at Chi-Chi's, a Mexican place in Greenbelt, a suburb not far from the university. Apoorva introduced us. It took me only a few minutes to realize that Ruchi was lovely and smart. I was very pleased with his choice.

As soon as I got home, Nalini asked me, "How is she? Will she make a good *bahu* for us?" A daughter-in-law is called *bahu* in India. "Yes!" I said. "You should get together with her as soon as possible." Nalini quickly asked Apoorva to have Ruchi come to our house for dinner. Both women were on their best behavior, each wanting to impress the other. Not long after the evening, Nalini received a note from Ruchi saying that she very much enjoyed the dinner and praised Nalini's cooking. That sealed the deal for Nalini. If any additional support were needed, Sona also chimed in: "I like Ruchi!" Apparently they knew each other through mutual friends at the university.

Once Apoorva and Ruchi had agreed to be married, the only thing left was to work out the logistics. Ruchi's parents came to our house to formally propose a wedding. Nalini and Rekha were overwhelmed with joy. Rekha could not contain her happiness. "Apoorva, now you belong to us," she exclaimed. "You are ours!" But working out the logistics was not easy. After some negotiation, the wedding date and venue were decided. It would take place on Labor Day, September 5, 1994, at Martin's Crosswinds in Greenbelt, Maryland. Indian weddings are an elaborate affair. It is not uncommon for 500 to 600 people to attend the event. Even the engagement ceremony can involve 100 to 200 people. Typically, the bride's mother makes a special visit to India to buy jewelry and sarees that the bride will wear at various times on her wedding day. Each side has its separate engagement ceremony.

On our side, Nalini wanted an elaborate wedding and to invite some 400 people, including those from different parts of the U.S. as well as India. She wanted a traditional Indian wedding with all the trappings that she had missed out on when we got married. I didn't want Nalini to go through what my mother had, so I let her have whatever she wanted regarding the ceremony and shopping. For her, this was the first major social event of a life that had been full of adversities and setbacks. She wanted to show off that we could afford an elaborate wedding. Above all, she wanted to bask in the glory of being the mother of the bridegroom. She wanted to be involved in every detail, including what Apoorva and Sona would wear at which occasion, and what names and details would be included on the invitation card. We had to make a day-long trip to Edison, New Jersey, to meet with an Indian printer specializing in wedding invitations. Nalini preferred a traditional wedding invitation of the sort generally sent out in India. My idea of an artistic, modern invitation was ruled out.

A point of major contention was who to invite. Apoorva wanted to invite some of his friends, as did Sona. And Nalini had her own list that took priority over everyone else's. Several relatives from around the country were invited, and they needed to be provided lodging at our home or those of friends. They couldn't be shoved into hotels. Further, Nalini's sister Tara was to come from India, so we had to arrange for her air travel and a month-long stay with us. We wanted to repay the debt of gratitude we owed her for what she had done for us in Mumbai. As noted earlier, Tara rented several sanitariums for us during our nomadic existence in Mumbai.

Both of us dearly wanted to invite my mother, who had left the U.S. earlier in the year, to the engagement ceremony and wedding. When we called her with the good news, she was overjoyed and started crying on the phone. "Your Kaka would have been very happy to hear this!" she said. My father had passed away by this time. My mother, however, declined to come, saying that the journey would be too much for her. "But bring them as soon as they are wed," she said. "We should take them to Kankai for her blessings!" My mother deeply believed in Kankai, our family goddess whose temple is some 200 miles from Mumbai.

———————

Local Indian guests were not always accommodating. Several of our friends had special dietary requirements beyond being vegetarian. They were on a strict vegan diet and ate before sundown, generally around 5 p.m. They said they would come to the wedding but only if we met their requirements. This meant arranging a special dinner for them, for which the caterer would charge extra. I agreed because Nalini wanted to accommodate them and I wanted to please her, given that this was her first big social event and she naturally didn't want a single guest at the wedding to go unfed. A few guests brought out-of-town visitors who were not on the invitation list, which messed up the seating arrangement at several tables. When the caterer learned this, he was unhappy—he was charging only for guests on the list and wondered how many more uninvited guests had sneaked in. The final count of wedding guests on our side was 350, and we expected an equal number on the bride's side.

Nalini insisted that Apoorva, who was busy working at a consulting company, attend the traditional ceremonies spread over weeks before the wedding. So he had to take time off from work and spend weekends in countless wedding-related activities. Needless to say, this annoyed him—he'd rather have spent time with Ruchi than with his mother and her friends performing all sorts of rituals. After one such event, Apoorva exclaimed, "Whose wedding is this, after all?"

I said to him, "Listen, please son. I know this is your wedding, but Mom wants you to do all the things that I did not do when she got married! If you want to blame anyone for this, blame me." I met with him weekly at a Ruby Tuesday's restaurant near where he worked and counseled him to let his mother do what she wanted.

Selecting a menu for the wedding feast also required intricate negotiations. Both sides had to agree about what should be served—appetizers, entrée, desserts. Only after agreement was reached would the caterer provide cost estimates. Representatives of both parties came to the tasting session to sample the agreed-upon dishes and suggest any changes. Both sides agreed that the menu should be vegetarian, with special dishes for the few guests who were strictly vegan.

Finally, the wedding day arrived. Apoorva and his friends drove to the wedding hall in our car, a Dodge Aspen, decorated with flowers. We went in a Toyota. Once at the hall, Apoorva was dressed as an Indian bridegroom in a traditional, elaborate wedding outfit bought in New Jersey. (Gujaratis living on the East Coast who don't go to India to shop for wedding things often go to Edison, New Jersey, where a number of Indian stores specialize in wedding merchandise such as gowns, sarees and jewelry.)

And then there was the horse for the groom to mount! His party procession began at one end of the wedding hall's parking lot with Apoorva on horseback followed by costumed revelers dancing and singing. Nalini led a dancing procession of ladies bedecked in beautiful sarees and expensive jewelry. I feared that with all of the noise from drums and singing, the horse might go berserk. But the horse's owner assured me, "Nothing to worry about, Mr. Gandhi. The horse is used to all this. He's been in numerous Indian weddings." Most Indian weddings in the area, it seems, had used the same horse. The ceremony and fanfare made up for what Nalini had missed at her own wedding nearly 40 years earlier, when the groom showed up at her brother's place confused and wearing simple, everyday garb.

For Apoorva and Ruchi's wedding, some 700 guests arrived and were seated in the hall. Some stood at the bar sipping cocktails and munching on appetizers while the wedding ceremony was performed. A Hindu priest, brought in from New Jersey, went through the traditional ceremony in Sanskrit, which the bride and groom, as well as most of the adults gathered there, did not understand. The ceremony was over in about two hours and was followed by an evening reception with loving speeches lauding the newlyweds and wishing them a long and happy married life. Then there was the feast, followed by dancing to Bollywood tunes that went on till midnight. By evening's end, Apoorva and Ruchi were married and left for their honeymoon the next day. Nalini and I were thoroughly exhausted, but I was gratified that Apoorva had gotten his bride and Nalini a wedding that she never had for herself. Now, at least, she'd had it for her son.

––––––––––

Unlike Apoorva, Sona looked beyond Indians for her choice of spouse. We tried to nudge her toward Indian boys, but she let it be known in no unclear terms that it was her decision and we should stay out of it. That independent streak again! She told us that she would make her own choice—when she was ready. When she did, she chose Josh Maltby, a classmate and business-fraternity brother at the University of Maryland. He was of Irish-Catholic descent. When Sona informed us about Josh, a crisis ensued. As suggested earlier, Indian parents—particularly mothers—generally disapprove of their children marrying Americans. There were arguments, lectures and, as Sona put it later, "an ocean of tears." This all went on for several years. She was already approaching 30 and we had no choice but to conclude that she was only going to marry Josh, the person of her choice whom she loved. We kept on reminding her that there were numerous Indian boys at the university—in fact, there was an Indian Student Association—and asked why she hadn't gone there and socialized with them. "Well," she replied, "if you go there and meet with any of those kids, you might not want to go there again based on their behavior. Besides, I love Josh, and he loves me." Then she turned to me and said with tinge of irony: "I thought, of all people, you would understand and approve my choice." She still wanted our approval. We decided that we shouldn't push the matter any further. During the time that Sona was dating Josh, he had been to our house several times and we were favorably impressed.

After we relented, Josh came upstairs to my home office. We exchanged a few pleasantries and then he said, "I would like to propose to Sona. Would you have any objection?"

"Do you love her?" I asked.

"Yes, very much," he said.

"Then go ahead and ask her!"

And that was it. There was no elaborate visit from parents as in Apoorva's case. Nalini was reconciled with Sona's choice and welcomed Josh into the family with open arms. He has proven to be an ideal son-in-law, of whom any Indian mother would be proud. Sona's marriage to Josh was relatively easy for us. She not only had a clear idea about who to marry, but also when, where and how. Further, Sona hired a wedding planner who relieved us of several logistical details. Apoorva and Ruchi were also there to lend a helping hand. All we had to do was to foot the bill.

Sona and Josh picked the wedding date: July 4, 2003. I wanted the venue to be in the city, since I was its CFO and wanted to invite Mayor Williams and other senior officials to the wedding. Sona agreed and selected the National Museum of Women in the Arts, in the heart of the city, as the venue. Its impressive marble interior and dazzling chandeliers made it an ideal, though expensive, place to hold a wedding.

Sona didn't want a traditional Hindu priest to perform a wedding ceremony that no one would understand. She chose Srimati Kamala, a highly informed American minister who was consecrated as a swami, to perform the ceremony. She was deeply versed in Hindu scriptures and presided over the Self-Revelation Church of Absolute Monism, where I used to take Apoorva and Sona to Sunday School, and which is dedicated to the spiritual heritage of India and the life of Mahatma Gandhi.

In many ways, Nalini deserves great credit for helping to arrange the elaborate weddings of our children. After each one, she and I looked back on the slipshod manner in which we got married and how I had ruined many of the pleasures and joys of a wedding not only for her but also for my mother. My father had remained hands-off about our wedding and left everything for me to do on my own. Poor and penniless, I did the best that I could. My father showed up on the wedding day and that was that. I wasn't going to repeat such behavior and was determined to see that Nalini and the children had everything they wanted, including the wedding of their dreams. Whatever they needed to make their weddings memorable, I was ready to provide. Only they can tell whether I succeeded.

On March 15, 2000, Ruchi had given birth to Gaurav, a name that means pride. And he is indeed the pride of the family. Nalini was ecstatic. This was a moment of great joy for her. Once again, she had something to be very proud about, as did I. One of my brothers never married. Another married but had no children, while the other married brother had only one daughter. Nalini said, "Let us call Baa. She will be very happy to know that it's boy—her first great grandson who will carry the family name forward!" So, we called Baa immediately. She was extremely happy and peppered us with questions: "How long before I see my great grandson? What is his name? Was Sona there to name him? You know, as Apoorva's sister that is her right. I want to see him, hug him, kiss him and love him before I die," she said crying.

Nalini was crying, too. "Well, Baa," she said. "You will have to come to America soon then."

"No, I am too old for that," Baa replied. "But bring the boy here. We will take him to Kankai, our family goddess." By the time her other great-grandchildren were born—

Apoorva's daughter, Shivani (February 12, 2002) and Sona's son, Kiran (February 11, 2008)—Baa had passed away. By the time Sona's daughter Tara was born on June 27, 2011, Nalini also had passed away.

To our great parental satisfaction, both Apoorva and Sona are settled in the Washington area with their own wonderful children. In addition to their son Gaurav, Apoorva and Ruchi have a daughter, Shivani, both of whom are rapidly growing into responsible young adults themselves. Ruchi, who has an MBA, deferred her professional career to stay at home to raise Gaurav and Shivani. She also has a large heart and deeply compassionate nature, so she pursued the adoption of Anisha, an infant from a Mumbai orphanage. A deaf girl, she is now growing up in this deeply loving family. When I see her bantering with Gaurav and Shivani and playing with other children, I am overwhelmed with gratitude that I have such a loving son and daughter-in-law.

Both Josh and Sona are model parents to their son, Kiran, and daughter, Tara. As Sona moves from place to place around the world in her highly demanding job, her ever-accommodating husband moves with her. Josh is an exceptional father who takes care of the children while pursuing his professional goals in diverse environments. He too earned a Wharton MBA.

Seeing Apoorva and Josh taking care of their children makes me feel inadequate as a father. They got their kids hooked on sports, particularly ice hockey. I delight in going to their games and seeing them score goals.

When Gaurav was 14, he started a computer-help company, Technolo-G, to help neighbors and others solve computer problems. He even prepared business cards naming him founder and CEO! No wonder he is specializing in computer science at the University of Maryland, where he began his studies in September 2018. His younger sister Shivani is an ice-hockey devotee like him and brave enough to play with boys. Even at her young age, she is socially sensitive and politically active. She helps friends in need. For example, she helped a transgender friend who was going through an especially hard time adjusting to a new reality. She also participates in women's marches and other causes.

Kiran, my other grandson, is the smartest child of his age I know. His sister Tara, named after Nalini's sister, is a precocious young beauty who instinctively knows how to pose for a picture. Looking at her numerous photographs I always wonder how she knows to strike the right pose each time. We all think that she will have a fabulous modeling career! Having lived in Guatemala, both Kiran and Tara are fluent in Spanish and act as my interpreters when I visit them there. Yes, this is shameless bragging by their grandfather, but only a very lucky man has such wonderful children and grandchildren.

––––––––––

On Sunday, December 7, 2008, I had taken the grandchildren and their parents to the Metropolitan Club for brunch with Santa, an annual Christmas event that kids and adults enjoy very much. Nalini was in the hospital with a bad heart, a genetic condition that she inherited. She'd insisted that I take the kids to the club—she didn't want to deny them the pleasure of meeting Santa. While they were having brunch and fun with Santa, I retreated to the club's phone booth every half hour to check on Nalini's condition. On my last call, I was told that things were serious and Nalini needed to be flown by helicopter to the Washington Hospital Center for an urgent operation. I went back to the party and told Apoorva and Ruchi what was happening, then left immediately for the hospital.

Nalini and I were married for 47 years. I wouldn't presume to say that it was always a happy one: a bumpy ride on occasion for both of us, but more for her than me. Our problems started right from the beginning. For what should have been a once-in-a-lifetime event, especially for Nalini—an orphan who had been raised by resentful relatives—sadly it was not. I obdurately insisted on a very simple, no-fuss wedding. The ceremony Nalini got was the signing of a few court papers attested to by a lowly court official in a crowded tenement in front of a few relatives and neighbors. The groom wore not the lavish, traditional Indian garb but ordinary work clothes—not even a jacket and tie. I insisted on a wedding ceremony devoid of rites and rituals and with no wedding feast, which to me would have been a waste of food while millions in our country were starving. Immediately after the wedding, I had to send her to Savarkundla to live with my parents, to live among strangers in a place without any of the amenities that she was used to in Mumbai, where I struggled to find a place for us to live. Then came the harrowing years in that city where we lived nomadically moving from place to place.

Even in the U.S., where I was perennially worried about making a career, Nalini bore the brunt of my frustrations and disappointments. After moving from place to place in Mumbai in search of a better job, I followed the same pattern in the U.S., dragging Nalini along with me in my peripatetic search for "perfect work" from Greensboro to Pittsburgh to Boca Raton for short job stints, and then to Baton Rouge for my doctoral studies. While I worked toward my Ph.D., we were again reduced to a hand-to-mouth existence, with me holed up in a library carrel till late every evening while Nalini was home alone. After three years at Pitt, we were on the move again, this time to Washington, where we began our lives anew.

Only in Washington did Nalini and I feel relatively settled, so we bought a suburban house. As I concentrated on my career (again in search of perfect work), Nalini devoted herself to raising our two children. As I attained higher-level positions in Washington, I worked long hours and neglected family duties, leaving numerous chores and responsibilities to Nalini.

One of her disappointments was that her lack of education prevented her from having a rewarding career. Most of the Indian friends with whom we socialized were from the upper-middle class and had college degrees. Some, including women, had professional degrees. A few were doctors. Most of the women were employed. At parties, when ladies talked about their days at the office, Nalini felt left out. After our children were grown, she struggled to find a job, but her lack of formal education and inadequate English proficiency prevented her from taking on even a clerical position. She tried hard to adjust to her new American reality. As soon as she came to the U.S., despite her difficulty with English, she joined a secretarial school where she learned typing. That skill came in handy when I needed someone to type an early draft of my dissertation, which she did on a manual IBM typewriter. This was a matter of great pride for her, as she felt that she contributed toward my getting a Ph.D.

We considered purchasing a 7-Eleven store or a laundromat, where she could mind the cash register, or buying a small motel, a popular occupation among Indians at the time. Her idea was that I would continue my work to finance the business while she managed operations. I ruled out these ideas on the grounds that I would wind up tending to them in my spare time and on weekends. Such businesses require 24/7 attention from owners. Moreover, cashiers in such places can be sitting-duck targets for intruders. We knew of cases in which Indian convenience-store attendants and motel clerks had been killed during robbery attempts.

Nalini worked for a while as an apprentice at a hair salon but did not become a full-fledged hairdresser. She finally got a job as an invoice-processing clerk with a consulting company where a friend worked. At last she could get dressed up in the morning and go to an office like her friends. And she was good at her job. In fact, some of our immigrant relatives got their first jobs at the same company based on her recommendation.

———————

As I look back on our long marriage, I can't help but feel an unending sense of remorse. Of many people whom I have failed in life—Kaka, Baa, my children, some dear friends—I have been most troubled by my failure as a husband to Nalini. In my endless search for a career and, again, that perfect work, I often neglected her. I failed not only to be a good husband but also a good father. The lion's share of the credit for our children turning out to be responsible adults goes to their mother. Nalini bore the burden of running the household—grocery shopping, ferrying the kids from hockey practices to swimming and ballet lessons, and the myriad other chores that go with raising a family in America. Their father was too often absent, pursuing his own goals.

As if this was not enough of a burden on Nalini, members of our extended families joined us in the U.S. My mother, sister, brother, his wife, Nalini's brother and his wife, and their three children all came in one fell swoop. Our children had to make room for them in the house. Nalini took care of them. She helped find jobs for my sister and brother, and her brother and his wife, and ferried them to their workplaces. She did all this while managing her job and running a busy household. Again I was absent, in Trenton, New Jersey, on special assignment in the office of Governor Jim Florio.

By contemporary standards, we made an odd pair. We were that proverbial couple where the husband worries about big things, like how to solve the Arab-Israeli divide and global climate change, while the wife takes care of the basics, such as grocery shopping and carpooling children to hockey practices. While I had four higher-education degrees, Nalini had barely finished high school. Having been orphaned at an early age, her elder brother paid no attention to her schooling. In fact, he took her out of school so she could help in the household chores and babysit his children. No wonder, when she arrived in the U.S., she did not speak, read or write English.

Beyond my professional career, I was deeply interested in literature, politics and social policy. I read whatever I could—there are hundreds of books in my library. Nalini, on the other hand, never read much of anything, even in our native tongue, Gujarati. She gained her limited English-language proficiency by watching TV.

After we settled in Washington, Nalini enjoyed socializing with other immigrant Indian families, while I was a relative recluse. I know that I disappointed her and our children on the social front. I was not a prized presence at parties—I played no musical instruments and did not sing, nor did I gossip, a further drawback. All of this created tension between us, of course. So why, some might ask, did we stay together? This is where Indian culture and tradition came to the fore. Professional and educational disparities among Indian couples are quite common given the differing opportunities afforded young men and women in India. Further, in Indian marriages, individual likes and dislikes are subordinated in favor of what is good for the family, particularly children.

———————

On that December Sunday in 2008, the heart specialist was waiting for me at the Washington Hospital Center. He briefed me and said he needed my permission to operate on Nalini. I agreed, and the heart team took her into the operating theater. After two hours, the doctor emerged and told me that things looked good for Nalini, but she would have to stay at the rehab center next door for two weeks before going home. Luckily, we found a private room there where she could recuperate. Though she came home in due time, her condition was precarious. She spent the next six months moving in and out of doctors' offices and hospitals.

On July 23, 2009, Nalini's heart gave way. She was 69. Within six months her younger brother, Vinod, followed her. He had migrated to the U.S. and was in his early

60s. All of their brothers and sisters passed away in their 50s or early 60s, all seeming to have inherited health problems, especially heart conditions and diabetes.

As I look back on the various parts of my life, particularly the harrowing Mumbai experiences, Nalini was the right person for me. What other woman would go through those hellish Mumbai days with me or live apart from her husband so soon after her wedding in a town she'd never been to and with in-laws who were virtual strangers? Even in America, during our early years we lived a wandering life, shuttling from place to place. And as I struggled through my various jobs and studies, Nalini was always there, taking care of our home and children. Only late in middle age did we feel settled. During all that time, Nalini gracefully put up with my idiosyncrasies. Above all, she raised two wonderful children practically on her own, and for that I will remain deeply and forever grateful to her.

Chapter 15

ON BEING AN AMERICAN

April 30, 1976, was a momentous day in the annals of India's judiciary. On that day in New Delhi, a lone dissenting judge of the Supreme Court of India, Justice H.R. Khanna, spoke out against the right of Prime Minister Indira Gandhi to imprison political prisoners.

"The power of the courts to issue a writ of habeas corpus is regarded as one of the most important characteristics of democratic states under the rule of law," he opined. "The principle that no one shall be deprived of his life and liberty without the authority of law is rooted in the consideration that life and liberty are precious possessions." Freedom of expression prevailed in my native country when Indira Gandhi was soundly defeated in a general election soon after the declaration of emergency under which she had imprisoned her political opponents.

That same day—in another court in another country some 8,000 miles away—a momentous event was being played out in my civic life. In a naturalization ceremony in Pittsburgh, I would be sworn in as a U.S. citizen. It was cooler than a normal April day, though the sky was clear. There was a lot on my mind. Here I was surrendering my Indian citizenship forever and becoming an American citizen. Unlike some countries, India does not allow dual citizenship; to become a U.S. citizen, I had no choice. As a green card holder, I'd had the best of both worlds: I could enjoy all the benefits of living in the U.S. and still maintain Indian citizenship. But no more.

That morning I put on my well-pressed blue suit, a white shirt and red tie. My shoes were nicely shined. Nalini, who would accompany me to the ceremony, donned her brilliant red saree. We left early for the courthouse downtown to make sure that we were on time for the ceremony, received by a group of volunteers who were there to welcome us and the other new soon-to-be citizens. To my surprise, one of the volunteers was an elderly lady who was a student in an evening accounting class that I taught. She congratulated me and offered to take me to the judge's chambers before the ceremony. I introduced her to Nalini and readily agreed to visit the judge.

Though I have a law degree from India, I had never set foot in an Indian court nor seen a judge's chambers. Learning the law in India was as bookish as everything else. You cram law books, pass the bar exam and, lo and behold, you are a lawyer! While the judge was getting dressed in the antechamber, Nalini and my student and I waited in his thickly carpeted, well-organized office. A secretary came in and offered us coffee. The walls were impressively lined with law books and pictures. Soon the judge appeared, a bald, clean-shaven man dressed in a flowing black gown.

"Your Honor," my student said, "this is Dr. Gandhi and his wife, Nalini. He is my accounting professor!" We shook hands and, after a few pleasantries, the judge said, "Let's go and swear you in. I know you're eager to become a U.S. citizen." It was a solemn ceremony. The crowd of would-be citizens and their families was large. We took the oath and pledged our allegiance to the flag with right hand on heart. The judge solemnly explained its meaning. He talked about the governing motto of the country: *e pluribus unum*—"Out of many, one." The judge's explanation wasn't necessary; all I had to do to understand the motto was to look around. There were people from all over, chiefly from Asia, Africa and Latin America. There were a few white European faces, but it was mostly a multicolored gathering of immigrants aspiring to become U.S. citizens. Here one could see the face of America's future.

After the ceremony, I invited my student to have lunch with us in a nearby restaurant. While the two women chatted, I let my mind wander. I was now a U.S. citizen! For most Indians, this is a practical thing to do. At the naturalization ceremony they take the pledge of allegiance and try to sing the national anthem, yet typically there is no overflowing patriotic love for America. Becoming a citizen opened up job opportunities, but most often it was done to bring blood relatives—parents, brothers and sisters—to the U.S. through so-called "chain migration." (Mr. Trump would have a heart attack if he knew that we were about to sponsor many of our relatives and they in turn would do the same.)

Nalini and I, of course, wanted to bring our immediate family members, who were clamoring to come to the Promised Land. To do so we needed to become citizens. I waited a few years after I became eligible and Nalini did so soon afterward. We sponsored our relatives, who came together—my mother and sister, my brother and his wife, Nalini's brother and his wife and three children. Our family grew overnight from four to 13. Our children got to know and live with aunts and uncles and a grandma whom they'd barely known.

What had held me back? Why hadn't I become a citizen as soon as I was eligible? As a green card holder, like many Indian Americans, I had a kind of bigamous identity. I lived happily in the U.S., enjoying all the benefits of an affluent society while maintaining my Indian citizenship. Some Indian Americans have fond hopes of spending their post-retirement life in India and thus don't want to give up their Indian citizenship. Some are sensitive to the criticism that they have betrayed India by leaving it and making their home in the affluent West. They were told that India needed them, not America. They wanted to go back and serve the motherland. Not I.

When I boarded that Air India plane for New York on the 10th of October in 1965, I vowed never to return to India except for brief visits. If I felt any sense of betrayal, it was of the reverse sort: I didn't leave India—it forced me out. Still, in becoming an American citizen, I kept asking myself: "Have I betrayed India, my motherland?" Why did I need to become a U.S. citizen? I could have carried on as a green card holder enjoying nearly everything the country has to offer. But after I became eligible for citizenship, I kept asking myself why I hadn't yet become a citizen. What's holding me back? I knew that I wasn't going back to India, so why not commit and participate fully in the civic life of the community and country that I lived in and loved?

America had always held an attraction for me—partly because it offered an affluent life that I could never afford in India. But my fascination with America was much more than that: I was attracted to the freedoms that America afforded its people, letting them—particularly the young—explore, experiment and in essence shape their life the way they want to live. That kind of freedom and flexibility were lacking in an ossified India, whose myriad customs and traditions inhibited its people and curtailed individual growth.

I felt guilty enjoying the benefits of being a green card holder in America and yet shying away from fully committing myself to the country. Thus becoming a citizen ultimately was an act of commitment to the country where I intended to live the rest of my life and raise my family—and, above all, that had been so good to me.

That commitment had its roots in my vision of America that I had in India. I knew in my bones that it was only in America that I could rise and realize my full potential. I also knew from bitter experience that had I stayed in India it would have crushed me, which it very nearly did. I have often wondered what would have happened to me had I not been able to escape the country. During those dark days in Mumbai, I carried on my daily life more like a zombie. With every hurt and humiliation that I suffered at the hands of undeserving people, it was like a daily death by a thousand cuts. Many a time I felt like striking back, but who would I strike back and to what end? I knew the reality was not going to change with my random outbursts. I still needed to get up in the morning and face the same people and suffer the same indignities. Life in Mumbai was that hopeless. Thus when I got a chance I took that leap of faith and crossed the ocean.

A few weeks after President John F. Kennedy's inauguration as the 35th president of the United States on January 20, 1961, I saw that majestic event in one of those newsreels that usually precede movies in India. I forget what movie I saw, but clearly recall the inauguration. I was quite taken by the young president's eloquence, handsome look and elegant demeanor on that wintry January day. It had snowed heavily the night before. Two things about the inauguration struck me most. First, the 87-year-old poet Robert Frost recited from memory his poem "The Gift Outright." He had written a special poem, "Dedication," for the occasion but, blinded by the dazzling sunlight, could not read it. Second, Kennedy spoke forcefully about a citizen's duty to his country. "And so, my fellow Americans," he declared, "ask not what your country can do for you—ask what you can do for your country." A senior in college in India, full of hopes and ambitions and patriotic fervor to help my motherland, I found this exhortation exhilarating. I went to see the movie again just to watch the inauguration and listen to Kennedy's moving oratory.

After a few harrowing years in Mumbai, however, I came to doubt the wisdom of Kennedy's words about a citizen's duty toward his country and wondered whether he'd gotten it right. What had changed? For starters, despite earning an accounting degree from what was arguably the best business college in India, I'd failed to land a job—any job—despite a hundred or more applications. There were just too many college graduates chasing too few jobs. One had to know the right people in the right places to get a job, and I did not meet that requirement. When I finally did find a job, it was nothing to write home about.

After Nalini and I married, I couldn't afford for the two of us to live in Mumbai, so I had to send my new bride hundreds of miles away to live with my parents for nearly two years while I lived and slept in the office where I worked. When she finally returned to Mumbai, we moved from place to place every three months. It was a miserable existence; if there was a scarcity of jobs, affordable housing was even scarcer.

My traumatic years in Mumbai washed away most of my hopes, ambitions and patriotic fervor. I came to a bitter realization that a country should be organized to help its citizens explore their potential. Well, forget about that in India. Despite Herculean efforts, I could barely eke out an existence. It became painfully clear that nearly everything in Indian society, particularly the Indian economy, rewarded the rich and punished the poor. India's Soviet-style five-year plans come and go but the masses still live in miserable conditions. Over 70 years after Indian independence in 1947, according to the United Nations, India is home to the largest number of poor people in the world: one third of the planet's 1.2 billion extremely poor people subsist in India without access to basic services such as education, health, water, sanitation and electricity. Yet India is among the 10 richest countries in the world with 245,000 millionaires and 111 billionaires. Even worse, it has the second-highest income inequality in the world with millionaires and billionaires living next to shanty towns and slums in big cities like Mumbai.

My only salvation, it seemed, was to leave the country of my birth for a new home where I could find a congenial environment and flourish: America. That's when I realized that even leaving the country was a rich man's game. It cost several hundred thousand rupees to go abroad—I didn't have even a few thousand. My meager monthly salary was already spent before it was received. I had no bank account. We lived hand to mouth—cash in, cash out. With my ambition, I simply couldn't reconcile myself to the realities all around me. Fortunately, with help from a college friend, I was able to leave India for the United States.

I was not alone. Soon after the liberalization of U.S. immigration policies in 1965, tens of thousands of young Indians left for America, where a better world awaited them. Many were professionals—mostly doctors and engineers who soon became valued residents of their adopted country. In America, they found a society that appreciated its citizens—even rich or poor immigrants—and where even ordinary citizens had the opportunity to explore their potential. Sadly, I never heard a lament from Indian politicians about this significant brain drain, much less any attempt to stop the hemorrhage of precious talent with a rapidly accelerating trend among the young to leave the country. I recall a cynical comment made by a wag concerning the acute grain shortages of the day: "Take our brains, but send us your grains!"

––––––––––

Indian immigrants have come to the U.S. in three waves. During the early decades of the 20th century, many came to work on railroads in Washington, Oregon and northern California. The second wave was in the late 1960s and '70s, when immigrants were allowed in based on skills deemed helpful to an expanding economy. This opened the immigration of highly skilled Asians, including Indian doctors, engineers and other professionals to the U.S. Asians who immigrated under the "skills provision" became citizens in due course and began bringing their families to the U.S., essentially changing the pattern of immigration. Roughly 87 percent of immigrants in 1960 were from Europe, but by 2010 some 90 percent were non-Europeans. This profoundly changed the nation's demographic profile. Alarmed by this unexpected result of the Immigration and Naturalization Act of 1965, attempts were made to restrict immigration under its family-reunification provision, which favored existing citizens over new immigrants. A bipartisan commission was led by the Reverend Theodore Hesburgh, then president of the University of Notre Dame, to reform policies with an eye toward solving the problem of illegal immigration. The commission played a significant role in helping Senator Alan K. Simpson (R-Wyoming) and Congressmen Romano L. Mazzoli (D-Kentucky) formulate major immigration-reform legislation known as the Simpson-Mazzoli Act of 1986.

I thought that Indians, along with other nonwhite minority communities, should try to preserve the family-reunification provision as Congress revisited the nation's immigration policy. This important legislation allowed us to bring our loved ones to the U.S. Along with leaders of the Indian community, in February and March of 1983 we visited Congress to lobby for maintaining the family-reunification provision. I drafted a statement and also led a delegation to the White House, where I spoke with Judge William P. Clark, Jr., then national security advisor to President Ronald Reagan.

"Judge, for us Indians, family has special meaning," I told him. "We come from a society with a tradition of 'extended family,' where children, parents and grandparents all live together. It is the duty of children to take care of their elderly until they die. If family reunification were to be denied, who would take care of our elders back home?"

Judge Clark appeared moved by my plea. "Tomorrow morning, in my daily briefing of the president," he told our gathering, "I will share your statement and brief him about the stakes involved in the family-reunification issue."

In testimony at hearings that Senator Simpson held on immigration reform on February 25, 1983, I again emphasized how important family reunification is to Indians. In the final analysis, despite strong attacks against it, the family-reunification provision remained essentially intact. The legislation that passed also included the legalization of some four million illegal immigrants.

The third wave of Indian migration occurred during the mid-1990s and the first decade of the 21st century. Most of it was skill-based. Indians came in large numbers under temporary visa provisions to meet the increasing need for high-tech professionals to solve the mammoth Y2K problem. Many of them found ways to stay. By 2015, Indian immigrants numbered around four million, constituting the third-largest group of Asians in the U.S., after Chinese and Filipino Americans.

———

My activities in the immigration arena were guided by my desire to advance the interests of Indian Americans. Beyond that community interest, however, I also firmly believed—and still do—that a continuous and judicious flow of immigration is good for the country. More working-age younger immigrants are needed because America is about to face a massive aging crisis. Japan and the countries of Western Europe are already struggling with it. The U.S. needs to provide adequate healthcare and social security for its fast-aging population. Indeed, 10,000 baby-boomers retire each day and join that group of Americans who will need all kinds of care and attention. For that it needs a continuous inflow of young immigrants and their offspring because the birth rate has been declining for quite some time in the U.S. As *The Economist* put it recently, "The future quality of life of this aging, shrinking population increasingly depends on two factors: sustained high fertility amongst minority groups already in the country—and continued immigration."

What is more, if the U.S. is to maintain its competitive edge, it will have to let in more immigrants. Tech companies of Silicon Valley and elsewhere depend upon highly skilled immigrants. Witness, for example, the substantial increase in immigration of young Indians trained in computer technology to resolve the Y2K problem. Similarly, at the other end of the skill spectrum, the U.S. needs immigrants to work in fields, farms, factories, restaurants and in construction industries where there is an acute shortage of people willing to work long hours in difficult conditions. Generally immigrants would do that kind of hard yet essential labor. Further, the U.S. will need younger immigrants to keep its economy humming, given their ever-increasing needs as they form households.

Fortunately, the U.S. can afford to open its doors widely. Just look at the sheer continental size of the country and its relatively small population; it is roughly three times the size of India and yet has only about a quarter of its population. It also has less than one-tenth of India's population density. Just one Mumbai suburb, Malad, holds about seven percent of the city's population, yet has more people (1.6 million) than vastly bigger mountain states like Montana (1.5 million) or Wyoming (0.6 million). Even densely populated American cities on the East Coast appear relatively empty to an Indian eye.

Asian immigrants are known for their industry, innovative skills and entrepreneurial zeal. Fully one quarter of all new business ventures are started by immigrants, mostly Asians. Instead of being a burden on the country, they soon become contributing citizens. Take the case of my family. My brother Dilip and Nalini's brother Vinod, who followed us to the U.S., were not professionally trained nor college educated. Yet they found jobs as soon as they came and got quickly settled. They did not hesitate to work at the nearby Jerry's sandwich shop and gas station despite their entrepreneurial careers in Mumbai. Their adult children started delivering newspapers in the morning and waiting tables at Pizza Hut in the evening. Their wives did not hesitate to work at whatever menial jobs they could find. It is the classic immigrant story multiplied a million times.

Most Indians who came here during the mid-1960s and '70s like myself were educated primarily in professions such as medicine, engineering, pharmacology, accounting and consulting. Presently they are among the most highly educated minorities in America: 70 percent of adult Indian Americans are college educated, the highest percentage among all Asians. They are also two-and-a-half times more likely to be college educated than the country as a whole.

With this level of education, they can be found excelling in every field from accounting to zoology. They can be found working hard and living quietly as a model community in practically every corner of America. It is hard to find a hospital without an Indian doctor, an engineering firm without an Indian engineer, a university without Indian professors, a highway without an Indian-run motel or a town without an Indian store. One seldom opens a professional journal without seeing an article written by an Indian. Indian immigrants are known for mixing scientific talents with entrepreneurial zeal, as evidenced in the tech worlds of Silicon Valley, Northern Virginia and Boston, where there are hundreds of Indian American millionaires and even a few billionaires. Several major American corporations—Google, Microsoft, Master-Card, Adobe and Harmon among them—presently have Indian Americans as CEOs. Though small in numbers, Indian immigrants are an extraordinarily productive and contributing community with their hard work, initiative, professional skills and a natural proclivity to form new businesses.

Even if first-generation Indian Americans have done well professionally and economically, not all feel at home in the larger American society. For one thing, their social mores are different. They are generally not at ease at such staple American gatherings as happy hours or with male-bonding rituals such as deer hunting. As a result, they have created small societies of their own in which they are entirely at home—Little Indias, as it were, much the same way that Chinatowns are found in most large American cities.

First-generation Indian Americans essentially live in cultural cocoons from which they step out daily to do their jobs, only to come back in the evenings and weekends. Many are 9-to-5 Americans. Only their work lives are lived in America. The rest is still Indian—the spicy food, melodious songs, old-time religion with its mysterious rites and rituals, exotic temples and gurus, lovely dresses and extravagant jewelry—the whole cultural fabric. It is a self-imposed isolation—part American, part Indian. Though many of them have been in the U.S. for years, if not decades, and nearly all of them have graduate degrees, they are still plagued by the emotional baggage they brought with them from India including superstitions. The most flagrant example of this blind faith surfaced on September 21, 1995, when many of them rushed to pray to Lord Ganesh for his blessing. On that day, the news of a miracle came from India and spread all over world—including particularly the U.S.—that statues of Lord Ganesh were actually drinking milk that was offered to them in prayer! Lord Ganesh is among the most widely revered gods in the Hindu pantheon. Hindus offer prayers to him because he is known to remove obstacles.

Our family was as much a part of this bifurcated culture as most of our friends. In all of our moves in the U.S., Nalini always wanted to make sure that she would be able to take care of our family and at the same time provide the children with an Indian social environment. Before we settled down in a new place, we searched for Indian, particularly Gujarati, families with whom we could socialize. Apoorva and

Sona also found their friends at Indian parties, which invariably involved children. They looked forward to weekend parties as eagerly as Nalini did. Their childhood friendships turned into lasting relationships, and several of their friends found their spouses as a result of this frequent socializing.

When we moved to Pittsburgh, we didn't hesitate to choose a random Indian household from the telephone directory and call to invite ourselves in. And we were welcomed with open arms. It is, after all, an Indian custom to treat an uninvited guest as if he or she were quite special. Inevitably, friendships are formed. These customs, rituals, temples, even Bollywood movies and songs, keep us bonded and socially integrated while we conduct our professional lives. These Little Indias give us the social comfort and safety networks needed to live in a different land that is socially as far away as it can be imagined. All minorities try to retain their identities, but few have resisted the inevitable process of Americanization to the extent that Indian Americans have. It is, in a way, an initial defiance of the melting pot, but does not work beyond the early generations.

There has been a consistent rant about non-European immigrants' failure to assimilate within the larger American society. It has come from august personages such as George F. Kennan, the famed diplomat, and Arthur Schlesinger, Jr., the distinguished historian. Both have worried about maintaining American character and values in the face of increasing diversity brought on by hordes of immigrants, particularly from Asia, Africa and Latin America. Similarly, at the other end of the spectrum, Michael Anton—in a *Claremont Review* essay, sees "the ceaseless importation of the Third World foreigners with no tradition of, taste for, or experience in liberty" casting a shadow on American democracy and constitutional order.

It should be noted, however, that approximately 150 years ago the same warnings were heard about the Jews, Italians and Poles who were arriving on American shores in the millions. Even at the founding of the republic, Benjamin Franklin had raised similar concerns about German immigrants. In these and many other anti-immigrant sentiments, I see a haughty white European conceit about the ownership of liberty and democratic values. But the idea of American citizenship is based upon anyone swearing by the American constitution and all that it contains. As the famous British writer G.K. Chesterton put it, "America is the only nation in the world that is founded on a creed," one set forth with "theological lucidity in the Declaration of Independence." Similarly, in 1944, the great Swedish sociologist Gunnar Myrdal defined this American creed as devotion to the principles of liberty, self-government and equal opportunity to all regardless of race, gender, religion and nation of origin. At its heart is the pursuit of happiness. As V.S. Naipaul put it, "It is an immense human idea.... It is an elastic idea; it fits all men."

Further, in much of the contemporary anti-immigrant rant, I see a failure to realize that America is no longer the domain of white Anglo-Saxon Europeans only. Presently, 43 million immigrants who are mostly from Asia, Africa and Latin America constitute nearly 13 percent of the U.S. population, three times as high as in 1970. With the equal number of their U.S.-born children, they already constitute about a quarter of the total population. Thus the country has already moved forward. Indeed, reflecting 2018 revisions of Census Bureau statistics, a Brookings Institution report confirms the emergence of "racial minorities as the primary demographic engine of the nation's future growth, countering an aging, slow-growing and soon to be declining white population. The new statistics project that the nation will become 'minority white' in 2045. During that year, whites will comprise 49.7 percent of the population in contrast to 24.6 percent for Hispanics, 13.1 percent for blacks, 7.9 percent for Asians and 3.8 percent for multiracial populations."

Yes, assimilation of first-generation immigrants—no matter where they come from—is nearly always difficult. It is like when a river merges with the ocean; at its mouth the water maintains its distinctive color and characteristics, yet as the river moves further into the ocean, it is overwhelmed and loses its distinct identity. Similarly, first-generation Indian immigrants, like any other, may retain their distinctive identity, but for their second and third generations and beyond, Americanization is a foregone conclusion. The melting pot works! No immigrants have been able to defy this inevitable fate of Americanization. I see this firsthand in our own family. Both Apoorva and Sona, and their children especially, are American first, Indian second. They have more in common with their American friends next door than with their cousins in India. Yes, they do not look like Americans of European descent, but their values and concepts of liberty, manners and mores are the same as those of Americans who trace their ancestry to Europe.

Presently, assimilation of new immigrants is in fact faster than with earlier generations. They have the advantage of ever-proliferating mass culture and its many means—TV, movies, music and social media of all variety—that the earlier generations did not have. Their children begin marrying beyond their community faster. More than half of U.S.-born Hispanics marry non-Hispanics. Similarly, about half of the offspring of Japanese immigrants marry outside their ethnic and racial community. Even among Indian Americans the rate of intermarriage is faster than what I had expected. My own daughter Sona married Josh, an Irish Catholic. Their children look like any in the neighborhood. As we have seen before, economic assimilation among Indian Americans, even in the first generation, is astonishingly high. With their advanced education and professional training, they are now among the top one percent of Americans in terms of their income and economic well-being. Temple University professor Sanjoy Chakravorty and his colleagues Devesh Kapur and Nirvikar Singh have studied this remarkable success of Indian Americans in a recent book aptly entitled, *The Other One Percent: Indians in America* (Oxford University Press, 2016).

As time passed even for Nalini and I, India gradually faded in the rearview mirror. At some point we felt more at home with our American neighbors than with relatives in India who had moved on. Every time we visited India, both Nalini and I felt that we no longer belonged there and couldn't wait to return after a few weeks! We felt much more at home in Washington than we had in Mumbai. Our Americanization was too evident to ignore. We had no choice but to accept the reality unfolding on the ground beneath our feet.

As immigrants remake their life, they also remake the country. They bring in fresh energy and creative vitality. We need them to maintain our competitive edge as well as do the work that we do not want to do ourselves. Fortunately, as indicated earlier, we have room to let them in. We should not be afraid of them. In this winter of our discontent, when a presidential candidate rode into the White House in part based on his anti-immigrant rhetoric, I join many in asserting that we must welcome immigrants.

The period between 1815-1914 was called the British Imperial Century in recognition of Great Britain's overwhelming international dominance with its far-flung empire. In a similar vein, Henry Luce, the publishing magnate and editor-in-chief of Time-Life magazines, declared the 20th century to be an American Century. In a *Life* magazine editorial on February 17, 1941, he urged America to assume the mantle of world leadership. He argued that the U.S. "must be sharing with all peoples our Bill of Rights, our Declaration of Independence, [and] our constitution...." Such was the making of the American Century in the aftermath of the Second World War. Luce's plausible declaration was based upon America's vast military arsenal as well as overwhelming worldwide cultural influence.

Given our present predicament and national confusion, some have argued that if the 20th century was an American Century, it has been short-lived. Yet as we continue to move into the 21st century, I suggest that it will be an American Century as well! Such a claim would appear audacious, if not preposterous, to anyone who looks at news headlines or glances at TV news reports, which are filled with the decline of American power and prestige abroad and disillusionment at home. Why then am I claiming the 21st century as an American one? For starters, America has provided an unprecedentedly high standard of living and freedom of expression to the majority of its heterogeneous people. No other country has done it as well and on such a vast scale. America has made good life possible even for the common people. It gives them a chance to make something of life by liberating them from the crushing burden of poverty that still plagues too many parts of the world. Any country that can do it within a mere 250 years of its formation should be called triumphant and not distressing as some would have it.

But it is more than what America has done for the material well-being of common men and women. It is the American idea of the pursuit of happiness, which as V.S. Naipaul says, lays "at the heart of the attractiveness of the civilization to so many outside it or on its periphery.... So much is contained in it: the idea of the individual, responsibility, choice, the life of the intellect, the idea of vocation and perfectibility and achievement. It is an immense human idea. It cannot be reduced to a fixed system. It cannot generate fanaticism. But it is known to exist; and because of that, other more rigid systems in the end blow away."

A hundred years ago when Italians, Jews, Poles and other Europeans were knocking at America's door, the great American commentator Walter Lippmann—unlike others—was not afraid of these hordes of new immigrants. In fact, he said these immigrants brought with them "a thousand unforeseeable possibilities.... The great social adventure of America is no longer the conquest of the wilderness but the absorption of 50 different peoples.... Immigration may swamp us; it may, if we seize the opportunity, mean the impregnation of our national life with new brilliancy."

Continued immigration—judicious and measured—is our ace in the hole. The best and the brightest as well as the tired and poor from around the world want to come to our shores above all, and no other country has the American tradition of accepting and absorbing them.

––––––––––

In the summer of 2017, I was driving along Wisconsin Avenue through Bethesda, Maryland, one of the most prosperous neighborhoods of suburban Washington. On my way to the nation's capital, I stopped at a light by the Bethesda Naval Hospital, a premier medical center that has served presidents, congressmen, senators and other Washington bigwigs since 1940—the year, incidentally, I was born. It is also near the headquarters of the National Institutes of Health, where cutting-edge medical research is conducted. A car pulled up on my right. I watched the window slide down and a man's face turn my way. Thinking that he needed assistance, perhaps directions, I pressed the button to open the window on my passenger side.

"Can I help you?" I asked.

"Yeah," he said, leaning toward me and shouting. "Get outta my country! Why don't you go back to where you came from?"

Shocked and tongue-tied, I froze and couldn't respond. He drove off, his mission accomplished. I just sat there, staring at the green light. As cars behind me started honking, I regained my composure and continued down the avenue. I reached for words that I wished I had said: "I have lived in America since 1965, probably before you were born!" Or "I am an American citizen, as are my two children and five grand-children." Or "This is my country. I came from Maryland just now and am presently going to Washington, DC. That is my home now."

———————

As I reflect on my checkered life, I have many regrets, but coming to America is not one of them. In fact, it is the best thing that happened to me. It was here in America that I found my life's calling. For me, America truly was—and is—*still the promised land.* Neither the racism I encountered in the South nor the academic politics I fought in the universities nor the greed and malfeasance I found in DC could diminish my rev-erence for the freedom and opportunities that I found within the shores of the United States. I grew to love America even as I feared for its well-being. I came to understand that America's strengths and weaknesses depend on the health of its families, a stabiliz-ing force in any society. As I made homes in Greensboro and Baton Rouge, Pittsburgh and DC, I witnessed the gradual disintegration of the American family. It troubled me. It also made me focus on seeing that my family stayed healthy and together. I made sure that my son and daughter got strong educations and were prepared to be successful in starting their own families.

Which brings me back to survival. And India. And Indian Americans. Growing up in that small village, I did not feel love from my parents. My father was a shopkeeper, my mother a housekeeper. They labored every day to keep the family sheltered and fed. There was little time left for anything else. In that environment, I learned how to survive. It toughened me and made me strong. As I confronted obstacles that could have blocked me in India and America, I reached for tools in that survival kit, persist-ed—and prevailed, even in the face of angry people who shout, "Go home!"

After 50-some years, I am still here. Indian Americans like me are succeeding in academia, business, technology and politics. We are surviving—and prospering— because we are Americans. As long as that spirit is alive and well, America will remain great. No demagogue can detract America from its manifest destiny, and no terrorist can make it lose its bearings. America is my home! And home for my children and grandchildren... and for many generations to come.

ACKNOWLEDGMENTS

Events described in this book go as far back as some 70 years. Much of the material here is drawn from the memory and some is subjective. Yet as the distinguished neurologist Oliver Sacks once suggested, "such subjectivity is built into the very nature of memory, and follows from its basis and mechanisms in the human brain. The wonder is that aberrations of a gross sort are relatively rare, and that, for the most part, our memories are relatively solid and reliable."

I am grateful to numerous people who have been variously helpful to me in writing, revising and promoting this book, among them especially:

- Alice Rivlin for writing a generous foreword and Charles A. Bowsher, Stephen Joel Trachtenberg and Anthony A. Williams for writing endorsements for the book. They also helped me in a variety of ways while I was the CFO of Washington, DC.
- At Arch Street Press, my highly diligent editor Robert Rimm who took personal interest in the book and ably shepherded it all the way to its publication and who, through his numerous insightful comments, penetrating questions and suggestions helped me to clarify issues and greatly improved the manuscript.
- Harry Jaffe, the distinguished reporter and contributing editor at *The Washingtonian*, who closely read and edited an earlier version of the manuscript, and helped me to rewrite and organize various sections. Essentially, he helped me to transform what was an academic tome full of footnotes and references into what has become, I hope, a readable memoir. Similarly, Kenneth DeCell, former editor at *The Washingtonian*, line edited the earlier manuscript and also made excellent suggestions.
- My son Apoorva and daughter Sona read through the entire manuscript and made excellent suggestions to make it more accurate and authentic, particularly relating to the family material.

- Angell Jacobs and David Tseng, two of the ablest civil servants in DC government and my colleagues in the office of the CFO, read the District-related and select other chapters and made helpful suggestions. Similarly, Helen Hsing and Ted Barreaux, two of my highly perceptive GAO colleagues, read GAO-related and other selected sections and helped me to correct errors and omissions.
- And above all, Panna Naik, my life partner, who reads everything I write and nearly always improves it.

Needless to say, despite all of the help I received from these good people, I am sure there are still unavoidable shortcomings in the book for which I hold only myself responsible.

ACKNOWLEDGMENT OF SOURCES

I am also grateful for quotations from the following sources:

Bradbury, Ray, "America: An Ode to Immigrants," *The Wall Street Journal*,
    May 17, 2006
Brookings Institution, "The US will become 'minority white' in 2045,"
    March 14, 2018
Gibran, Khalil, *The Madman* (Dover, 1918)
Hartley, L.P., *The Go-Between* (Hamish Hamilton, 1970)
Hemingway, Ernest, *A Moveable Feast* (Scribner, 2009)
Naipaul, V.S., *A Writer's People* (Knopf, 2008)
    ——*A Bend in the River* (Knopf, 1979)
    ——"Our Universal Civilization," *City Journal*, Summer 1991
Sacks, Oliver, *On the Move, A Life* (Vintage, 2015)
Talese, Gay, *A Writer's Life* (Knopf, 2006)
White, E. B., *Here Is New York* (Harper, 1949)
Zangwill, Israel, *The Melting Pot* (1908)

GLOSSARY OF INDIAN TERMS

Baa—the author's mother, Shantabahen

Bahu—daughter-in-law

Bandi—a sleeveless jacket that most Indian men wear over a shirt

Bania—a trader community, generally Gujarati

Bapa—the author's grandfather, Jivanlal

Bhajans—Hindu prayer songs

Bidis—cheap, handmade local version of cigarettes

Brahmins—priests and teachers considered the epitome of the Indian caste system

Chapatti—a leavened Indian bread

Chappals—a footwear like sleepers

Dalits—untouchables, often at the bottom of the Indian caste system

Desh—a term used to refer to provinces or native villages

Dhoti—a rectangular piece of unstitched cloth wrapped around the waist and legs and
    knotted at the waist

Eid (or Eid al-Fitr)—marks the end of Ramadan, which is a month of fasting
    and prayer

Ghatis—people who come from ghats (mountains) and work as servants in the
    Mumbai shops, stores and homes

Harijans—a term used by Mahatma Gandhi for untouchables, literally meaning
    children of God

Kafani—a loose shirt worn under a sleeveless jacket

Kaka—the author's father, Mohanlal or Mohanbhai

Kankai—family goddess

Krishna—the most popular Hindu god

Kshatriyas—warriors and rulers

Kurta—a loose Indian shirt

Laxmi—goddess of wealth

Lengha— loose pajama-like pants

Maa—the author's grandmother, Manibahen

Maharaja—a great king

Mama—author's maternal uncle

Mami—Mama's wife

Mandakranta—a Sanskrit meter with a deep elegiac tone

Masa—a maternal uncle

Masjid—a mosque, or place of worship for Muslims

Maya—Sanskrit word for illusion

Mumbaiwala—a householder in Mumbai

Natu, Nat—shortened version of author's first name, Natwar

Pughree—a lump sum paid up front to rent a dwelling followed by monthly rent

Samaj—generally a social association

Shudras—laborers.

Vaishyas—farmers, traders and merchants

INDEX OF PEOPLE INFLUENTIAL TO AUTHOR AFTER HIS MIGRATION TO THE U.S.

CPSIA information can be obtained
at www.ICGtesting.com
Printed in the USA
FFHW021928180619
53088088-58702FF